Fundamentals of SQL Server 2012 Replication

Sebastian Meine, Ph.D.

First published by Simple Talk Publishing August 2013

Technical Review: Kalen Delaney and Robert Sheldon
Editor: Robert Sheldon
Cover Image: Sebastian Meine
Typeset: Peter Woodhouse and Gower Associates

Table of Contents

Foreword

Replication is the oldest of the high availability technologies in SQL Server. Introduced in SQL Server 6, replication synchronizes data between SQL Server instances, typically copying data from a Publisher, which is the source of the data, to a Subscriber, which hosts the copied data. If the Publisher fails, the Subscriber can take over data operations. Unlike other high availability technologies, replication gives the DBA full control over how much or how little of the data should be replicated. The DBA can choose which tables to replicate from the Publisher to one or more Subscribers and even decide which columns within those tables to replicate.

As a very mature technology, replication is also very robust and, in most cases, very straightforward to set up and manage. This book will get you started with SQL Server replication even if you've never worked with any kind of high availability feature, and if you've already been working with replication, the discussions about troubleshooting could still prove invaluable.

Replication lends itself very nicely to a step-by-step tutorial of the sort presented in this book. Sebastian guides you through setting up a complete replication scenario. Subsequent chapters then drill into more details about Publishers and Subscribers, as well as publications, subscriptions and articles. Following a set of chapters that discuss transactional replication are several on merge replication.

Sebastian Meine has been working with SQL Server for over a decade. I first met him as a student in a SQL Server Internals class I was teaching for the company he worked for. I noticed immediately that Sebastian was not one to be satisfied with simple explanations. He wanted to know as much as he could about every detail of the SQL Server engine, including not just what and how, but also why. I was not always able to answer every question he had, and many were about issues I had never thought of before, which inspired me to do more digging on my own.

Since that class, Sebastian and I have kept in touch. I was delighted to offer him the opportunity to write the original Stairway on which this book is based and even more delighted when he accepted.

If you've wanted to learn the what, how and why of SQL Server replication, you've come to the right place! I hope you enjoy reading and learning from this book as much as I enjoyed editing it.

Kalen Delaney, www.SQLServerInternals.com

Poulsbo, WA – July 2013

About the Author

Sebastian Meine is the SQL Stylist at sqlity.net llc (HTTP://SQLITY.NET). After receiving his PhD in Computer Science at the University of Linz, Austria, he spent several years at a global Fortune 50 company as software architect responsible for code quality and the performance of dozens of large-scale database installations nationwide.

In 2010, to fully engage in his passion for SQL Server, he founded sqlity.net. Since that time he has been helping his clients to boost their SQL Server health, enhance their T-SQL coding skills and tighten their SQL Server security.

Sebastian is a sought-after trainer, speaker and author who shares his knowledge regularly within the worldwide SQL community through his writings and public speaking engagements. Additionally, he is co-author of *tSQLt, the Database Unit Testing Framework for SQL Server*. tSQLt is open source and available at HTTP://TSQLT.ORG.

Sebastian is also the CTO of TSTS Inc., a company that provides online personalized training and workout solutions.

About the Technical Reviewer

Kalen Delaney has been working with SQL Server for 25 years and provides performance consulting services as well as advanced SQL Server training to clients around the world, using her own custom-developed curriculum. She has been a SQL Server MVP since 1993 and has been writing about SQL Server for almost as long. Kalen has spoken at dozens of technical conferences, including every US PASS conference since the organization's founding in 1999. Kalen is a contributing editor and columnist for *SQL Server Magazine* and the author or co-author of several of the most deeply technical books on SQL Server, including *SQL Server 2008 Internals* and the upcoming *SQL Server 2012 Internals*, both from Microsoft Press. Kalen blogs at WWW.SQLBLOG.COM and her personal website and schedule can be found at WWW.SQLSERVERINTERNALS.COM.

Acknowledgements

This is the place where people write that they could not have done this alone. This book is no exception, and a lot of people helped and worked hard on making it possible. I am grateful for all the help I received, especially from the team at Red Gate.

Of all the people who helped, there are two who stand out. The first is my good friend Kalen Delaney, who got me into the SQL Server Central Stairway project in the first place and then spent numerous hours reviewing and editing the original *Stairway to SQL Server Replication*. The second is Robert Sheldon. He spent countless hours reviewing and editing to make sure that the book stayed on a consistent technical and linguistic level throughout.

Thank you both for working with me on turning this "small project" into the book you are holding in your hands today.

Sebastian Meine

August 2013

Introduction

Many of my clients need to make data that lives on one server available on another server. There are many reasons for such a requirement. You might want to speed up cross-server queries by providing a local copy of the data. Or you might want to make the data available to resource intensive reporting queries without impacting the OLTP load, maybe even with an intentional delay so you're always reporting against complete days only. Finally, you might be looking to implement high availability. In all these situations, SQL Server Replication is a viable option to look at when planning for the implementation of such a requirement.

With this book, I want to introduce you into the vast world of SQL Server Replication and show you its most important strengths and weaknesses. After working through the exercises, you will be able to make an informed decision whether replication is the right feature to use and which type of replication is the most advantageous in your situation. You will also know when to stay away from replication and use other features such as simple log shipping or the new "Always On" feature set.

What This Book Covers

Fundamentals of SQL Server 2012 Replication provides a hands-on introduction to SQL Server replication. The book begins with a short overview that introduces you to the technologies that make up replication. In the following chapters, the book will walk you through setting up different replication scenarios. All hands-on exercises are designed with security best practices in mind. When you're finished working through the exercises, you will be able to implement your own multi-server replication setup while following the principle of least privilege (HTTP://EN.WIKIPEDIA.ORG/WIKI/ PRINCIPLE_OF_LEAST_PRIVILEGE).[1]

---

[1]

Chapter 1: Overview of SQL Server Replication

Chapter 1 gives a high level overview of the different components that together make up SQL Server Replication. All the terms that you will encounter throughout the book, such as *Publisher* and *Subscriber*, are introduced and explained here. This chapter also gives a small glimpse outside of the boundaries of this book by introducing replication terms such as *Queue Reader Agent* that we won't cover in later chapters.

Chapter 2: Configuring a Basic Replication Setup

Chapter 2 gives a quick run-through of a very basic replication setup involving only a single server. The purpose of this chapter is to get you up and running as quickly as possible, so you can get a feel for the power of SQL Server Replication. For that, we'll be taking a few shortcuts that you will rarely encounter in a real-life setup. While walking through these exercises, you will get a better understanding of the three main parts of any replication setup: The Publisher with its publication, the Distributor, and the Subscriber with its subscription.

Chapter 3: The Role of the Distributor

The most important and most undervalued component of SQL Server Replication is the Distributor. In many real-world setups, the Publisher gets tasked with also playing the role of the Distributor. However, this can cause a significant overhead on the Publisher, particularly if you have published a very busy database, or if you have many Subscribers. Chapter 3 will show you how to set up the Distributor as a stand-alone system, allowing for the least amount of additional load on both the Publisher and the Subscriber. You will also learn about the most important settings that are provided by the Distributor and their impact on your replication setup.

Chapter 4: Transactional Replication – the Replication Agents

Replication is executed by a set of processes that are not part of the SQL Server core itself. These processes are called replication agents. While they are usually executed with the help of SQL Server Agent, it is important to understand that they are independent of, not related to, the latter. Chapter 4 gives an overview of the agents that are involved in transactional replication.

Chapter 5: Transactional Replication – the Publication

The publication is the part of replication that defines what part of the data is made available to others. Chapter 5 provides a detailed walk-through of setting up a publication for transactional replication. You will learn about articles and filters. We will also touch on article properties, which allow you to fine-tune the behavior of a single article. This is also the first chapter that will look at security and the principle of least privilege. You will learn how to apply this principle to the replication agents that are defined by the publication.

Chapter 6: The Publication Access List

Chapter 6 is all about security. Here you will encounter the Publication Access List and learn how it controls who can access your publication, for example, to create a subscription. While it is written in the context of transactional replication, everything covered here works the same way for merge replication, so be sure not to skip this chapter.

Chapter 7: Transactional Replication – the Subscription

Chapter 7 walks you through the steps involved in setting up a subscription to your publication. You will learn about the differences between pull and push subscriptions and when one might better suited to your needs than the other. This chapter also covers the access control aspects of setting up a subscription.

Chapter 8: SQL Server Agent Jobs for Transactional Replication

By default, SQL Server Replication makes extensive use of SQL Server Agent jobs. Chapter 8 shows all jobs that are created for transactional replication and explains the purpose of each one.

Chapter 9: Merge Replication – the Replication Agents

Most of the preceding chapters are geared towards transactional replication. The next few chapters (9 to 12) cover merge replication. Before you read on, make sure you have read *Chapter 3: The Role of the Distributor* and *Chapter 6: The Publication Access List*.

Similar to transactional replication, merge replication is driven by a set of replication agents. Chapter 9 covers those agents and explains how merge replication differs from transactional replication.

Chapter 10: Merge Replication – the Publication

Like transactional replication, merge replication requires that you set up a publication first. Chapter 10 walks you through the steps of creating a merge replication publication. As in Chapter 5, we will also cover the security settings that you need to know about when setting up your own publication.

Chapter 11: Merge Replication – the Subscription

Chapter 11 shows how to set up a subscription for merge replication. In addition to selecting a push or pull subscription model as covered in Chapter 7, merge replication requires that you also pick between a client and a server subscription. This chapter shows how all these selections can be done. And, as before, you will learn how to tighten security around the merge replication agents.

Chapter 12: Merge Replication – Conflicts

Merge replication is designed to be used in an environment in which the data on each of the connected systems might be changed. New data might be loaded into the publication database while, at the same time, updates to the existing data are applied at the Subscribers. Merge replication will synchronize all those changes bi-directionally across all servers, Publisher and Subscribers alike. However, in any bi-directional synchronization system, conflicts can occur when the same piece of data is changed in more than one place between two synchronizations.

Chapter 12 details how merge replication deals with such conflicts either automatically or by soliciting human intervention.

Chapter 13: Replication Monitor

SQL Server Replication is made up of many components that work together to provide the desired functionality. With so many pieces involved, there are many things that can go wrong. The SQL Server Replication Monitor provides an easy means to see if your setup is working as desired, or if any components need attention.

Chapter 13 introduces this tool and shows where to find the pertinent information for your Publication or Subscription.

Chapter 14: Troubleshooting

Chapter 14 shows how to troubleshoot a replication setup that is not working as designed. It is based on an example setup in which the account security is completely messed up. This example demonstrates where the difficulties in diagnosing replication problems lie. It points to the shortcomings of the Replication Monitor and shows how to find the information required for fixing the problem. It also touches on problems you might encounter later, such as an update conflict in a transactional replication setup, and shows where to find further information to help troubleshoot those problems.

The Book's Intended Audience

If you're new to replication, or you just inherited a replication setup and want to understand the process better, this book is for you. You'll be introduced to various replication concepts and shown how the different components work. This book is not intended for people already well versed in SQL Server replication. For example, we do not cover such specialized topics as peer-to-peer replication, manually scripting replication creation scripts, or setting up topologies such as insert-only replication.

System Requirements

This book shows how to set up a real life replication scenario. As those rarely live on a single SQL Server instance, most of the examples and exercises in this book require three separate servers with their own SQL Server instance installed on them. While you can follow many examples using just one instance or multiple instances on a single server, you will get most out of the exercises if you follow them exactly and use three separate machines. Those machines should live in the same domain, but if you don't have access to a domain controller, you can still follow the examples by creating the required user accounts on all three machines instead of just the domain controller.

Finally, as this book is about SQL Server 2012 Replication, you need an instance of that SQL Server version on each of your machines. You can use the Standard, BI, Enterprise or Developer edition of SQL Server. (The Subscriber could also be the Web or the Express edition.)

The easiest way to get those machines is to open an account with Amazon AWS or Microsoft Azure and create four Windows virtual machines, one as the domain controller and three for the SQL Server instances. You can then install SQL Server as a trial version on each of them. That gives you half a year to work through this book. If you go down this route, make sure to shut down the machines every time you have to step away for an extended time period, as you will be charged for each hour during which the virtual machines are running.

Feedback, Errata and Code Download

We've done our very best to ensure that this book is accurate and that we've presented the concepts as clearly as possible. If you have suggestions for improvements, or if we've erred in some way, we'd love to hear about it. Please post all feedback and errata to the following URL:
HTTPS://WWW.SIMPLE-TALK.COM/BOOKS/SQL-BOOKS/FUNDAMENTALS-OF-SQL-SERVER-2012-REPLICATION-BY-SEBASTIAN-MEINE/ [2]

At the same location, you will find a link to the code download file, containing the various scripts used throughout the book to demonstrate the techniques for working with SQL Server replication in its various forms.

2

Chapter 1: Overview of SQL Server Replication

Main Entry: rep-li-ca-tion
Pronunciation: \ˌre-plə-ˈkā-shən
Function: noun
Date: 14th century

The word *replication* comes from the Latin word *replicare,* which means to repeat. Replication describes the process of reproducing or duplicating (HTTP://WWW.MERRIAM-WEBSTER.COM/DICTIONARY/REPLICATION[1] and *Chambers Dictionary of Etymology,* Chambers, 1999).

Replication in SQL Server does exactly that; it reproduces or duplicates data. You can use replication any time you need to create a copy of your data. That copy can exist in the same database as the source data, in a different database on the same instance, or in a database on a separate instance or server.

But SQL Server replication is about more than just copying data. You can set up replication to continuously synchronize the source data with the copied data or set it up to synchronize the data at scheduled intervals. Plus, replication supports both one-way and bi-directional synchronization, and lets you keep several datasets in sync with each other.

In this chapter, we look at how you can use SQL Server replication to synchronize your data across multiple SQL Server instances. We also cover some of the possible scenarios in which you can use replication. In addition, we examine the components that make up SQL Server replication and show how they work together to allow you to replicate your data and your data changes. Finally, we review the different types of replication and how they use the components in a replication setup.

---

[1]

Putting SQL Server Replication to Work

There are several scenarios in which using SQL Server replication is a good choice. For example, you can use replication to copy your data to a different machine in order to support ad hoc reporting or to provide a source for an Analysis Services cube. Using replication in this way offers two main benefits. First, you're separating your expensive reporting queries from your online transaction processing (OLTP), keeping the write-intensive OLTP load on one system and the read-intensive reporting load on the other.

The second benefit comes from the fact that replication can be scheduled to run at certain intervals. For example, you can run replication nightly to provide a data **snapshot** to the reporting environment. As a result, your reports will contain data from completed days only, rather than containing data from a part of a day. That means you don't have to build extra logic into your system to deal with today's incomplete data.

On the other hand, you can set up **transactional replication** to transfer data in near real-time to your reports. Although SQL Server doesn't offer synchronous replication, there is usually only a short delay for changes in the source data to show up in the replicated data. Of course, latency depends on a lot of factors, but most of the time it is in the range of only a few seconds.

A second scenario in which replication is often utilized is that of a traveling sales force. Salespeople usually carry their own laptops, which can contain important company data, and they often update that data throughout the day. The new information is then fed into the database back at headquarters. Because the laptops are often not connected, a continuous replication setup is not an option. What further complicates the issue is that the same data can sometimes be updated in different places, creating conflicts that must be resolved. With **merge replication**, SQL Server provides a replication topology that was built for exactly this type of scenario.

Replication can also be used for data archival and high availability (HA) purposes. You can, for example, maintain a copy of your complete database on a second server and automatically keep it in sync with the main database. You can even combine your HA standby server and database copy with your reporting server and database, saving on hardware and licensing costs. Before SQL Server 2012, this was the only way to maintain a synchronized copy of your database that was accessible for read requests.

However, SQL Server 2012 introduced the **Always-On** feature, which combines clustering and mirroring into one flexible HA solution. **Always-On** lets you maintain a one-to-one copy of your database (or database group) that is automatically kept in sync with the master copy. This feature utilizes technology that was introduced with the snapshot isolation levels in SQL Server 2005 to provide read-only access to the secondary databases. It also allows the synchronization to be either synchronous, to maximize protection, or asynchronous, to reduce the impact on the primary database.

With the **Always-On** feature, you can also implement more than one secondary server. For example, you might set up your first secondary server in the same datacenter as the primary server. You can configure the secondary server to be updated synchronously for fast failover. You might then implement another secondary server in a remote location (such as across the ocean) to ensure maximum disaster recoverability. This one you can configure to be updated asynchronously to minimize the impact on the main database.

What all this means is that, if your goal is to create an exact copy of the database, replication in SQL Server 2012 is not necessarily the way to go because **Always-On** offers advantages such as synchronous data transfer and the guarantee that the two databases are identical.

On the other hand, if your goal is not to have a one-to-one copy, replication offers a lot more flexibility. You can replicate just a subset of tables. You can even filter out rows. You can have two subscriptions of publications in separate databases write to the same database, thereby collecting data from different sources into one place. You can also synchronize multiple data sources bi-directionally, allowing for data to change in more than one place. Finally, you can even do things such as change the replicated data on the fly or replicate only data inserts and updates, while ignoring deletes.

SQL Server can replicate data from one database to another database on the same server or on another server. That second server can be in the same building or on the other side of the world. SQL Server also allows you to replicate data to and from other database management systems such as Oracle.

Replication Components

Replication requires a number of components to work properly. Figure 1-1 provides a high-level overview of the pieces involved in a replication setup.

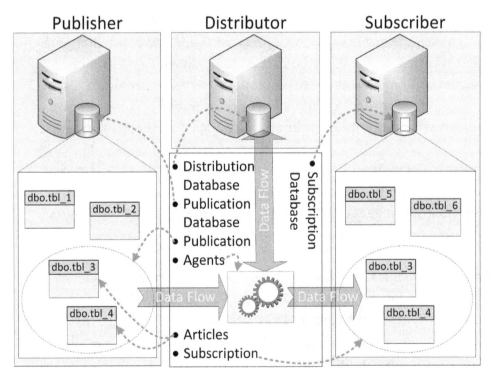

Figure 1-1:   The components that make up a replication setup.

The components in the replication setup shown in Figure 1-1 include a **Publisher** and its **publication database**. The publication database contains a **publication** that includes two **articles**. The setup also includes a **Distributor** and its **distribution database** as well as a **Subscriber** and its **subscription database**, which contains the **subscription**. Finally, the setup includes the **replication agents** necessary to drive these processes. (A replication setup also includes a few maintenance jobs, but they are not displayed in Figure 1-1.)

Let's dig deeper into each of these components.

Articles

For each SQL Server object that should be replicated, an article needs to be defined. Each article corresponds to a single SQL Server object. For example, in Figure 1-1, the tables dbo.tbl_3 and dbo.tbl_4 are the articles.

The objects that are replicated most often are tables, views, and stored procedures. (For a complete list of objects that can be replicated, check out the topic, *Publishing Data and Database Objects* in SQL Server Books Online.)

An article's properties determine whether that article contains the entire object or a filtered subset of its parts. For example, an article can be configured to contain only some of the columns of a table.

With some restrictions, multiple articles can be created on a single object.

Publications

A publication is a collection of articles grouped together as one unit. In Figure 1-1, the dotted circle that surrounds the two articles represents the publication.

Every article is defined to be part of exactly one publication. However, you can define different articles on the same object in separate publications.

A publication supports several configurable options that apply to all its articles. Perhaps the most important option is the one that lets you define which type of replication to use.

Publication database

Any database that contains objects designated as articles is called a publication database. When you set up a publication on a database, SQL Server modifies the inner workings of that database and creates several replication-related objects. A publication database is also protected against being dropped.

A publication can contain articles from a single publication database only.

Publisher

The Publisher is the SQL Server instance that makes a publication available for replication; however, the Publisher itself doesn't actually have an active role in a replication setup. After the publication is defined, the Distributor and sometimes the Subscriber do all the heavy lifting.

The entire left-most column in Figure 1-1 represents the Publisher with its publication database, publication, and two articles.

Distributor

Each Publisher is linked to a single Distributor. The Distributor is a SQL Server instance that identifies changes to the articles on each of its Publishers. Depending on the replication setup, the Distributor might also be responsible for notifying the Subscribers that have subscribed to a publication that an article has changed. The information about these changes is stored in the distribution database until all Subscribers have been notified or the retention period has expired.

The Distributor can be configured on a SQL Server instance separate from the Publisher, but often the same instance takes the role of the Publisher and the Distributor.

In Figure 1-1, the top part of the center column is the Distributor. There are no table details shown because you don't usually have to directly access a replication's internal objects.

Distribution databases

Each Distributor has at least one distribution database. The distribution database contains a number of objects that store replication metadata as well as replicated data.

A Distributor can hold more than one distribution database; however, all publications defined on a single Publisher must use the same distribution database.

Subscriber

Each SQL Server instance that subscribes to a publication is called a Subscriber. The Subscriber receives changes to a published article through that publication. A Subscriber does not necessarily play an active role in the replication process. Depending on the settings selected during replication setup, it might receive the data passively.

In Figure 1-1, everything related to the Subscriber is displayed in the right-hand column. Here you can find the subscription database and the subscription, which is represented by the dotted circle that surrounds the two replicated articles.

Subscriptions

A subscription is the counterpart of the publication. Each subscription creates a link, or contract, between one publication and one Subscriber.

There are two types of subscriptions: **push subscriptions** and **pull subscriptions**. In a push subscription, the Distributor directly updates the data in the Subscriber database. In a pull subscription, the Subscriber asks the Distributor regularly if any new changes are available, and then updates the data in the subscription database itself.

Subscription databases

A database that is the target of a replication subscription is called a subscription database. As in the case of the publication database, SQL Server modifies the subscription database during the first initialization. The most obvious change is the addition of a few replication-related objects. However, unlike publication databases, SQL Server doesn't prevent a subscription database from being dropped.

Replication agents

The replication processes are executed by a set of replication agents. Each agent is an independent Windows executable responsible for one piece of the process of moving the data. In a default installation of replication, each agent is executed by its own **SQL Server Agent** job. Most of those agents usually run on the Distributor, although some can run on the Subscriber. The Publisher houses replication agents only when the Publisher and Distributor are the same instance.

Instead of relying on the SQL Server Agent, you can execute any replication agent manually or by some other scheduling means. However, in most cases, these approaches provide little advantage and often make troubleshooting more complex.

The following sections briefly introduce each replication agent type. The replication agents are described in more detail in later chapters.

Snapshot Agent

In all replication topologies, the **Snapshot Agent** provides the data required to perform the initial synchronization of the publication database with the subscription database. Transactional replication and merge replication use other agents to keep the data in sync afterwards. For both topologies, replication will use the Snapshot Agent again (after the initial synchronization) only when you request a fresh resynchronization.

Snapshot replication, on the other hand, uses the Snapshot Agent exclusively to replicate data. It works by copying all the data every time from the publication database to the subscription database.

Log Reader Agent

The **Log Reader Agent** reads the transaction log of the publication database. If it finds changes to the published objects, it records those changes to the distribution database. Only transactional replication uses the Log Reader Agent.

Distribution Agent

The **Distribution Agent** applies the changes recorded in the distribution database to the subscription database. As with the Log Reader Agent, only transactional replication uses the Distribution Agent.

Merge Agent

The **Merge Agent** synchronizes changes between the publication database and the subscription database. It is able to handle changes in both the publication database and the subscription database and can sync those changes bi-directionally. A set of triggers in both databases support this process. Only merge replication uses the Merge Agent.

Queue Reader Agent

The **Queue Reader Agent** is used for bi-directional transactional replication. Bi-directional transactional replication is an advanced topic that won't be covered in this book. For more information, see the topic, *Replication Agents Overview*, in SQL Server Books Online.

Replication maintenance jobs

In addition to the SQL Server Agent jobs that run the replication agents, a replication setup includes a few additional jobs that are responsible for cleaning up old data and for other monitoring and maintenance tasks.

How Terms Are Used

Not surprisingly, you'll find the terms *Distributor, Publisher,* and *Subscriber* used throughout this book. Each one always refers to a SQL Server instance together with the machine it is on. So if you see the phrase "database on the Subscriber," it refers to a database on the instance that plays the role of the Subscriber. If you see the phrase "file on the Distributor," it describes a file on the machine that hosts the instance of SQL Server that is used as a Distributor.

The databases that participate in replication are referred to as the *publication database, distribution database,* and *subscription database,* depending on the role each plays in the replication context. Each lives on its respective SQL Server instance.

Be aware that a single SQL Server instance can play more than one role in the replication context. For example, the Publisher and the Distributor are often the same instance.

Publication, distribution, and *subscription* are logical replication concepts rather than physical objects; they are not referring to database objects or databases. Instead, you will find a phrase such as "a table that is part of the publication." For more detailed definitions, refer back to the previous section.

A replication agent is always called an *Agent,* and a SQL Server Agent job is always called a *job,* so the term, *Distributor* never refers to a Distribution Agent or the SQL Server Agent job that is used to execute the Distribution Agent. Rather, the term always refers to an instance of SQL Server or to the machine running that instance.

Replication Types

SQL Server supports three types of replication: **snapshot**, **transactional**, and **merge** replication. There is also **peer-to-peer** replication, which is transactional replication with a few enhancements that allow for bi-directional updates.

Snapshot replication

Snapshot replication creates an identical copy of the replicated objects and their data each time it runs. There is no synchronization capability available for snapshot replication; subsequent executions always copy the entire dataset again, overwriting any external changes that might have been applied to the target database.

Snapshot replication uses SQL Server's bcp utility to write the contents of each table into the snapshot folder. The snapshot folder is a shared folder set up on the Distributor when replication is configured. Each component that participates in snapshot replication needs to have access to the snapshot folder.

Every time snapshot replication runs, all articles and their data are again copied from scratch, which can require significant bandwidth and storage resources. During their initial setup, all other replication types use, by default, a single replication snapshot to sync the Publisher to its Subscribers.

Snapshot replication is rarely used by itself and therefore will not be covered further. However, its mechanisms are an integral part in the initialization process of the other replication types, so you will see it being mentioned in several places throughout the book.

Transactional replication

Transactional replication copies data uni-directionally from the source database to the target database. This replication type uses the log files associated with the source database to keep data in sync. If a change is made to the source database, that change can be immediately synced to the target database, or the synchronization can be scheduled. Transactional replication, however, is sensitive to external changes to the target database. Any such change can potentially break replication so, for all intents and purposes, the target database should be considered read-only. There are exceptions to this rule, however. For example, you can modify objects in the target database that are not part of the replication setup.

Transactional replication works, as the name suggests, on a transaction basis. The Log Reader Agent scans the transaction log of the publication database and examines each committed transaction to determine whether any changes affect the replicated articles. If they do, those changes are logged to the distribution database. The Distribution Agent then replicates those changes to the Subscriber.

Transactional replication allows for close to real-time synchronization and leaves only a small footprint on the Publisher. There are several options to allow for bi-directional data movement in transactional replication, as in the case of peer-to-peer replication. However, uni-directional transactional replication is the most commonly used form, and we will not cover the other forms in this book.

For transactional replication to work, every table you want to publish must be configured with a primary key.

Merge replication

Merge replication allows two or more databases to be kept in sync. Any change applied to one database will automatically be applied to the other databases – and vice versa.

Merge replication was designed to allow for data changes on the Publisher as well as the Subscriber, but merge replication also allows for disconnected scenarios. For example, if a Subscriber is disconnected from a Publisher during part of the day, the Subscriber and Publisher are synchronized when they are reconnected.

The Merge Agent is responsible for synchronizing the changes between the Publisher and its Subscribers. It utilizes a set of triggers to identify articles that have changed and to record those changes.

Because data can be modified on both the Subscriber and Publisher, it's possible for a row to be updated in two different places at the same time, which can result in data being in conflict. Merge replication comes with several built-in options to help resolve such conflicts.

Merge replication identifies rows across the different servers by using a `uniqueidentifier` column with the `ROWGUIDCOL` property set and a unique constraint defined on that column. If you publish a table that does not have such a column already, a properly configured `uniqueidentifier` column will be added automatically.

Summary

In this chapter, you learned about the basic components that make up SQL Server replication. Objects in a publication database that are marked for replication are called articles. Articles are grouped together into publications. If changes occur to those articles, the changes are propagated to the Subscriber, as defined by a subscription. The data flows through the distribution database, which resides on the Distributor. The Publisher, Distributor, and Subscriber can be on the same SQL Server instance or on separate instances, either on the same or on different machines. The source and the target database can be the same (if the Publisher and Subscriber are on the same SQL Server instance), but the distribution database has to be separate from the others.

Chapter 2: Configuring a Basic Replication Setup

The best way to get a feel for how SQL Server replication is implemented and how it works is to see it in action. In this chapter, we perform a set of exercises that walk you through a simple replication setup. The exercises demonstrate how to configure replication to copy a single table from one database to another database. To keep this setup simple, we'll use transactional replication and a single SQL Server instance to play the roles of Publisher, Distributor, and Subscriber. We'll also create the two publishing and subscribing databases as part of the exercises.

To set up replication, you must configure the Distributor and create a publication and a subscription. The easiest way to perform these tasks is by using SQL Server Management Studio (SSMS). It's possible instead to use Transact-SQL scripts to set up and control replication. In fact, some advanced options necessitate the use of scripts. However, even the simplest setup requires a set of stored procedures that, together, have over 200 non-optional parameters. So it makes sense to start out by using SSMS. (A discussion of these stored procedures is beyond the scope of this book. For information about them, refer to SQL Server Books Online.)

The exercises in this chapter were developed on a single SQL Server 2012 instance. However, you can also follow these steps on a SQL Server 2005, 2008, or 2008 R2 instance.

Setting Up the Distributor

The Distributor lies at the core of transactional replication. It must be available when you set up the other components, so you need to configure it first. Although the Distributor can reside on its own SQL Server instance, often the Publisher and the Distributor are set up on the same machine. This is called the *local distributor* model and it is what we'll do in this first exercise.

The following steps walk you through the process of creating the Distributor:

1. Open SSMS and connect to the SQL Server instance that you want to use.

2. In **Object Explorer**, right-click the **Replication** folder (listed beneath the server/instance name), and click **Configure Distribution**, as shown in Figure 2-1.

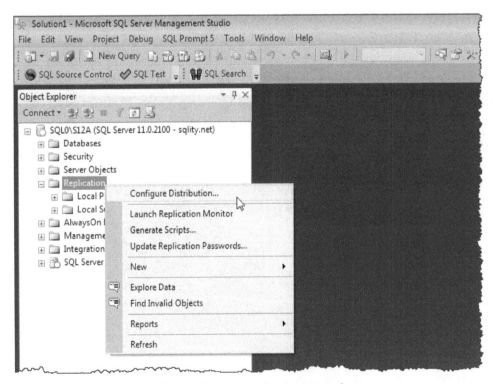

Figure 2-1:   Launching the Configure Distribution Wizard.

After clicking **Configure Distribution**, the first page of the **Configure Distribution Wizard** appears (shown in Figure 2-2). The page provides general information about setting up a Distributor.

Figure 2-2:   Opening page of the Configure Distribution Wizard.

The **Configure Distribution Wizard** has two purposes. First, it lets you set up a SQL Server instance to be a Distributor. Second, it lets you select an existing Distributor to be used when setting up a Publisher. When using the local distributor model, these two steps occur with one execution of the wizard. Later chapters will provide more details about these two actions and their implications.

3. You can select the **Do not show this starting page again** option if you don't want the page to appear when you start the wizard. Or you can ignore the option and simply click **Next** to go to the next page.

4. On the **Distributor** page (shown in Figure 2-3), you can choose to set up the current instance to be a Distributor or select another instance that's already been configured as a Distributor.

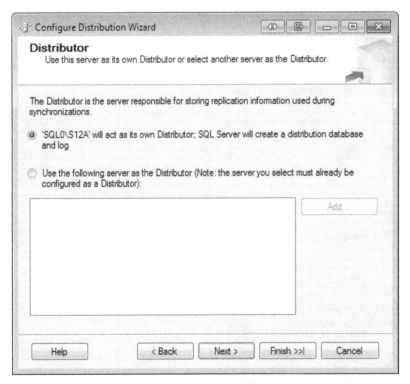

Figure 2-3:   Selecting the server that will be used as the Distributor.

Because you'll be installing the Distributor on this SQL Server instance, leave the default settings, and click **Next**.

5. If the SQL Server Agent is not set up to start automatically with the operating system, you'll get an additional page here that lets you change SQL Server Agent's configuration. That page, **SQL Server Agent Start**, is shown in Figure 2-4.

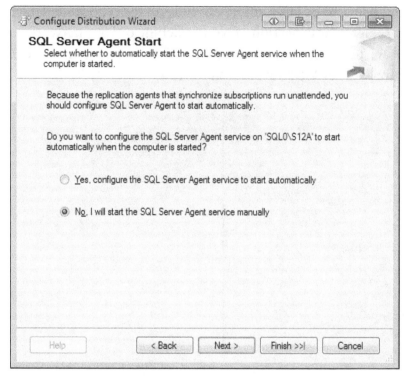

Figure 2-4:   Warning that SQL Server Agent is not set to start automatically.

To be able to select the **Yes** option, the SQL Server service account needs to have administrative privileges in Windows. However, because this is not a recommended security best practice, you most likely will not be able to select the **Yes** option so, if this page appears, take it as a warning, then select the **No** option, and adjust the setting manually.

For our exercises to work, it's not necessary that the SQL Server Agent be set to auto-start. However, it will need to be running, so this is a good place to start the SQL Server Agent service if needed.

After you're finished on the **SQL Server Agent Start** page, click **Next**.

6. On the **Snapshot Folder** page (shown in Figure 2-5), you specify the location for the snapshot folder. The snapshot folder is used during the initial synchronization of transactional replication and needs to be large enough to hold all the replicated data. You can place the snapshot folder in any location on your machine or your network. For performance reasons, it makes sense to create a network share on the Distributor. The example shown in Figure 2-5 uses \\SQL0\ReplDataS12A.

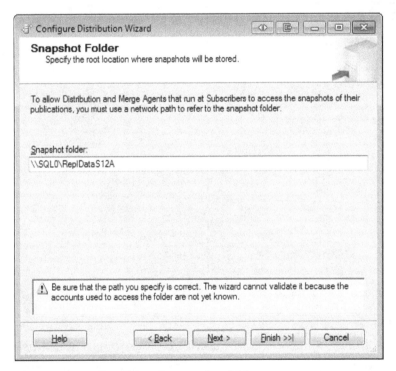

Figure 2-5: Specifying the snapshot folder.

When you set up the snapshot folder, you must also ensure that the appropriate rights have been granted on that folder. To keep this example simple, simply grant write access to the **Authenticated Users** group, as shown in Figure 2-6. Note, however, that this approach is not a recommended security best practice, and you should grant this access only for the purposes of these exercises.

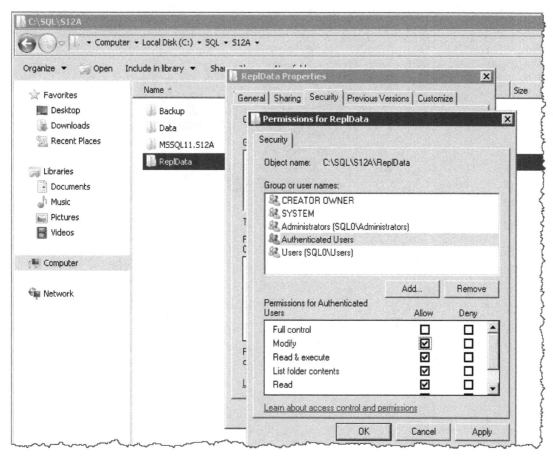

Figure 2-6: Granting access to the snapshot folder.

In addition, you must ensure that file sharing has been enabled on the snapshot folder and that read access to that share has been granted to the **Everyone** group, as shown in Figure 2-7. In a later chapter, you'll learn more about how to tighten security in this area. (To keep this entire exercise simple, there are a few other places in this chapter where you will select options that are not security best practices. All those will be tightened up in later chapters as well.)

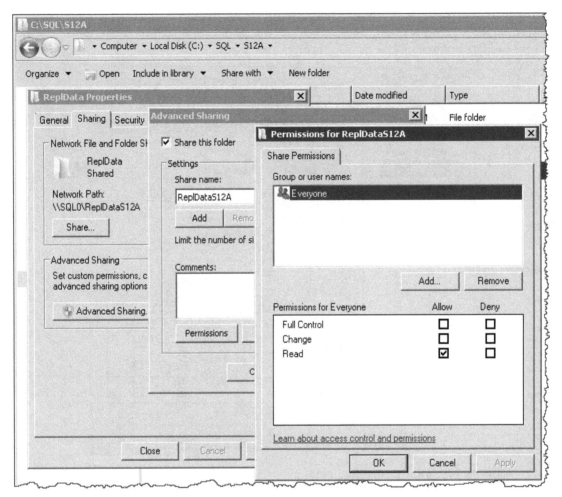

Figure 2-7: Granting access to the snapshot folder share.

If these folder security settings are not set up correctly, you'll have to deal with silent failures, that is, failures that don't generate obvious or even easy-to-find error messages, so double-check that you got them right. There are no completely silent errors in replication. However, sometimes everything looks fine at first glance and you have to really dig to see that there is a problem.

After you've set up your snapshot folder and its share, click **Next** on the **Snapshot Folder** page of the Configure Distribution Wizard. This takes you to the **Distribution Database** page, shown in Figure 2-8.

Figure 2-8:   Creating the distribution database.

7.   Specify the name of the distribution database and the folders where the data and log files should be located. The distribution database will be created based on these parameters. Be aware that this step will fail if a database with the selected name already exists.

After filling in the three fields, click **Next** to advance to the **Publishers** page, shown in Figure 2-9.

Figure 2-9:   Enabling Publishers to use this Distributor.

8. On the **Publishers** page, you specify the Publishers that should have access to the
    Distributor. Every SQL Server instance that you want to set up as a Publisher and
    that is going to use this Distributor needs to be added to this list. Note, however, that
    being on a Distributor's access list does not make a server a Publisher. It merely grants
    the server access to that Distributor.

You will always find the local instance preselected in this list. That is due to the fact that
a SQL Server instance that is set up to be a Distributor can use only itself as a Distributor
for publishing. Therefore the wizard automatically suggests the local instance to be
a Publisher on this list. Because we're actually going to use the local instance as our
Publisher, you can leave the default setting.

Click **Next** to advance to the **Wizard Actions** page, shown in Figure 2-10.

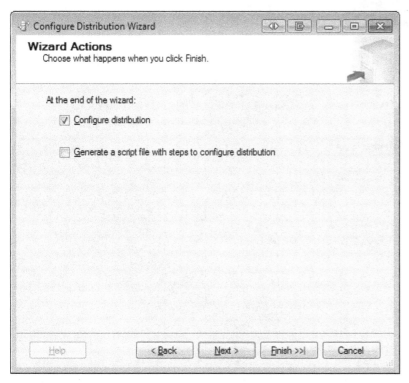

Figure 2-10:   Configuring the Wizard Actions page.

9. On the **Wizard Actions** page, you choose whether you want the wizard to execute your selections immediately or whether you want the wizard to create a script that you can execute at a later time. Ensure that the **Configure distribution** option is selected, and then click **Next** to move on to the **Complete the Wizard** page, shown in Figure 2-11.

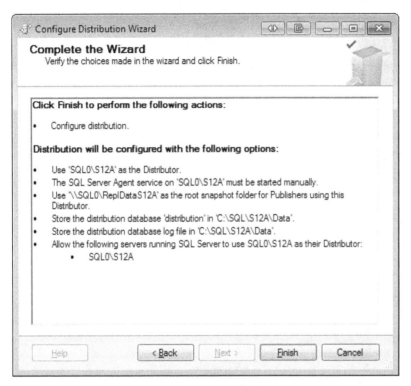

Figure 2-11: Reviewing your configuration options.

10. Review your configuration options, and then click **Finish** to create your Distributor.

As the wizard is creating the Distributor, it displays the **Configuring** page, shown in Figure 2-12. Here you'll find information about the wizard's progress as it works through each step.

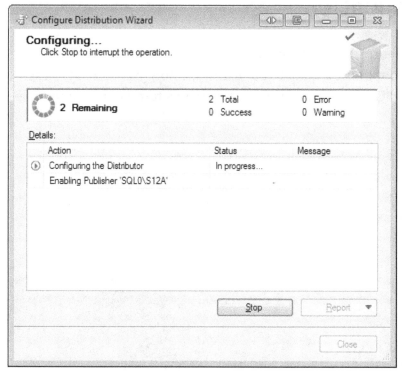

Figure 2-12: Reviewing the execution status.

After the wizard has created the Distributor, the **Configuring** page should show that the process has been successful. If the process was not successful, that information will be displayed instead.

Setting Up a Publication

Once you've set up your Distributor, you can create a publication; however, before you do that, you need a database containing a table to publish. So, before you start the next exercise, execute the Transact-SQL script in Listing 2-1 to create a test database and table for the publication.

```
USE MASTER;
GO
EXECUTE AS LOGIN = 'SA';
GO
CREATE DATABASE ReplA;
GO
USE ReplA;
GO
IF OBJECT_ID('dbo.Test') IS NOT NULL DROP TABLE dbo.Test;
GO
CREATE TABLE dbo.Test(
  Id INT IDENTITY(1,1) PRIMARY KEY,
  Data INT CONSTRAINT Test_Data_Dflt DEFAULT CHECKSUM(NEWID())
);

GO
INSERT INTO dbo.Test DEFAULT VALUES;
GO 1000
USE MASTER;
GO
REVERT;
GO
```

Listing 2-1:   Creating a test database and table for the publication.

Now you're ready to set up your publication. The following steps walk you through that process:

1. In **Object Explorer**, expand the **Replication** folder, right-click **Local Publication**, and then click **New Publication**, as shown in Figure 2-13.

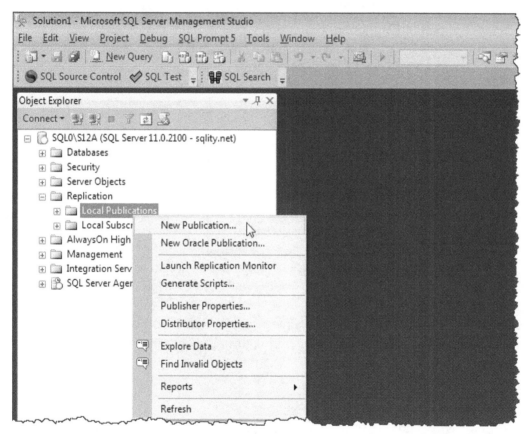

Figure 2-13:   Launching the New Publication Wizard.

The welcome page of the **New Publication Wizard** appears and provides information about creating a new publication, as shown in Figure 2-14.

Figure 2-14: The opening page of the New Publication Wizard.

You can select the **Do not show this starting page again** option if you don't want the page to appear when you start the wizard. Alternatively, you can ignore the option and simply click **Next.**

2. When the **Publication Database** page appears (shown in Figure 2-15), select the Rep1A database (the one you just created), and click **Next**.

Figure 2-15: Selecting the publication database.

3. On the **Publication Type** page (shown in Figure 2-16), you select the publication type, which corresponds to the type of replication you're implementing. For this exercise, select **Transactional publication**, and click **Next**.

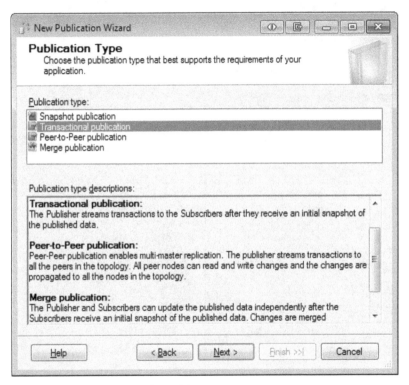

Figure 2-16:   Selecting the publication type.

4. On the **Articles** page (shown in Figure 2-17), you choose which articles should be part of this publication. Notice that the **Articles** page includes the **Objects to publish** pane. The pane lists the database objects hierarchically, similar to the way **Object Explorer** in SSMS displays database objects. Also, notice that the dbo.Test table you created earlier is included in that hierarchy. Select that table, and click **Next**.

Figure 2-17:   Selecting the articles to include in your publication.

5. The next page in the wizard is **Filter Table Rows** (shown in Figure 2-18). Here you define any filters that should be applied to your articles. You'll learn about filters in a later chapter, so for now, skip this page by clicking **Next**.

Figure 2-18:   Creating filters on a publication's articles.

6. On the **Snapshot Agent** page (shown in Figure 2-19), you specify when to run the Snapshot Agent. The Snapshot Agent creates that initial snapshot that is used to start the synchronization process. For this exercise, select the option **Create a snapshot immediately and keep the snapshot available to initialize subscriptions**, and then click **Next**.

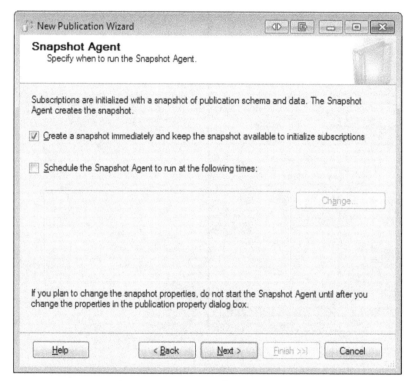

Figure 2-19: Specifying when to run the Snapshot Agent.

7. On the **Agent Security** page (shown in Figure 2-20), you specify the account to use to run the Snapshot Agent. For this exercise, you can use the SQL Server Agent account. Click the **Security Settings** button to select that account.

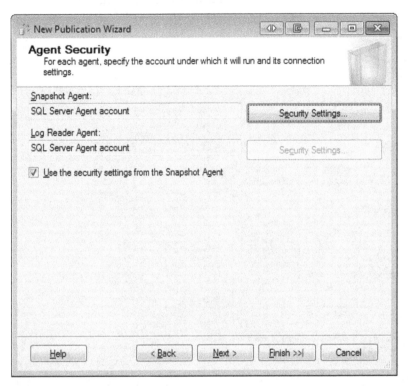

Figure 2-20:   Assigning a security account to the Snapshot Agent.

8. When the **Snapshot Agent Security** dialog box appears, select the option **Run under the SQL Server Agent service account**, as shown in Figure 2-21.

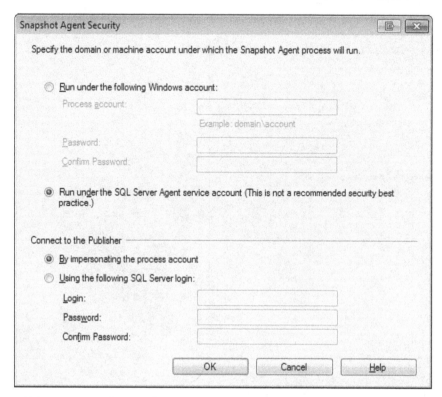

Figure 2-21: Selecting the security account for the Snapshot Agent.

9. Click **OK** to close the **Snapshot Agent Security** dialog box. You'll be returned to the **Agent Security** page of the **New Publication Wizard**. Click **Next** to continue to the **Wizard Actions** page, shown in Figure 2-22.

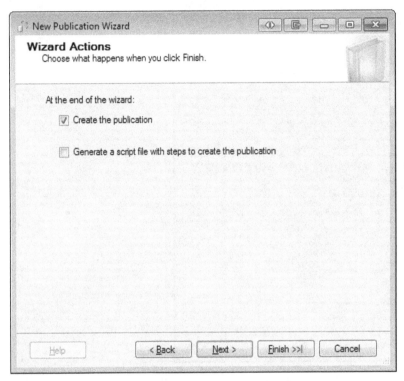

Figure 2-22:   Choosing what happens when you click **Finish**.

10. On the **Wizard Actions** page, you choose whether you want the wizard to create the publication immediately or to create a script you can execute at a later time. For this exercise, ensure that the **Create the publication** option is selected, and then click **Next** to move on to the **Complete the Wizard** page, shown in Figure 2-23.

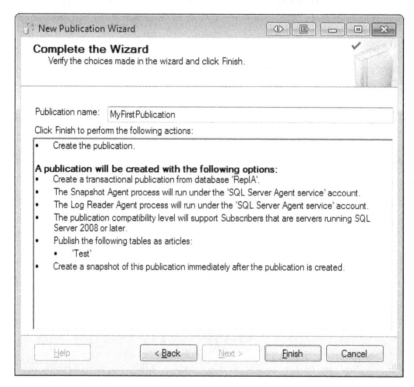

Figure 2-23: Reviewing your configuration options.

11. In the **Publication name** text box, type `MyFirstPublication`, review your
    configuration options, and then click **Finish** to create the publication.

As the wizard is creating the publication, it displays the **Creating Publication** page,
shown in Figure 2-24. Here you'll find information about the wizard's progress as it works
through each step of the process.

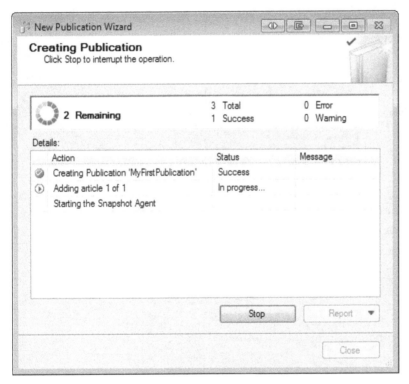

Figure 2-24: Viewing the execution status of the New Publication Wizard.

After the wizard has created the publication, the **Creating Publication** page should show
that the process has been successful. If the process was not successful, that information
will be displayed instead.

Setting Up a Subscription

The final step in setting up replication is to create the subscription. In most cases, the subscription will be on a different machine from the Publisher, but there are scenarios in which you want it to be on the same instance. To keep this exercise simple, you'll be creating your subscription on the same instance as well. But first, you must create your subscription database. To do so, use the Transact-SQL code in Listing 2-2 to create the **ReplB** database.

```
USE MASTER;
GO
EXECUTE AS LOGIN = 'SA';
GO
CREATE DATABASE ReplB;
GO
REVERT;
GO
```

Listing 2-2:   Creating the target database.

After you've created the database, you're ready to create your subscription. The following steps walk you through that process.

1. In **Object Explorer**, expand the **Replication** folder if necessary, right-click **Local Subscriptions**, and then click **New Subscriptions**, as shown in Figure 2-25.

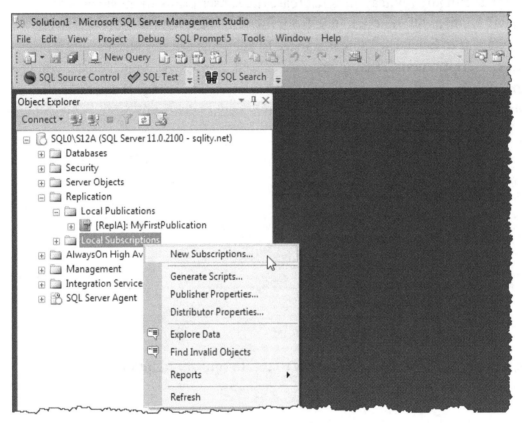

Figure 2-25:   Launching the New Subscription Wizard.

2. The Welcome page of the **New Subscription Wizard** appears (shown in Figure 2-26) and provides information about the wizard.

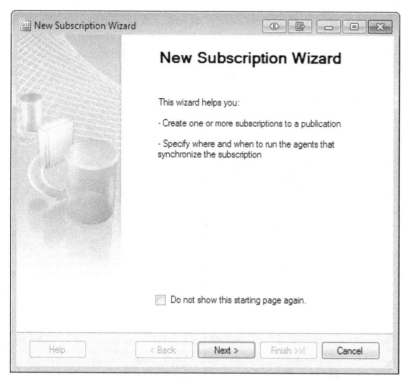

Figure 2-26: Opening page of the New Subscription Wizard.

You can select the **Do not show this starting page again** option if you don't want the page to appear when you start the wizard. Or you can ignore the option and click **Next**.

3. On the **Publication** page (shown in Figure 2-27), you select a publication you want
    to associate with your subscription. The publications are listed hierarchically in the
    Databases and publications pane. Select the publication you created in the previous
    section, and then click **Next**.

Figure 2-27: Selecting the publication for your subscription.

4. On the **Distribution Agent Location** page (shown in Figure 2-28), you specify whether this is a push or a pull subscription. In this exercise, you'll create a push subscription, which is the default setting. So all you need to do is to click **Next**.

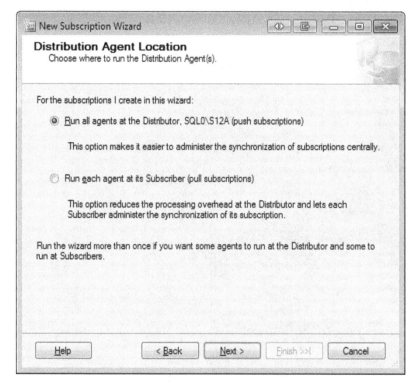

Figure 2-28: Choosing between a push or pull subscription.

5. On the **Subscribers** page (shown in Figure 2-29), you choose one or more Subscribers and the subscription database associated with each one.

For this exercise, select your server and the Repl1B database from the **Subscription Database** drop-down list, and then click **Next**.

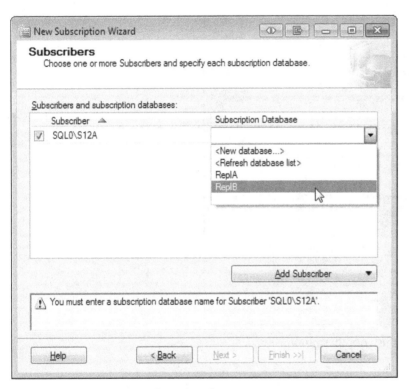

Figure 2-29:   Setting up the Subscriber.

6. The next screen is the **Distribution Agent Security** page (shown in Figure 2-30). The Distribution Agent is responsible for moving the data from the distribution database to the subscription database. To do so, it has to connect to the Distributor and the Subscriber. On the **Distribution Agent Security** page, you specify a security account for the Distribution Agent as well as connection details for the two required connections.

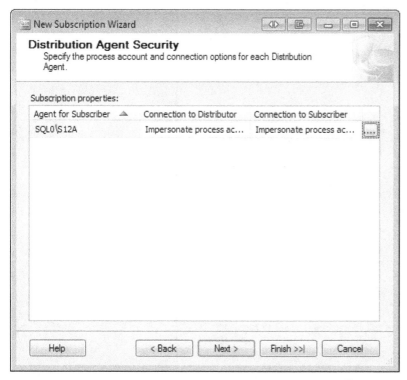

Figure 2-30:   Configuring the Distribution Agent's security.

Click the ellipsis button on the right side of the first row in the **Subscription properties** grid. This launches the **Distribution Agent Security** dialog box, shown in Figure 2-31.

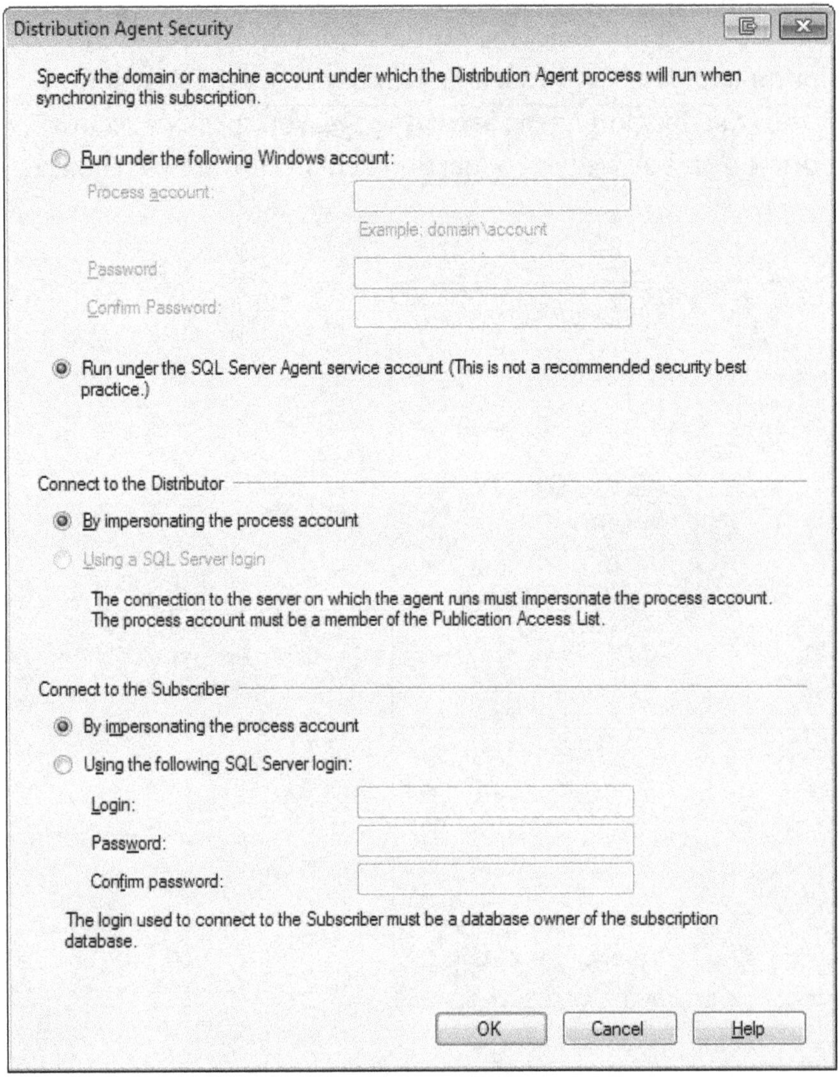

Figure 2-31: Selecting a security account for the Distribution Agent.

7. Select the option **Run under the SQL Server Agent service account**, and then click **OK**. You're returned to the **Distribution Agent Security** page of the **New Subscription Wizard**.

8. Click **Next** to continue to the **Synchronization Schedule** page, shown in Figure 2-32.

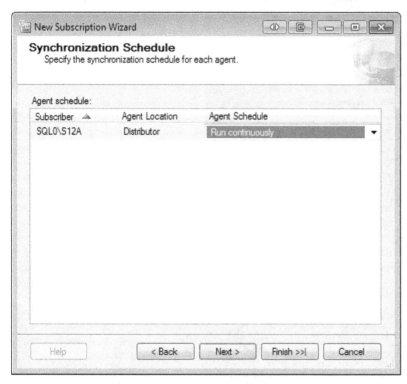

Figure 2-32: Setting up the synchronization schedule.

9. In the first row of the **Agent schedule** grid, select **Run continuously** from the **Agent Schedule** drop-down list, and then click **Next** to move on to the **Initialize Subscriptions** page, shown in Figure 2-33.

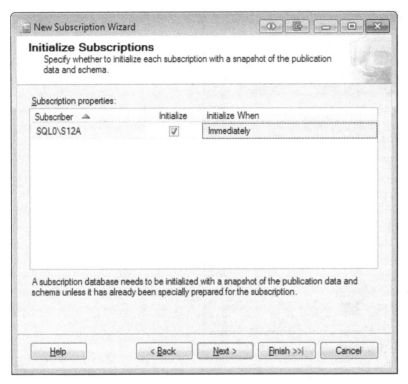

Figure 2-33: Initializing your subscription.

10. For this exercise, you want to initialize your subscription immediately, so use the default settings, and then click **Next** to continue to the **Wizard Actions** page, shown in Figure 2-34.

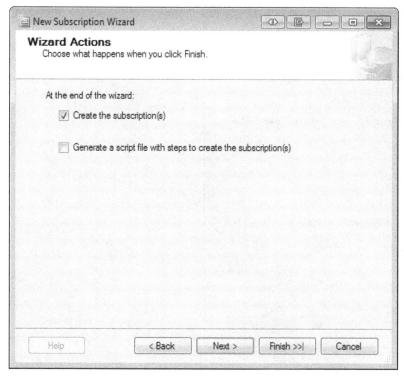

Figure 2-34: Determining what actions the wizard should take.

11. Ensure that the **Create the subscription(s)** option is selected, and then click **Next**. The **Complete the Wizard** page appears, as shown in Figure 2-35.

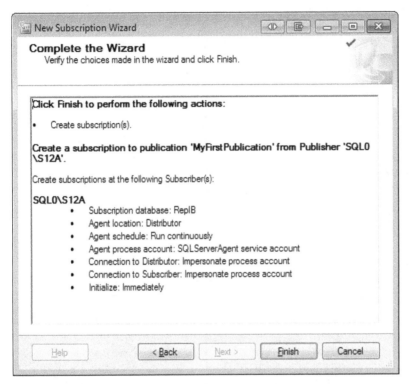

Figure 2-35: Reviewing your configuration options.

12. Review the configuration options, and click **Finish** to create the subscription.

As the wizard is creating the subscription, it displays the **Creating Subscription(s)** page, shown in Figure 2-36. Here you'll find information about the wizard's progress as it creates the subscription.

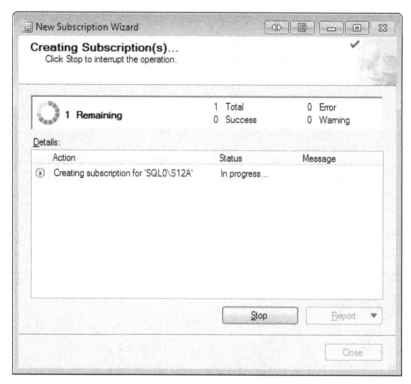

Figure 2-36: Viewing the execution status.

After the wizard has created the subscription, the Creating Subscription(s) page should show that the process has been successful. If the process was not successful, information to that effect will be displayed instead.

Success!

When you created the Test table in the ReplA database, you inserted 1,000 rows into it. After the initial snapshot is transferred over to the subscription database, the Test table in the ReplB database will also contain the same 1,000 rows.

A couple of minutes after you set up the Subscriber, you can run the script in Listing 2-3 to verify that replication pushed all the data to the Subscriber as expected. This script joins the ReplA.dbo.Test and ReplB.dbo.Test tables to show which rows were replicated correctly.

```
SELECT TOP ( 20 )
        A.Id AS [ReplA.Id],
        A.Data AS [ReplA.Data],
        B.Id AS [ReplB.Id],
        B.Data AS [ReplB.Data]
FROM    ReplA.dbo.Test A
FULL OUTER JOIN ReplB.dbo.Test B
        ON A.Id = B.Id
ORDER BY A.Id DESC;
```

Listing 2-3:   Comparing data in the Publisher and Subscriber.

You can also run further tests of your own, such as inserting and updating rows in ReplA.dbo.Test in order to watch the changes magically appear in ReplB.dbo.Test.

Summary

In this chapter, we worked through several exercises that stepped you through the process of configuring a simple replication setup. In this case, our setup was a transactional replication configuration. To keep the exercises simple, we configured our Distributor, Publisher, and Subscriber on the same instance of SQL Server 2012. Chances are, in a real-world scenario, you'll want to set up at least some of those components on different instances and different servers. As we progress through the book, you'll see how to do just that. In the meantime, you should now have a sense of how to basic replication setup works.

Chapter 3: The Role of the Distributor

The Distributor is the core component in a SQL Server replication setup. The Distributor controls and executes the processes that move the data from one server to another. SQL Server comes with a set of Windows executables that carry out the processes that make replication work. These programs are called replication agents. In a default setup of replication, most (or potentially all) replication agents run on the Distributor. The Distributor also stores metadata about publications and subscriptions in the distribution database.

Distribution Components

A number of specific components are important to the Distributor and replication in general. They include the distribution database, snapshot folder, and replication agents. Although Chapter 1 covers these components, this chapter provides more details about how they apply to the Distributor and the distribution process.

The distribution database

When you set up distribution, SQL Server creates a distribution database. The distribution database is classified as a system database so, to find it in **Object Explorer**, you need to drill down into the **System Databases** subfolder of the **Databases** folder. You can access **Object Explorer** through SSMS.

You can install multiple distribution databases on a Distributor. If multiple Publishers use the same Distributor, you can reduce contention if each Publisher uses a separate distribution database. However, the selection of which distribution database to use is a Publisher-wide setting, so different publications on the same Publisher must share the same distribution database.

The distribution database contains metadata about a Publisher's publications and their articles. In addition, the database contains metadata about the progress and state of the replication process. In the case of transactional replication, the database also contains any Transact-SQL commands that were executed on the Publisher and that need to be replicated. For each command, all the data necessary to re-execute that command is also stored in this database.

Because of the amount of data that the distribution database must store, it can become quite large, so make sure you have enough room on your hard drive to accommodate its projected growth.

The size required for the distribution database is dependent on many factors. For example, assume that our database includes the dbo.MyProc stored procedure, which inserts data into seven tables published in a transactional replication setup. If the procedure itself is published, the data needed to re-execute it on the Subscriber will be stored in the distribution database. If, on the other hand, the procedure itself is not published, or if the seven inserts get executed ad hoc by the application, each INSERT statement with all the column values will be stored. Not surprisingly, this approach requires a lot more space in the distribution database than the stored procedure, although both approaches accomplish the same thing.

That means the distribution database size is affected by the number of statements, their frequency, and the type of statements that are executed by your application to insert or update data. Other factors affecting the size of the distribution database are the time it takes to get the data to the Subscribers (latency) as well as the different retention times, as we'll see later in the book.

The snapshot folder

Although we don't cover snapshot replication in any detail in this book, it's important to understand how the snapshot folder works. By default, the first initialization and data synchronization of a replication setup, regardless of the replication type, utilizes the mechanisms of snapshot replication. Any re-initialization also makes use of this infrastructure. Because the snapshot folder lies at the heart of this process, it's important to set it up correctly and plan for enough space on the drive.

The snapshot folder is used by snapshot replication to hold a snapshot of the replicated tables. Every time snapshot replication runs, a snapshot of all the replicated tables is saved to the snapshot folder. This is accomplished by using the SQL Server bcp utility.

The snapshot folder can be a share anywhere on the network. The snapshot folder can also be an unshared local folder on the Distributor, but this significantly restricts other available options, so we won't pursue this strategy any further. Going forward, we'll use the term "snapshot folder" specifically to mean a folder that is accessible via a share over the network.

The Windows account that is used to execute the Snapshot Agent needs to have write permission on this folder, and most other agents need to be granted read access. Information about setting up replication agent security is covered at the appropriate places throughout the rest of the book.

The replication agents

By now, you should have a clear picture of what the term "replication agent" represents, so let's quickly rehash the most important points. The SQL Server database engine does not execute the replication process. In fact, the term "replication" actually refers a set of technologies made up of components independent of the database engine. Many of those components are the replication agents.

If you follow the standard setup for replication, as described in this book, SQL Server will create SQL Server Agent jobs that execute and control the replication agents. However, you do not have to follow that pattern; the agents are independent executables, so you can also execute them from the command line.

With the exception of a pull-subscription setup, all agents reside on the Distributor. For pull subscriptions, the Subscriber executes its own Distribution Agent in order to pull the data from the distributor. Chapter 7 explains pull subscriptions in more detail. Chapters 4 and 8 cover the roles of all the agents in more detail.

Best Practices

A replication setup often follows the local distributor model, in which all parts of the Distributor live and run on the Publisher. This model is easier to implement than other models; however, it takes a measurable toll on the Publisher's performance. If the impact becomes too great, you should move distribution to its own server. With the Distributor and all its processes on a separate machine, the impact on the Publisher is minimal.

If you have a lot of Publishers using the same Distributor, the distribution database might become a bottleneck. To alleviate this, you should install one distribution database per publishing SQL Server instance. This also significantly simplifies backup and recovery planning.

Setting up Distribution

The exercises in this and the following chapters attempt to show security best practices and point out the requirements for a full-scale installation of replication. To that end, the exercises assume that the Publisher, Distributor, and Subscriber are three distinct machines. If you plan to try out these exercises – and I encourage you to do so – you need to identify the three servers now. Although the exercises in this chapter are concerned primarily with setting up the Distributor, some of the steps require actions on the other machines.

Again, I encourage you to use three separate machines for these exercises. There are several pages in the wizards that won't show if you're on a single machine. Also, to see the difference between push and pull subscriptions, the Distributor and Subscriber must be different machines. Finally, combining two or more machines can hide mistakes that don't show up unless you set up replication on separate machines. To make sure you get the most out of this and the following chapters, using three machines is indispensable.

Because most enterprise networks are set up with a Windows domain, we'll assume that the three machines are part of a Windows domain. While it's possible to set up replication outside of a domain, it is not recommended. This book will therefore not go into any details on how that works. However, if you're forced to work outside of a domain, you must ensure that each user account used for replication exists on every machine and is configured with the same password, instead of existing just on the domain controller.

The rest of this chapter walks through how to set up a Distributor. We will go through this setup in more detail than we did in Chapter 2. When you have completed the exercises, you'll have prepared a SQL Server instance to act as a Distributor in a full-scale replication setup. You will know what the different settings mean and how to set them based on your requirements.

As you work through these exercises, you might notice that some of the screenshots seem to be repeated from Chapter 2. Although we use some of the same interface components, such as the **Configure Distribution Wizard**, we won't be using those components in exactly the same way, so be aware that there are differences.

Removing replication

To be able to follow along with the exercises in the next sections, you need to start with SQL Servers on which replication is not yet installed. If replication has been set up on any of your servers – maybe because you followed the steps in Chapter 2 – you need to remove it now. However, before you continue, make sure that the existing replication setup is not needed. It can be very time consuming to reconfigure a replication setup if you've accidentally dropped it.

The easiest way to remove replication is to connect to the SQL Server instance in **Object Explorer** and generate a script to delete replication, as described in the following steps:

1. Right-click the **Replication** folder and then click **Generate Scripts**, as shown in Figure 3-1.

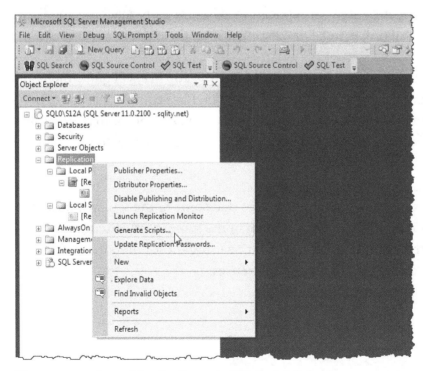

Figure 3-1:   Launching the Generate SQL Script dialog box.

This launches the **Generate SQL Script** dialog box (shown in Figure 3-2). Using this dialog box, you can generate scripts that either create or delete replication components.

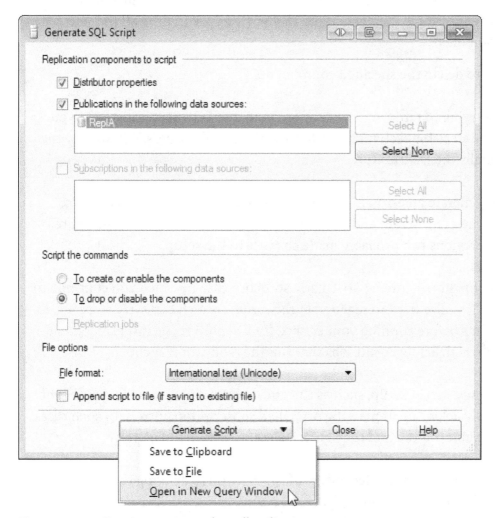

Figure 3-2:   Creating a script to drop all replication components.

2. In the **Script the commands** section, select the option **To drop or disable the components**.

3. Select all available components that are listed. That means the Distributor, all publications, and all subscriptions that are not grayed out.

4. At the bottom of the screen, click **Generate Script**, and then click **Open in New Query Window**. A script is then generated that you can use to drop all the selected replication components.

5. Run the script to delete the specified components.

If the setup you're trying to remove involves more than one SQL Server instance, you have to repeat these steps for each instance. Start with the Subscribers, followed by the Publishers, and finally the Distributor.

If any of the steps generate an error, make sure you're removing the instances in the correct order, and then regenerate and run the new scripts. You'll need to regenerate them because the previous run probably made changes to the setup.

In some cases, you might run into a particularly stubborn case in which you continue to receive errors even if you've tried to regenerate the script. In such cases, try stopping all the replication agents before running your scripts. (In a default replication setup, that means stopping the SQL Server Agent jobs that run the replication agents.)

6. If you have a single server setup, such as the one described in Chapter 2, you might have to manually delete any remaining orphaned subscription entries. In such cases, right-click the subscription, and then click **Delete**, as shown in Figure 3-3.

When prompted to confirm your deletions, confirm that you're deleting the correct object, and accept the changes accordingly.

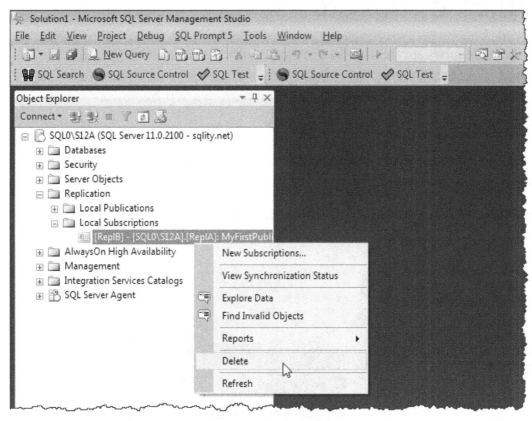

Figure 3-3:   Dropping orphaned subscription entries.

Setting up the Distributor

Once you've ensured that any previously installed replication components have been removed from your SQL Server instances, you're ready to set up your Distributor. The following steps walk you through the process of configuring a SQL Server instance as the Distributor:

1. Open **Object Explorer**, if necessary, and connect to the SQL Server instance that you plan to set up as your Distributor.

2. Right-click the **Replication** folder and then click **Configure Distribution**, as shown in Figure 3-4.

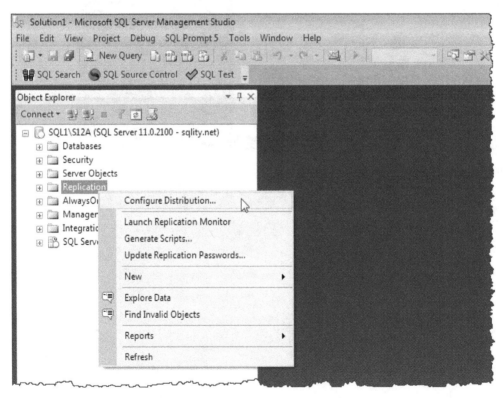

Figure 3-4:   Launching the Configure Distribution Wizard.

3. This launches the **Configure Distribution Wizard**. If the first page to appear is the Welcome screen, click **Next** to go to the **Distributor** page (shown in Figure 3-5).

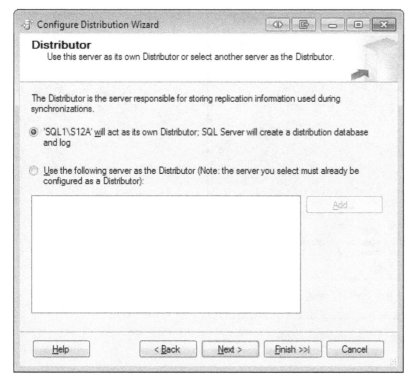

Figure 3-5:   Selecting the current SQL Server instance as the Distributor.

Because we're setting up the Distributor on the current SQL Server instance, select the first option on the **Distributor** page, and then click **Next**.

4. The **Snapshot Folder** page appears and asks for the snapshot folder location, as shown in Figure 3-6.

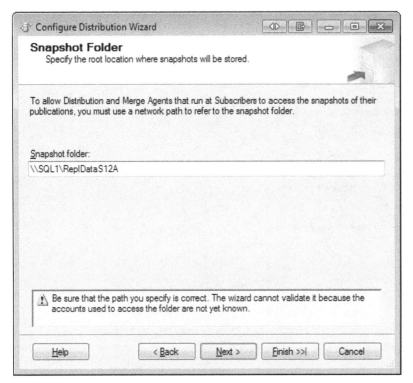

Figure 3-6:   Specifying the location of the snapshot folder.

Most processes that access the snapshot folder run on the Distributor. For this reason, it's considered a best practice to create a network share on the Distributor itself. That gives direct and therefore fast access to the local processes while also allowing for scenarios such as pull subscriptions that require remote access. (Pull subscriptions are covered in Chapter 7.)

Wherever you place the snapshot folder, make sure that the drive has enough room to hold a bcp copy of all replicated tables. The details on who needs to have which type of access to the snapshot folder are discussed in later chapters.

Enter the full path to the network share you want to use, and then click **Next**.

5. The next page of the wizard is the **Distribution Database** page. Here, you provide details about the distribution database, as shown in Figure 3-7.

Figure 3-7: Providing details about the distribution database.

Depending on the number of Publishers using this Distributor, the number of articles published and, most importantly, how often those articles change, the distribution database can become quite large and busy. Follow the standard best practices for placing and sizing busy databases when picking a location for the distribution database files.

While it's often a good idea to do so, the Configure Distribution Wizard does not allow you to create multiple distribution databases. The section, *Implementing multiple distribution databases*, later in the chapter, provides detailed information on why it might be a good idea to have multiple distribution databases, and on how to set them up.

Provide a name for the database and the folder locations for the data and log files, and then click **Next**.

6.   On the next page of the wizard, **Publishers**, you specify which servers can use the Distributor when they become Publishers. Figure 3-8 shows the **Publishers** page.

Figure 3-8:   Registering a Publisher to use the Distributor.

Every Publisher needs to be registered with the Distributor. This page shows a list of all registered Publishers. Because we're just setting up this Distributor, the list will contain only the Distributor itself when the page first appears.

To enable the instance you selected as Publisher to use this Distributor, click the **Add** button, and then select SQL Server Publisher in the drop-down list that appears. A standard SQL Server **Connect to Server** dialog box appears and lets you pick your publishing server instance. After you've connected to that instance, it will appear in the list, as shown in Figure 3-8.

For the Distribution Database option associated with the new Publisher, you'll find that the distribution database is automatically selected and you can't change it. You can find more information about how to use multiple distribution databases later in this chapter.

There are a few other settings that are automatically selected as well. You can get to them by clicking the ellipsis button at the end of the row that lists your Publisher. Chapter 5 provides more information about those settings.

7. After adding your Publisher, uncheck the Distributor itself, as this server will not be used as a Publisher in this example.

Once you've added the Publisher and deselected the Distributor, click **Next**.

8. When you add a SQL Server instance that is not the Distributor, as you've just done, the next page to appear in the **Configure Distribution Wizard** is the **Distributor Password** page (shown in Figure 3-9).

Figure 3-9:   Providing a password for connecting to the Distributor.

On this page, you specify the password that remote Publishers must use to access the Distributor. Every time you set up a Publisher and connect it to the Distributor, you must provide this password. Be sure to pick a secure password and store it somewhere safe.

Enter the password (twice), and then click **Next**.

9. The next few pages of the **Configure Distribution Wizard** are the finalizing pages that you saw in Chapter 2. Be sure to select the **Configure distribution** option (on the **Wizard Actions** page), review the configuration steps, and let the wizard do its magic.

Setting up distribution on the Publisher

In the previous section, you learned how to register the Publisher with the Distributor. However, that step alone is not enough to set up distribution. You must also register the Distributor with the Publisher, as outlined in the following steps:

1. In **Object Explorer**, connect to the SQL Server instance that you've designated as your Publisher.

2. Right-click the **Replication** folder and then click **Configure Distribution** to open the **Configure Distribution Wizard**. Refer back to Figure 3-4 if you're unsure about this step.

3. When the wizard appears, skip to the **Distributor** page. Select the option **Use the following server as the Distributor**, and then click the **Add** button.

4. A standard **Connect to Server** dialog box will appear. Select the SQL Server instance that you set up as your Distributor in the previous exercise.

5.   When you're returned to **Configure Distribution Wizard**, the **Distributor** page should look similar to what is shown in Figure 3-10. After you review the information, click **Next**.

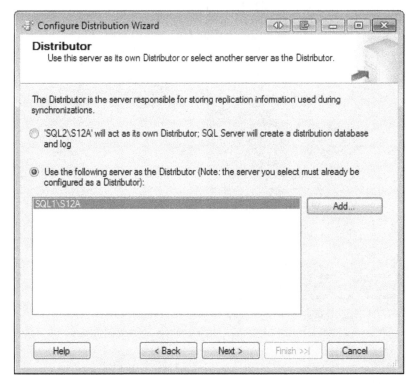

Figure 3-10:   Selecting a remote Distributor.

6.   The next page in the **Configure Distribution Wizard** is the **Administrative Password** page (shown in Figure 3-11).

Figure 3-11: Specifying the administrative password.

The password asked for here is the same password that we picked for the Distributor in the previous exercise on the **Distributor Password** page.

Enter the password (twice), and then click **Next**.

7. The remaining pages let you pick whether the wizard should create a script or should run the setup immediately. For this exercise, you should run the setup immediately. You'll be able to review the steps that the wizard will take when performing that setup. Once the wizard has completed running, the distribution setup is complete.

Implementing multiple distribution databases

If you want to use one Distributor to support several Publishers, you should consider creating a distribution database for each Publisher. This not only reduces contention on each distribution database, but it can also improve your ability to troubleshoot problems and recover from a disaster. The following steps describe how to create an additional distribution database:

1. In **Object Explorer**, connect to the SQL Server instance that you've set up as the Distributor.

2. Right-click the **Replication** folder, and then click **Distributor Properties**, as shown in Figure 3-12.

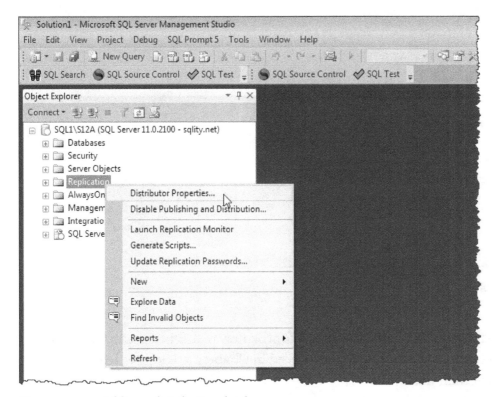

Figure 3-12:   Adding a distribution database.

This will open the **Distributor Properties** dialog box. On the **General** page, you'll see a list of the installed distribution databases.

3. Click the **New** button beneath the list of distribution databases. This opens the **New Distribution Database** dialog box, shown in Figure 3-13.

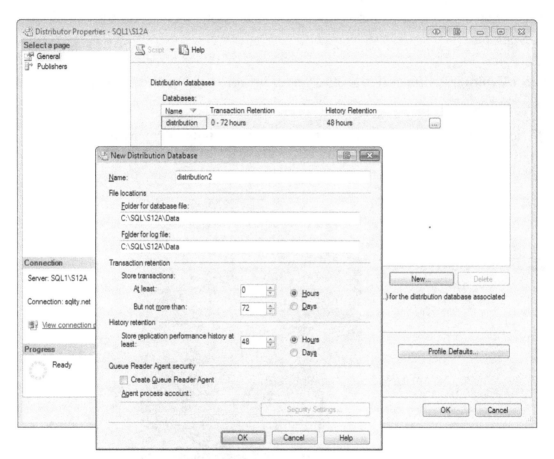

Figure 3-13: Adding a distribution database.

Here you specify the name and folder locations for the new distribution database. You can also specify retention values, which are covered in Chapter 7. For now, leave these retention options at their default values.

4. Click **OK** to create the new distribution database, and then close the **New Distribution Database** dialog box. You'll be returned to the **Distribution Properties** dialog box, which will now list both distribution databases.

5. Switch to the **Publishers** page of the **Distribution Properties** dialog box.

6. Click the **Add** button, and then click **Add SQL Server Publisher**. A **Connect to Server** dialog box appears (shown in Figure 3-14). This lets you register additional Publishers with this Distributor.

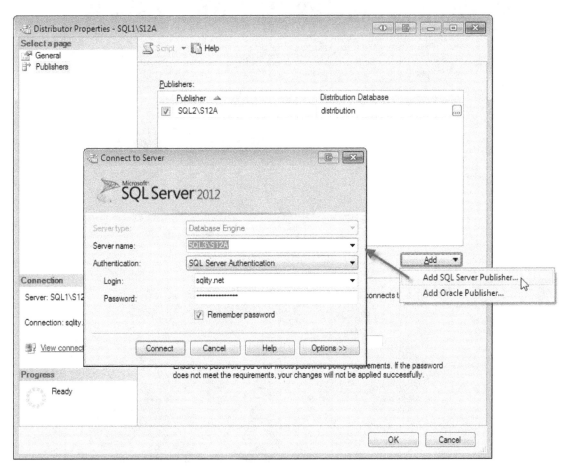

Figure 3-14:   Registering Publishers with the Distributor.

7. Select the SQL Server instance that you want to add as a Publisher. Then select an authentication type and, if applicable, a login and password. Next, click **Connect**. The Publisher will be added to the list of registered Publishers on the **Publishers** page of the **Distributor Properties** dialog box.

8. In the row for the new Publisher, select the distribution database you want to use for that Publisher from the **Distribution Database** drop-down list (next to the Publisher's name), as shown in Figure 3-15.

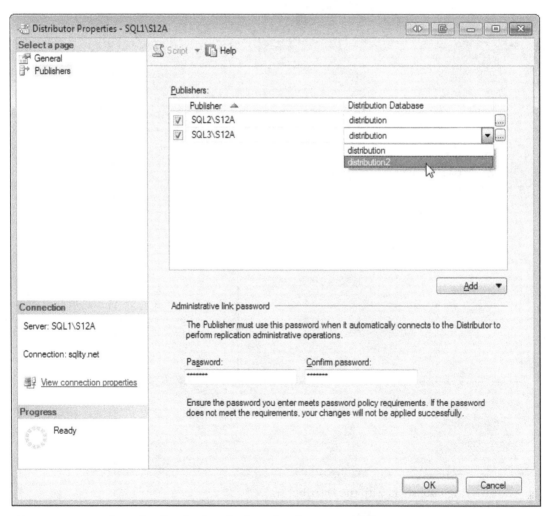

Figure 3-15:   Picking the distribution database for the new Publisher.

Make sure you select the correct database, because once you click **OK**, this selection cannot be changed. The only way to change the distribution database for an existing Publisher is to drop all publications on that Publisher and then delete the Publisher from the list of registered Publishers on the Distributor. You'll then need to set everything up again. So make sure you select the right distribution database in the first place.

9.   Click **OK** to close the **Distributor Properties** dialog box.

For more details on how to handle multiple distribution databases, check out the SQL Server Central article, *Scaling out the distribution database* at HTTP://WWW.SQLSERVERCENTRAL.COM/ARTICLES/REPLICATION/69663/.[1]

Summary

In this chapter, we prepared a SQL Server instance to be a Distributor for replication. We also prepared another SQL Server instance to use that Distributor. We will set up the Publisher for transactional replication in Chapter 5, followed by a Subscriber in Chapter 7.

At this point, there is not much to see on the Distributor. None of the agents are running yet, and nothing else will show any activity. Although there are now distribution databases on the server, they're well hidden amongst the system databases.

The only visible change is to the context menu of the **Replication** folder in **Object Explorer**. The menu now includes the **Distributor Properties** option, instead of **Configure Distribution**. This might feel a little disappointing – spending so much effort and having nothing to show for it. Keep in mind, however, that the Distributor is the most important piece of a transactional replication installation. Without it, no data would move anywhere. The reward for this work will come soon, so let's get started setting up the Publisher.

---

[1]

Chapter 4: Transactional Replication – the Replication Agents

Once you've configured the Distributor, you're ready to set up the other replication components. The way in which you configure them depends on the type of replication you plan to implement. In the next few chapters, we'll examine how to set up transactional replication. Before we get into the specific configuration details, however, you should have an understanding of the main components that drive replication: the replication agents. This chapter explains how the replication agents are used in transactional replication to carry out the various replication-related actions. Transactional replication utilizes three different agents, and in this chapter we cover each one in detail.

Replication Agents

The SQL Server Database Engine does not carry out the tasks associated with executing transactional replication. Instead, the replication process is driven by several external services known as replication agents. Replication agents are Windows programs that connect to the replication servers and facilitate data movement.

At first glance, there seems to be an overwhelming amount of moving parts required to make transactional replication work. However, when you look more closely, you'll find that there are really only three main players: the Snapshot Agent, the Log Reader Agent, and the Distribution Agent. Figure 4-1 provides an overview of the three primary replication agents. (Bi-directional transactional replication also utilizes the Queue Reader Agent, which applies changes made on a Subscriber to the Publisher. For more information about the Queue Reader Agent, check out SQL Server Books Online.)

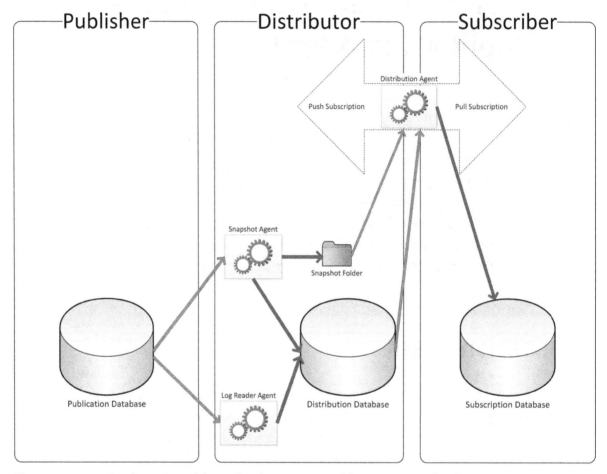

Figure 4-1:   Configuration of the replication agents used for transactional replication.

The arrows in the figure show how the replication agents work with the data. The arrows indicate the direction of the data flow; the lighter arrows indicate read access, whereas the black arrows indicate write access. For example, the Log Reader Agent reads data from the publication database and writes data to the distribution database.

The Snapshot Agent and the Log Reader Agent reside on the Distributor. The Distribution Agent, however, can live either on the Distributor or the Subscriber, depending on whether the subscription has been set up to follow the push or the pull model. Let's take a closer look at each of these agents to get a better sense of how they work.

Snapshot Agent

The Snapshot Agent is the main player in snapshot replication. However, in transactional replication as well as all other replication types, the Snapshot Agent performs the initial synchronization of the replicated objects. Although this is not the only way to execute the initial synchronization, it is certainly the most convenient way.

Generating a snapshot involves two steps. First, the Snapshot Agent generates the scripts necessary to drop and create the replicated objects on the Subscriber. After that, the agent uses the bcp utility to generate files that contain copies of the data from all the published tables. The Snapshot Agent places the files in the snapshot folder and maintains a record of each file in the distribution database.

If, after creating the snapshot, you run the SELECT statement shown in Listing 4-1 against the distribution database, you'll see that the MSRepl_commands table contains one record for each file that was generated. (The table also contains records for other replication-related activity, such as changes to the data, so don't be surprised to see a lot of other records in there.)

```
SELECT  publisher_database_id,
        xact_seqno,
        type,
        article_id,
        originator_id,
        command_id,
        partial_command,
        CAST(command AS NVARCHAR(MAX)) AS command_text,
        command,
        hashkey,
        originator_lsn
FROM    dbo.MSrepl_commands;
```

Listing 4-1:   Retrieving information from the MSRepl_commands table about the data files.

During snapshot replication, SQL Server places a shared lock on the published tables while the bcp utility generates the data files. This allows the Snapshot Agent to guarantee transactional consistency of the data; however, it blocks other requests trying to write to those tables while the locks are in place. Depending on the size of the tables, the time it takes to create the snapshot can be substantial, but this is the only way to guarantee transactional consistency in snapshot replication.

In transactional replication, the shared table locks are not required. Starting with SQL Server 2005, if you set up transactional replication through SQL Server Management Studio (SSMS), SQL Server uses a different method to generate snapshots. This method allows changes to the published tables during the snapshot generation process.

When the process starts, SQL Server places a table lock on all tables involved in the publication and then writes a marker to the log file associated with the publication database. The marker indicates the beginning of the snapshot process. Right after the marker is written, SQL Server releases the locks. The Snapshot Agent then generates the bcp files without taking further table locks, but be aware that SQL Server maintains fine-grained, short-lived locks at the page and row levels.

After the Snapshot Agent creates the bcp files, SQL Server writes another marker to the log file of the publication database, recording the end of the snapshot process. These markers are then used by the Log Reader Agent to copy any changes committed to the published objects (as recorded in the log file between those two markers) to the distribution database.

When it is time to apply the snapshot, the Distribution Agent uses the scripts generated by the Snapshot Agent during the first step to drop and re-create the tables in the subscription database. It then bulk-loads the data from the bcp files in the snapshot folder into those tables. During the load process, SQL Server maintains table locks on all subscription tables affected. With the table locks still in place, as the last step, the Distribution Agent uses the log data that captured the activity during the snapshot generation to bring all tables into a transactionally consistent state.

Log Reader Agent

The Log Reader Agent copies the transaction log records from the publication database to the distribution database for all transactions that modified published database objects.

Each time a database object changes, SQL Server first writes a record to the database's transaction log. After that, SQL Server applies the changes to the actual data pages. When the transaction is committed, SQL Server forces the log records to be written to disk before signaling success. This process is an integral part of any ACID-compliant relational database management system. (An ACID-compliant system is one that conforms to the principles of atomicity, consistency, isolation, and durability.)

During this process, SQL Server records all the information necessary to apply or reapply the changes to the data pages. For example, if a power outage occurs before all data pages have been written to disk, but after the transaction committed, these log records allow SQL Server to redo the changes and finish the write operations upon restart.

Transactional replication uses the same information to apply changes made to published objects in the publication database to the target objects in the subscription database.

If a data manipulation language (DML) statement such as INSERT, UPDATE, or DELETE or a data definition language (DDL) statement such as ALTER TABLE modifies a published object in the publication database, SQL Server marks the log file record of that change with a replication flag. SQL Server does not mark changes to non-replicated objects, even if they are in the same transaction as published objects.

The Log Reader Agent connects to the Publisher, searches the log file for records that are marked with the replication flag, and copies to the distribution database the information necessary to apply the changes to the subscription database. Because of this process, replication can have a significant impact on the log file size of the publication database.

One reason for this has to do with Virtual Log Files (VLFs). A log file is split into VLFs, and as long as one is required, that VLF and the ones that logically follow cannot be reused. For example, a VLF might be required for a lengthy period of time for long-running transactions or outstanding log backups. Only after SQL Server does not need a VLF to warrant transactional consistency will it be reused. SQL Server manages this process automatically.

With replication, however, there is an additional reason that can prevent VLFs from being reused. Because the Log Reader Agent has to process every log record in the publication database, reuse cannot occur until the Log Reader Agent processes all records in the VLF. Several situations can prevent the agent from processing log records in a timely manner. The most obvious ones are the Distributor being down or the Log Reader Agent not running. An overloaded Distributor can also cause a delay in log record processing.

When the VLFs cannot be reused, the log file must grow to continue to function, and the file fills up. Depending on the log file's autogrow setting, this operation can take a significant amount of resources. If the log file has reached its configured maximum size or the drive is full, SQL Server will prevent any further write access to that database until the issue is resolved.

After you've set up replication, keep an eye out for the size of the log file associated with your publication database. You can use the query in Listing 4-2 to verify whether replication is preventing log record reuse. If the log_reuse_wait_desc column contains the value REPLICATION over an extended period of time, replication is the reason for unexpected log growth.

```
SELECT   log_reuse_wait_desc,
         Name
FROM     sys.databases
```

Listing 4-2:   Querying sys.databases to discover issues related to VLF reuse.

Distribution Agent

The Distribution Agent moves data from the distribution database to the subscription database. The Distribution Agent connects to the Distributor and reads the recorded changes. Then it connects to the Subscriber and applies those changes in the order they occurred. That order is guaranteed within a single subscription and single publication, but not across publications. In some cases, this can lead to logical inconsistencies. For example, if you have two tables that have a foreign key relationship on the Publisher and those two tables are published in separate publications, two inserts into the two tables could get executed in the wrong order on the Subscriber, leading to a temporarily orphaned record in the child table. However, replication by default does not copy foreign key constraints to the Subscriber, so you will not receive an error if a logical inconsistency should occur. To be safe, tables that have a foreign key relationship should always be published in the same publication.

If the subscription is a push subscription, the Distribution Agent runs on the Distributor. That means that the Distributor is in control of when the distribution to each Subscriber occurs. For a pull subscription the agent is located on the Subscriber, in which case the Subscriber controls the synchronization schedule. In most cases, you'll want to use the push subscription model, but if you have several Subscribers and you need to start and stop the data flow to each of them at different times (such as having to wait for a nightly reporting process), you're better off using the pull subscription model.

Summary

In this chapter, we discussed the internals of the replication agents. We looked at the purpose of each replication agent in detail and discovered what steps each is taking to make replication work. We also recognized that a replication process that is running slow can have a significant impact on the size of the publication database's log file.

After all this theory, let's now move on to actually setting up transactional replication. In Chapter 5, we'll create a publication, in Chapter 6 we'll set up the permissions necessary to set up a subscription, and in Chapter 7 we'll subscribe to that publication. Chapter 8 will close out the section on transactional replication with an in-depth look at the different SQL Server Agent jobs involved in transactional replication.

Chapter 5: Transactional Replication – the Publication

A publication is a set of articles made available as a unit for others to subscribe to. The articles are associated with objects in a database on the Publisher. In transactional replication, each transaction that changes one or more of these objects is recorded in the log. The information required to replay those changes is then made available to the Subscribers so they can apply the changes to their copy of the published objects.

A Publisher, then, is any SQL Server instance that hosts a database with a defined publication. You can define one or more publications on a Publisher, and you can define one or more articles on each publication. All articles within a single publication must reside in the same database, with each article corresponding to a single database object. However, articles in multiple publications can map to the same database object.

In this chapter, we'll take a deeper look at what is involved in setting up a transactional publication and walk you through a set of exercises that demonstrate the process. After working through these exercises, you'll be able to create your own transactional publication and configure the available options in an optimal way for your environment. You'll also be able to tighten security around your own replication setup.

Preparing to Create a Publication

Before setting up the actual publication, there are a few prerequisites that must be addressed. The first is to ensure that a Distributor and a Publisher have been configured. This chapter assumes that you performed the exercises in Chapter 3 in order to set up your Distributor. As part of those exercises, you should have also designated a separate SQL Server instance as your Publisher and associated the Publisher with the Distributor.

If you have not done so yet, please visit Chapter 3 for details about setting up distribution on both the Distributor and the Publisher.

Once you've set up your Distributor and your Publisher, you need to identify a database on the Publisher that you want to configure for replication, and then you must enable that database to support replication.

Creating a database

For the exercises in this chapter, we'll build our own database rather than use an existing one. Listing 5-1 shows the T-SQL script that you can run to create the ReplA database on your system.

```
USE MASTER;
GO
EXECUTE AS LOGIN = 'SA';
GO
CREATE DATABASE ReplA;
GO
USE ReplA;
GO
IF OBJECT_ID('dbo.Test') IS NOT NULL DROP TABLE dbo.Test;
GO
CREATE TABLE dbo.Test(
  Id INT IDENTITY(1,1) PRIMARY KEY,
  Data INT CONSTRAINT Test_Data_Dflt DEFAULT CHECKSUM(NEWID()),
  Data2 INT CONSTRAINT Test_Data2_Dflt DEFAULT CHECKSUM(NEWID()),
  Data3 INT CONSTRAINT Test_Data3_Dflt DEFAULT CHECKSUM(NEWID())
);


GO
INSERT INTO dbo.Test DEFAULT VALUES;
GO 1000
```

```
GO
CREATE PROC dbo.Proc1
AS
BEGIN
  INSERT INTO dbo.Test DEFAULT VALUES;
END;
GO
CREATE VIEW dbo.View1
AS
  SELECT  Id, Data
  FROM    dbo.Test
  WHERE   Id > 500;
GO
CREATE VIEW dbo.View2 WITH SCHEMABINDING
AS
  SELECT  Id, Data
  FROM    dbo.Test
  WHERE   Id < 500;
GO
CREATE UNIQUE CLUSTERED INDEX [dob.View2(Id):CI] ON dbo.View2(Id);
GO
CREATE FUNCTION dbo.Func1()
RETURNS INT
AS
BEGIN
  DECLARE @r INT = (SELECT MAX(Id) FROM dbo.Test);
  RETURN @r;
END;
GO
USE MASTER;
GO
REVERT;
GO
```

Listing 5-1:   Creating a test database for the publication.

Notice that the script, in addition to the database itself, creates several objects: a table, a stored procedure, a view, an indexed view, and a function. We can replicate any of these objects from our Publisher to our Subscriber.

Enabling a database for replication

Any member of the db_owner fixed database role can define a publication in a database. However the database must first be enabled for replication by a member of the sysadmin fixed server role.

If a member of the sysadmin fixed server role is setting up the publication, that user can skip this step. It is required only to allow members of the db_owner fixed database role who do not have elevated server privileges to create a publication in one of their databases.

The following steps walk you through the process of enabling a database for replication:

1. Open SQL Server Management Studio (SSMS), and connect to the SQL Server instance that has been designated as the Publisher. Make sure it is already linked to your Distributor, as mentioned earlier.

2. In **Object Explorer**, right-click the **Replication** folder, and then click **Publisher Properties**, as shown in Figure 5-1.

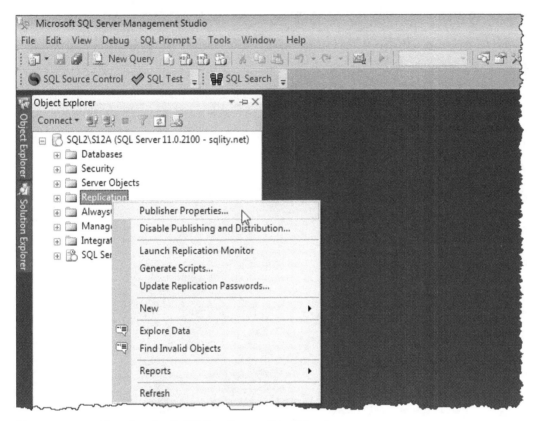

Figure 5-1: Opening the **Publisher Properties** dialog box.

This launches the **Publisher Properties** dialog box, which has two pages:

- The **General** page allows you to specify a new administrative password for the connection to the Distributor in the event it was changed there.

- The **Publication Databases** page (shown in Figure 5-2) lets you enable databases for publishing. For each database, you can select whether transactional replication, merge replication, or both are allowed.

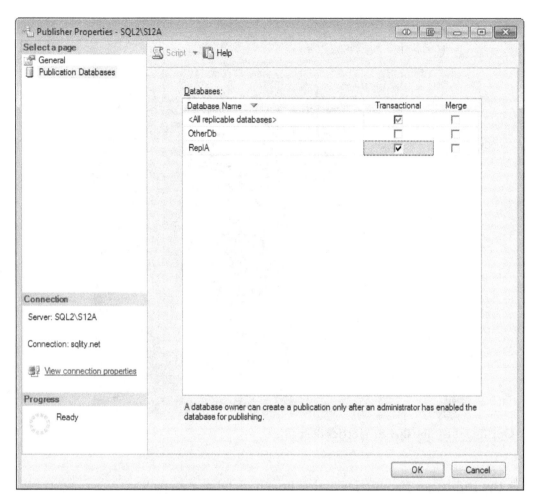

Figure 5-2: Enabling databases for publishing.

On the **Publication Databases** page, select the **Transactional** option associated with the
Rep1A database.

3.   Click **OK** to confirm your change and close the **Publisher Properties** dialog box.

That's all there is to enabling transactional replication on the Rep1A database. You're now
ready to create your publication.

Creating a Publication

The easiest way to create a publication is to use the **New Publication Wizard**. Except for configuring the security accounts themselves, you can use the wizard for the entire setup process. However, to make the process more manageable, we've broken down the exercise into several tasks: configuring the database for replication, selecting which articles to replicate, setting up the initial snapshot, and configuring security.

Setting up your database

To start the process of setting up a publication, you'll need to launch the **New Publication Wizard**, select a database on which you want to define the publication, and then specify the type of publication, as described in the following steps:

1. In **Object Explorer**, expand the **Replication** folder, right-click the **Local Publications** folder, and then click **New Publication**, as shown in Figure 5-3.

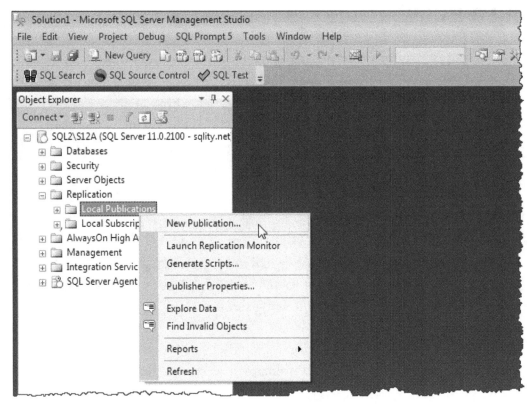

Figure 5-3:   Launching the **New Publication Wizard**.

2.   When the **New Publication Wizard** appears, advance to the **Publication Database** page, shown in Figure 5-4.

Figure 5-4:   Choosing the publication database.

If you started the wizard as a member of the **db_owner** fixed database role instead of as a **sysadmin**, the page will list only the databases that you own and that have been enabled for publishing. There will also be a note advising you that not all databases might be included in the list, as shown in Figure 5-5.

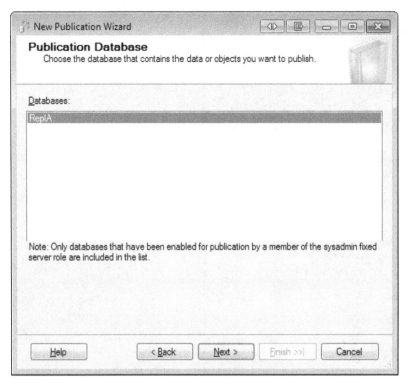

Figure 5-5: Choosing the publication database as a db_owner.

If, instead, you get the message box shown in Figure 5-6, refer back to the previous section about enabling a database for replication.

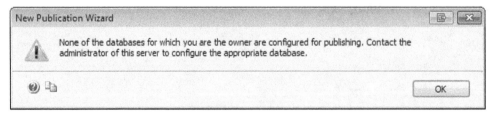

Figure 5-6: Receiving a warning that no database is enabled for replication.

3. From the list of databases shown in the **Publication Database** page, select the database that you want to publish (in this case, Rep1A), and then click **Next** to advance to the **Publication Type** page, shown in Figure 5-7.

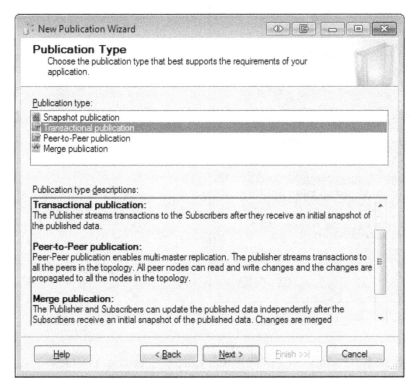

Figure 5-7: Selecting the publication type.

4. From the list of publication types, select **Transactional publication**.
   If you are only a member of the db_owner role, you might now see the error shown in Figure 5-8. It informs you that the selected database is not enabled for the type of replication selected, and it prevents you from continuing. Again, check back to the previous section for information about enabling a database for transactional replication.

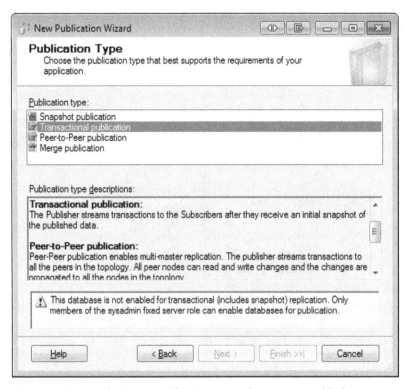

Figure 5-8: Selecting a publication type that is not enabled.

5. After selecting the publication type, click **Next**. This will take you to the **Articles** page, which we'll review in the next section.

Setting up your articles

After you select the publication type, you can define the articles for the publication. An article is always based on a single object in the publication database. You define your articles as part of the process of working through the **New Publication Wizard**. The following steps describe walking through the article-related pages of the wizard:

1. If you have not already advanced to the **Articles** page, do so now. The page lists all objects that can be replicated, as shown in Figure 5-9. The list of objects includes tables, stored procedures, views, indexed views, and user-defined functions.

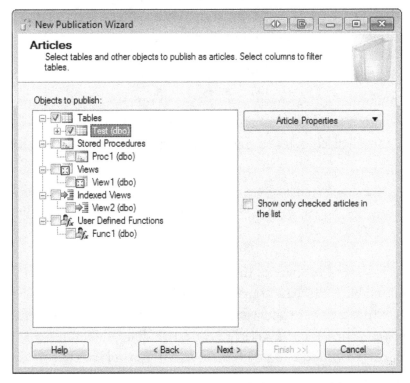

Figure 5-9:   Specifying the articles to include in your publication.

You configure the articles by using the **Article Properties** dialog box (described in the next step). The options available for configuring an article depend on the associated object type:

- By default, a table article replicates the data in the table as well as any schema changes to the table. However, you have the option to replicate only the data and ignore changes to the table schema.

- For a stored procedure, you can choose to replicate the procedure definition or the definition and each execution. Replicating an execution in this context means that each time the procedure runs on the Publisher, it will be called with the same parameters on each Subscriber. Data changes to underlying tables that happen during the execution of the procedure will not be replicated separately. This can be a great performance benefit because potentially a lot less data has to be moved.

- Views and functions always replicate the schema only.

- Indexed views are schema only by default. However, they can get replicated as tables; that means on the Subscriber side a table is created instead of a view. All schema changes to the indexed view as well as changes to the underlying data will be applied to that table.

For a complete list of articles and their restrictions, check out the topic, *Publish Data and Database Objects*,[1] in SQL Server Books Online.

2. Associated with each article is a set of properties that you can view or reconfigure. To access the properties associated with the Test table, select the table in the **Objects to publish** list, and then click the **Article Properties** button. This opens a drop-down list that lets you choose between showing the **Article Properties** dialog box for the highlighted article only, or showing the dialog box for all table articles in the

[1]

publication. The second option allows you to change the properties of all articles of a single type (the type of the highlighted object) in one shot. For this exercise, select the first option to open the **Article Properties** dialog box for the Test table only, as shown in Figure 5-10.

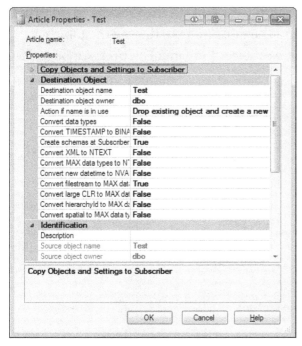

Figure 5-10:   Properties associated with the Test table article.

The list of properties changes depending on the type of article you have selected. For example, depending on the article, you can specify the name of the target object, what to do if the target object already exists, whether to replicate each stored procedure execution along with the definition, etc. For a detailed list of the available options and their explanations, refer to the topic, *Publish Data and Database Objects*,[2] in SQL Server Books Online.

2

3. For now, we'll stick with the **Test** table's default property settings, so click **Cancel** to close the **Article Properties** dialog box.

4. For table articles, there is one more option to be aware of. You can choose to publish the entire table or a subset of columns within that table. If you refer back to Figure 5-9, you'll notice a plus sign next to the Test table in the **Objects to publish** list. By clicking the plus sign, you can expand the table node to display the table's columns, as shown in Figure 5-11. Here, you can select individual columns to be replicated or to be excluded.

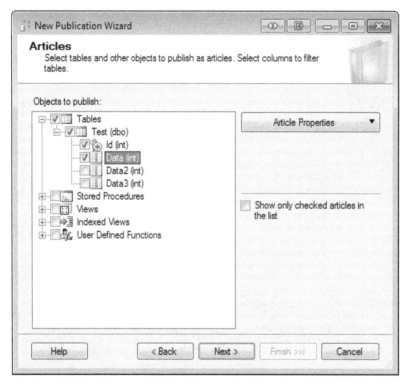

Figure 5-11: Selecting columns in a table article.

When selecting columns to be replicated, you must always include the primary key. All other columns can be omitted. In such cases, when you select individual columns, you're creating a *vertical filter*.

For the rest of this chapter, we'll assume you did not choose to exclude any columns. So make sure all columns are selected, and click **Next** to advance to the **Filter Table Rows** page. This page appears only if you selected at least one table article on the previous page, as we have done in the example.

5.   Click **Add** to open the **Add Filter** dialog box, which is shown in Figure 5-12.

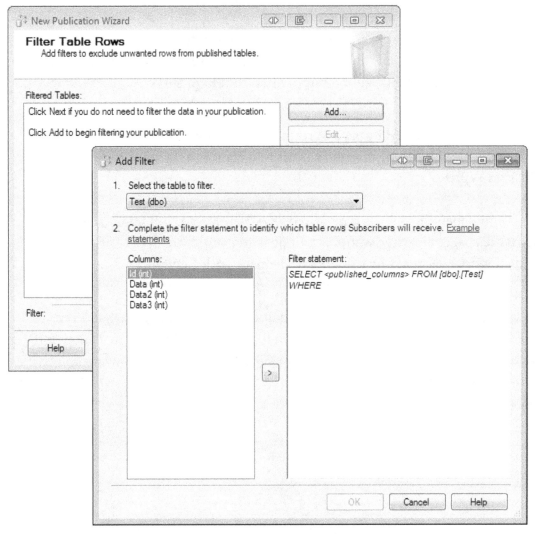

Figure 5-12:   Defining a horizontal filter on the Test table.

The **Add Filter** dialog box lets you create a filter that specifies which rows to replicate in your selected table article. This type of filter is known as a *horizontal filter* and looks like a `SELECT` statement that includes a `WHERE` clause. The part of the `SELECT` statement before the `WHERE` keyword is automatically supplied and cannot be changed. After the `WHERE` keyword, however, you can specify the clause's condition. For example, if you define the `WHERE` clause as `WHERE Data > 42`, only rows with a `Data` column value greater than 42 will be replicated.

Be aware that a horizontal filter uses significant additional resources because every row that was changed on a filtered article has to be inspected to see whether or not it matches the filter. For more details on horizontal filters, check out SQL Server Books Online.

6. Click **Cancel** on the **Add Filter** page to return to the **Filter Table Rows** page without creating a filter, and then click **Next** to advance to the next page of the **New Publication Wizard**.

7. At this point, depending on the type of articles you selected, you might see the **Article Issues** page. The page warns you of potential issues that could arise from your selection. Figure 5-13 shows an example of the page with a couple of issues listed.

This page does not mean that there is a problem. It only points out areas that often cause problems later. If it appears, make sure you look thoroughly through each point listed and then make the necessary changes, if any. Usually you can just advance to the next page by clicking **Next**. This will get you to the **Snapshot Agent** page, which we cover in the next section.

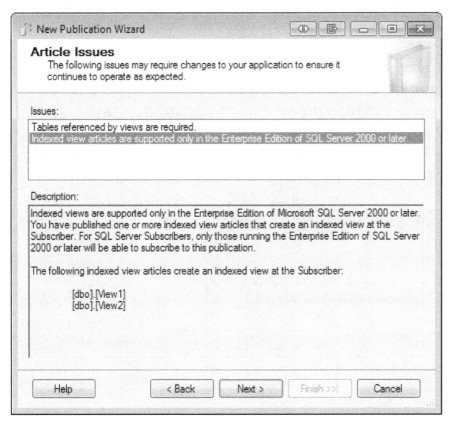

Figure 5-13: Potential issues with the article selection.

Setting up the initial snapshot

After you've defined the articles, the next step in setting up a publication is to schedule a snapshot for the initial synchronization from source to target. The snapshot is a copy of the object definitions and the data stored in those objects. When you create a new subscription for the publication, replication by default uses that snapshot to create and initialize the published objects on the Subscriber.

The Snapshot Agent creates the snapshot and stores it in the snapshot folder on the Distributor. The following steps describe how to configure the Snapshot Agent:

1. On the **Snapshot Agent** page of the **New Publication Wizard**, you can choose to have the Snapshot Agent create the snapshot immediately after the publication has been created, or you can schedule the agent to run at a later time, as you can see in Figure 5-14. If you choose to schedule the agent to run at a later time, you're presented with the SQL Server Agent **New Job Schedule** dialog box, which lets you create a schedule for running the Snapshot Agent.

Figure 5-14: Setting up the Snapshot Agent to create a snapshot.

If you're setting up a publication that will have only one Subscriber, you should probably create the snapshot immediately. On the other hand, if you'll need to resynchronize multiple Subscribers often, you should consider setting up the agent to refresh the snapshot regularly so you're always working with fresh data. Remember, however, that a snapshot is needed only when adding a new Subscriber to a publication or when an existing Subscriber needs to be resynchronized, such as when it has been disconnected for too long.

Also keep in mind that creating a snapshot – particularly if large tables are involved – can be quite resource intensive. Depending on the size of the tables and the network speed, generating a snapshot can take several hours.

With all this in mind, you usually do not want to schedule the Snapshot Agent to run at regular intervals. However, because of the impact that taking a snapshot can have, it might be a good idea to schedule it to run during off-hours instead of right away.

2. For this exercise, select the "immediate" option, as shown in Figure 5-14, and then click **Next** to advance to the **Agent Security** page, which is covered in the next section.

Setting up security

The next step on our way to a working publication is to set up replication agent security. Remember that replication agents are independent Windows programs responsible for actually moving the data. Transactional replication uses a Snapshot Agent, a Log Reader Agent and Distribution Agents. This section shows how to select the accounts that the first two agents execute under. You will also see how to specify the connection credentials for the agents to use to connect to the Publisher and the Distributor. Distribution Agents will be covered in Chapter 7 when we look at setting up a subscription.

It is a general security best practice to have each Windows service or service-like executable run under its own Windows account. That way, you can grant just the minimal set of required permissions to each account. That practice greatly reduces the surface for a potential malicious attack. It also reduces the amount of damage that can be done should an attack be successful.

The replication agents run automatically and unattended, which puts them into this category. Therefore, each one should be given its own account to run under. In this exercise, we follow this best practice and show you how to set up separate accounts. You'll also learn what permissions are required for each account.

The following steps walk you through the process of setting up agent security:

1.   If you haven't already advanced to the **Agent Security** page of the **New Publication Wizard**, do so now. On this page, you assign security accounts to the two agents used to process a transactional publication: the Snapshot Agent and the Log Reader Agent, as shown in Figure 5-15.

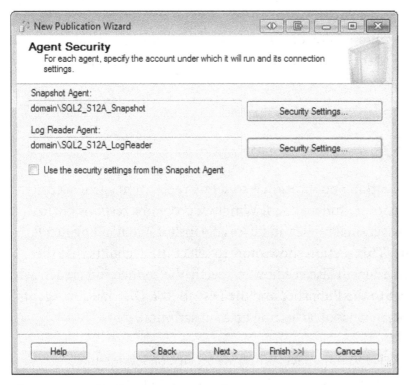

Figure 5-15:   Configuring agent security.

2.   To set the security configuration for the Snapshot Agent, click the **Security Settings** button associated with that agent. This opens the **Snapshot Agent Security** dialog box, shown in Figure 5-16. Here you can provide a Windows login, or you can use the SQL Server Agent service account. Microsoft documentation, however, warns that the latter is not a recommended security best practice, so you should provide a Windows login.

Figure 5-16:   Assigning a security account to an agent.

The **Connect to the Publisher** section of the **Snapshot Agent Security** page lets you to specify how the agent should connect to the publisher. You can either use Windows authentication (by selecting the option **By impersonating the process account**), or you can provide a SQL Server login for the connection to the Publisher.

For the connection to the distribution database, the agent always uses Windows authentication.

Click **OK** when you are done configuring the security settings for the Snapshot Agent.

3. For the Log Reader Agent, you have the same security options to choose from if you click the agent's associated **Security Settings** button. However, instead of taking this approach, you can use the same settings that you provided for the Snapshot Agent. To do so, select the **Use the security settings from the Snapshot Agent** check box on the **Agent Security** page but, as mentioned earlier, it's not recommended to do this.

Although replication provides a Snapshot Agent per publication, there is only one Log Reader Agent for each publication database. That means that if you already have a publication defined in your database, you cannot change the Log Reader Agent account here. However, you can still specify a different SQL Server login for the Log Reader Agent to use to connect to the publication database for the new publication.

4. After you select the account and connection settings for both agents, the next step is to grant the appropriate permissions to each applicable Windows account and SQL Server login. The Snapshot Agent is responsible for moving data from the publication database to the snapshot folder as well as to the distribution database. As a result, you must make the Windows account assigned to the Snapshot Agent a member of the db_owner fixed database role in *both* the publication database and in the distribution database. The account also needs to have write permission on the snapshot folder.

If you set up the Snapshot Agent to not use integrated security to connect to the publication database, but instead use SQL Server authentication, the provided SQL Server login also needs to be a member of the db_owner fixed database role in the publication database. In that case the Snapshot Agent Windows account itself does not need to have access to the publication database.

For this exercise, we're using the domain\SQL2_S12A_Snapshot Windows account for the Snapshot Agent. To ensure the necessary access rights, we must configure our accounts as follows:

- A SQL Server login must be associated with this Windows account on both the Distributor and the Publisher.

- The distribution and publication databases must each include a user that is associated with the login.

- Each user must be member of the db_owner fixed database role in that user's database.

- The domain\SQL2_S12A_Snapshot Windows account must also be granted write access to the snapshot folder, in this case \\SQL1\ReplDataS12A.

You should consult SQL Server and Windows documentation as necessary for details about how to set up these accounts.

5. The Log Reader Agent also copies data from the publication database to the distribution database, but it does not make use of the snapshot folder. The Windows account assigned to the Log Reader Agent needs to be a member of the db_owner fixed database role in the distribution database. In addition, the Windows account (or the SQL Server login, if you're using SQL Server authentication to connect to the publication database) needs to be a member of the db_owner fixed database role in the publication database.

For this exercise, we're using the domain\SQL2_S12A_LogReader Windows account for the Log Reader Agent. To ensure the necessary access rights, we must configure our accounts as follows:

- A SQL Server login must be associated with this Log Reader Agent account on both the Distributor and the Publisher.

- The distribution and publication databases must each include a user that is associated with the login.

- Each user must be a member of the db_owner fixed database role in that user's database.

Once again, you should consult SQL Server and Windows documentation as necessary for details about how to set up these accounts.

6. After you have configured the security settings for both agents and made sure the appropriate rights have been granted to these accounts, click **Next** to proceed to the **Wizard Actions** page, where we'll finish the setting up of the publication.

Completing the publication setup

The remaining steps let you assign a name to your publication and specify when to create the publication:

1. On the **Wizard Actions** page, you can specify that the wizard should create the publication as soon as you've completed the wizard or, instead, create a script that you can execute at a later time. For this exercise, select the **Create the publication** option, and then click **Next**.

2. On the **Complete the Wizard** page, shown in Figure 5-17, type a name for the publication in the **Publication name** text box. The name needs to be unique within each publication database.

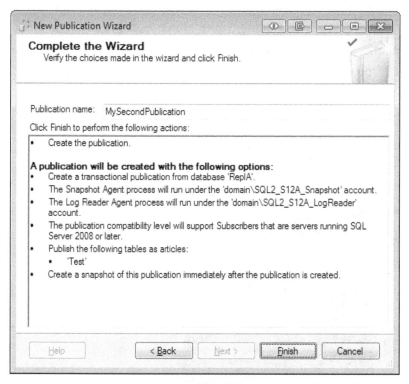

Figure 5-17: Assigning a name to the publication.

If you create two publications on different databases, you can use the same name for both of them. However, if you have multiple publications, I strongly recommend that you use meaningful and distinguishable names. A replication setup has a lot of moving parts. There is no need to cause additional confusion by choosing the same or similar names for multiple publications.

3. Type **MySecondPublication** into the **Publication name** text box, review the summary on the **Complete the Wizard** page, and then click **Finish**. The wizard will create the publication while displaying progress information on the **Creating publication** page. Once this step is complete, click **Close**.

These are all the steps necessary to create a publication. To see if everything worked correctly, we need to first create a subscription. The next two chapters will cover the steps for doing just that. In the meantime, you can check that the publication was actually created, by returning to **Object Explorer**, expanding the **Replication** folder and then expanding **Local Publications** folder, as shown in Figure 5-18.

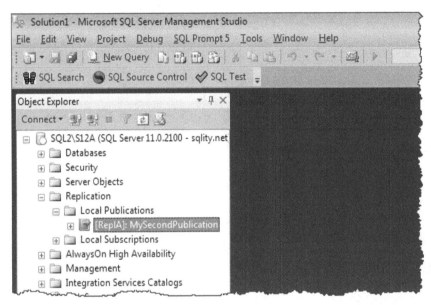

Figure 5-18: Verifying that your new publication exists.

Your new publication should now be listed under the **Local Publications** folder, which means you can now create a subscription. But first, let's look at several issues that could arise when setting up your publication.

Potential Problems

Because there are so many steps to take and decisions to make when configuring replication, you might run into issues during the setup. The most common problem is an account that does not have the appropriate rights. If something does not seem to work as expected, review all applicable accounts and make sure that they're configured with the correct permissions.

Another issue that might complicate matters is that error messages do not always point you in the right direction. For example, the message, `The remote server "SQL1\S12A" does not exist, or has not been designated as a valid Publisher` really means that the Snapshot Agent does not have the necessary permissions to access the distribution database. It has nothing to do with the Publisher. What makes matters even more difficult is that finding the error messages is not always a straightforward process.

You should also take into account several other considerations when implementing replication. (Chapter 14 will provide more details about how to troubleshoot replication.)

- If you're using a snapshot share that is located on the Distributor, you might have to grant write access to the Snapshot Agent account on both the share and the underlying folder.

- If you've assigned Windows domain accounts to the replication agents and use impersonation to connect to the other servers in your replication setup, you might have to grant the Windows account that is executing the SQL Server service read access to Active Directory. This is a best practice anyway. Check out SQL Server Books Online and Windows documentation for details on why and how to do this.

- In general, you should use a SQL Server login (such as `SA`) to execute the replication wizards, instead of a Windows account. A full discussion of why you should do this is beyond the scope of this book. However, you'll usually run into fewer issues – not only with replication, but with other functionality as well – if the objects you're dealing with are owned by a user associated with a SQL Server login and not a Windows account.

Summary

In this chapter, you learned how to create a publication for transactional replication. The chapter explained who is allowed to create a publication and what permissions the replication agents involved in a publication require to do their jobs successfully. In addition, the chapter described how to add articles to the publication and what object types you can select as articles. You also learned how to schedule the Snapshot Agent in order to generate the initial snapshot. Finally, the chapter pointed out potential problems you might run into when implementing replication.

Using this information, you should now be able to set up your own publication. Once you do, any modifications to the publication articles are recorded in the distribution database. However, because Subscribers have yet to be set up, no one is collecting that data from there, which means the distribution database will steadily grow, potentially a lot. The next step is to set up a Subscriber, which we'll cover in the following chapters.

Chapter 6: The Publication Access List

In the previous chapters, we set up distribution and created a publication. With those two pieces in place, all changes to the articles of that publication are recorded and held in the distribution database for later use.

To make use of this collected data, we have to set up a subscription. Before we can create a subscription, however, we need to make sure the necessary permissions are in place.

Setting Up a Subscription

As you learned in Chapter 5, to create a publication in a database, two requirements must be in place:

- The login used to execute the setup needs to have at least db_owner level permissions in the publication database.

- The database itself needs to be enabled for publishing. Enabling a database for publishing requires sysadmin privileges. However, it needs to be done only once per database.

The requirements for a new subscription are a little more complex. During setup, information needs to be gathered from the distribution database and changes need to be applied to that database, the publication database, and the subscription database. Additionally, you must provide an account to run the Distribution Agent. As a result, all three locations require a substantial list of permissions.

SQL Server supports two subscription models: pull subscriptions and push subscriptions. Chapter 7 provides information about both models and explains the differences between them. For now, however, know that in a pull subscription the Subscriber is responsible to collect data changes from the publication, whereas in a push subscription the Distributor actively *pushes* the data to the Subscribers. A push subscription requires the complex permission set mentioned above, but a pull subscription requires a significantly reduced set of permissions.

A discussion of the permissions required to set up a push subscription is beyond the scope of this book (although you can use an account with `sysadmin` privileges to simplify matters). For more details about the required permissions, see SQL Server Books Online. The easier case of the pull subscription is, however, worth spending time on.

To be able to set up a pull subscription, your account needs to fulfill only two requirements:

- Be a member of the `db_owner` database role in the subscription database.

- Be added to the Publication Access List (PAL) of the publication.

Before we continue, make sure that your login is mapped to a user in the subscription database that is a member of the `db_owner` role. Check SQL Server Books Online for details on how to do this.

Configuring the Publication Access List

The Publication Access List (PAL) is a security measure that prevents unauthorized users from accessing replication data. It is independent of the other permissions maintained by SQL Server. Instead, it is maintained as internal information in the publication database and cannot be directly accessed with Transact-SQL. It provides for an easy way to control who can subscribe to a publication without having to worry about other SQL Server permissions.

Only logins that meet the following three requirements can be added to the PAL for a specific publication:

- the login must exist on the Distributor

- the login must exist on the Publisher

- a user associated with that login must exist in the publication database.

You do not need to grant any permission to the user in the publication database. The user in the publication database is required only because the PAL information is stored in that database. Login information, on the other hand, is stored in the master database, so that information might not be accessible in all situations. However, database user information is readily available within each database, as it is stored at the database level.

The following steps walk through adding an account (in this case, DOMAIN\SQL3_PAL) to the PAL:

1. The PAL is maintained on the Publisher. Therefore the first step is to connect to it in SSMS.

2. In **Object Explorer**, expand the **Replication** folder and then the **Local Publications** subfolder.

3. Right-click your publication and then click **Properties**, as shown in Figure 6-1.

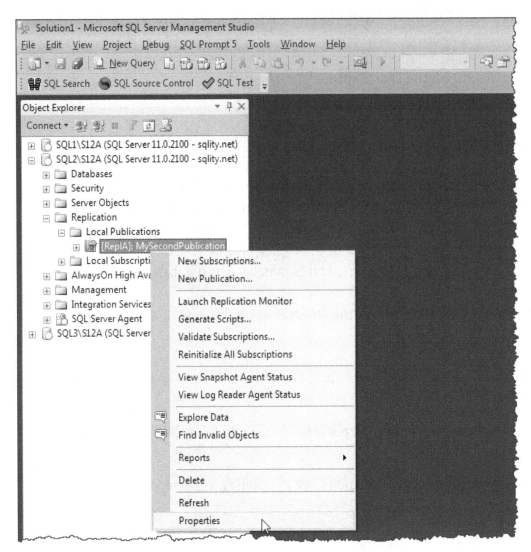

Figure 6-1:   Accessing a publication's properties.

4. When the **Publication Properties** dialog box appears, go to the **Publication Access List** page, as shown in Figure 6-2. The page contains a list of the logins that are already members of the PAL.

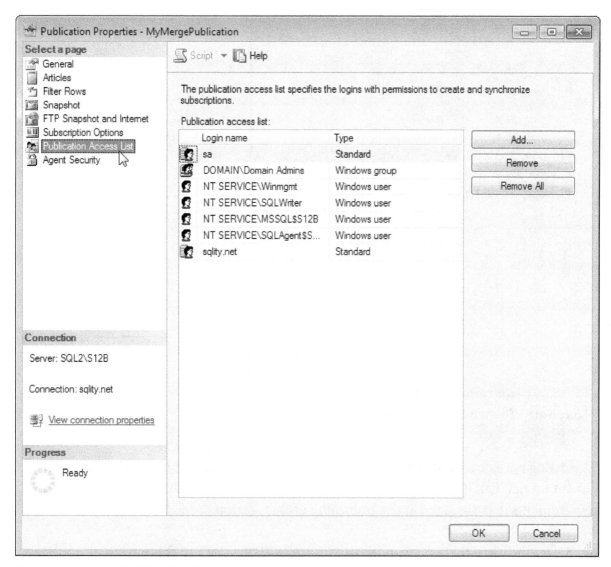

Figure 6-2: The **Publication Access List** page.

5. Click the **Add** button on the right-hand side to add a new login to the PAL. This opens the **Add Publication Access** dialog box, as shown in Figure 6-3.

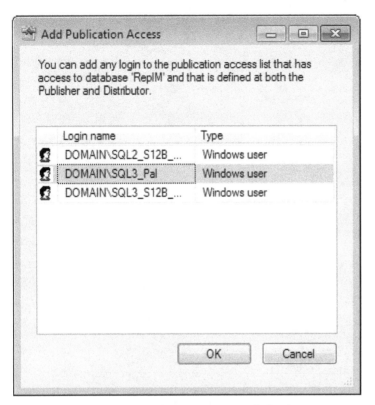

Figure 6-3: The **Add Publication Access** dialog box.

The dialog box contains all logins that are eligible to be a member of the PAL, but that are not yet on that list. If your login is not included here, make sure that it meets the three requirements that are listed at the beginning of this section.

6. Select the login that you want to add (DOMAIN\SQL3_Pal in this example), and click **OK** to close the **Add Publication Access** dialog box. Then click **OK** to close the **Publication Properties** dialog box. This is all you need to do to add a login to the PAL.

Creating the Subscription

A login that is a member of the PAL and also of the db_owner role in the subscription database can be used to execute the **New Subscription** wizard. You can find the details of how to use that wizard in Chapter 7. When you follow the steps in that chapter, you'll find that you need to provide a Windows account to execute the Distribution Agent. That account needs the same set of permissions as the account setting up the subscription, with one addition: the account must also have read access to the snapshot folder. Check out Chapter 7 for more details on how this works.

The example in this chapter is based on transactional replication. However, everything said also holds true for merge replication. The only difference is that a Merge Agent is used instead of a Distribution Agent.

Summary

In this chapter, we learned about the minimal security requirements for an account used to create a pull subscription. We also discovered how to configure the PAL. We'll encounter the PAL a few more times during the rest of the book, as it is a requirement for the accounts running the Distribution Agents or Merge Agents.

Chapter 7: Transactional Replication – the Subscription

In Chapter 6, you learned about the security considerations to take into account before creating a subscription. Now it's time to actually set up that subscription. A subscription's main purpose is to specify the database that the recorded changes will be applied to. Although you can define a publication without a subscription, the publication can live up to its potential only if there is a subscription in place. In fact, you can implement multiple subscriptions for a single publication.

A SQL Server instance that has a subscription defined in one of its databases is called a Subscriber. The Subscriber hosts the subscription database to which the published changes are applied.

In this chapter, we walk through the steps required to set up a subscription. You'll learn how to use the New Subscription Wizard to create and configure the subscription, what permissions are required for the account used for the Distribution Agent, and how to configure retention to control how long data is maintained. In addition, when setting up the subscription, you'll learn about the differences between push and pull subscriptions, which will help you decide which type is appropriate in your situation. You'll also learn how the different retention settings can affect your business requirements.

This chapter assumes that you've performed the exercises in the previous chapters and have set up the Distributor and the Publisher and configured a publication to which you can now subscribe. To get the most out of this chapter, you should designate a separate SQL Server instance to use as your Subscriber, as we did with the Publisher. The Subscriber should be on a machine separate from the Distributor as well as the Publisher.

Setting up a Subscription

The easiest way to create and configure the actual subscription is to use the **New Subscription Wizard**. The wizard walks you through each step necessary to set up the subscription. However, this process can be a bit overwhelming, so we've broken it down into several tasks: connecting to the Publisher, selecting the subscription type, specifying the Subscriber and subscription database, and configuring security on that database.

Connecting to the Publisher

Your first task in setting up a subscription is to select the publication that you want to subscribe to. For that, you need to launch the **New Subscription Wizard**. The following steps walk through that process of launching the wizard and connecting to your Publisher:

1. In SSMS, connect to the SQL Server instance that you want to use as the Subscriber. To be able to run the wizard, you need to use a login that has access to the Subscriber, the Distributor and the Publisher. In Chapter 6, we discussed the permissions required to set up a pull subscription. However, in this chapter we will be working with a push subscription because it is a more common setup in transactional replication. As mentioned during the previous chapter, we are not going to discuss the required permissions to set up a push subscription in detail. The easiest way to get through this chapter is to use a single Windows account that has `sysadmin` privileges on all three instances.

2. In **Object Explorer**, expand the **Replication** folder for your instance, right-click the **Local Subscriptions** folder, and then click **New Subscription**, as shown in Figure 7-1. This will launch the **New Subscription Wizard**.

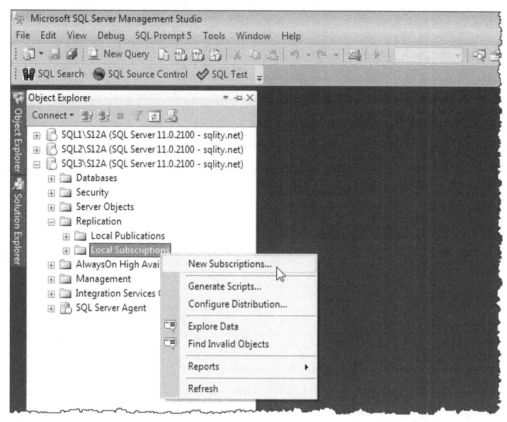

Figure 7-1: Launching the **New Subscription Wizard** from **Object Explorer**.

3. If a Welcome page appears, advance to the **Publication** page, shown in Figure 7-2. Here we identify the Publisher, the publication database, and the publication itself.

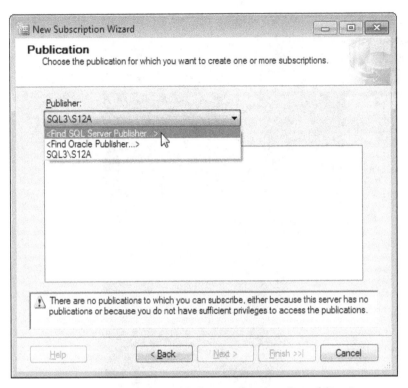

Figure 7-2:   Selecting the Publisher on the wizard's **Publication** page.

First, we need to select the Publisher using the **Publisher** drop-down list. If – as previously suggested – you are using a separate instance for your Subscriber, your Publisher
won't be listed here. Click the **Find SQL Server Publisher** option to open a standard SQL
Server connection dialog box, where you can connect to the SQL Server instance that is
your Publisher.

4. After you connect to your Publisher, it will be automatically selected in the **Publisher**
    drop-down list. Additionally any publication databases and publications defined on
    that Publisher are listed in the **Databases and publications** window, as shown in
    Figure 7-3.

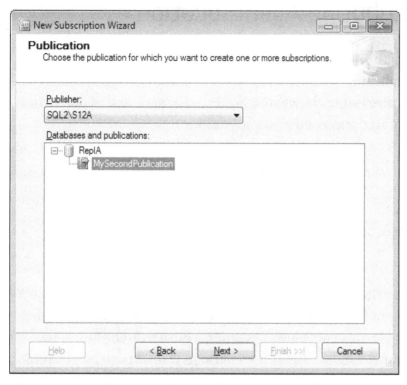

Figure 7-3:   Selecting a publication database and a publication.

If you performed the exercises in Chapter 5, the publication **MySecondPublication** will be listed beneath the RepIA publication database.

5.   Select the **MySecondPublication** publication, and then click **Next** to advance to the **Distribution Agent Location** page, which we cover in the following section.

Selecting the Distribution Agent location

To create a subscription (unlike the steps involved in creating a publication), you do not need to select which type of replication you want to use. The replication type is defined by the publication. However, there is one choice that needs to be made at this point: you must choose between a push subscription and a pull subscription.

When data is being replicated, the Distribution Agent moves data from the distribution database to the subscription database. Each subscription uses its own Distribution Agent. The difference between a push subscription and a pull subscription lies in where this agent runs and, as a direct consequence, which server has control over when the data movement occurs.

For a push subscription, the Distribution Agent runs on the Distributor and pushes the data to the Subscriber. If you need the data to move from the Publisher to the Subscriber in the shortest timeframe possible, in a continuous manner, a push subscription is the best way to go. This is also by far the most common scenario in transactional replication.

For a pull subscription, the Distribution Agent runs on the Subscriber, pulling the data from the Distributor. This option might be better than a push subscription if the Subscriber needs to steer the data flow. For example, the Subscriber might not always be connected to the network, or the data should not change on the Subscriber until a given process has completed. A pull subscription gives the Subscriber full control over when the data flow occurs.

For this exercise, we'll go with a push subscription. The following steps walk you through the process of selecting the subscription type:

1. If you haven't already done so, advance to the **Distribution Agent Location** page of the **New Subscription Wizard** (shown in Figure 7-4).

This page lists two options. **Run all agents at the Distributor** will configure the subscription as a push subscription. **Run each agent at its Subscriber** will configure the subscription as a pull subscription.

Figure 7-4:   Selecting the subscription type.

2.   Select the first option (as shown in Figure 7-4), and then click **OK** to continue to the **Subscribers** page, which we cover in the next section.

Note that, if you set up your subscription as a pull subscription instead of push, you'll see differences from what we show here when you get to the **Distribution Agent Security** page later in the wizard. However, the differences are minor, so you should still be able to follow along if you go with a pull subscription.

Specifying the Subscriber and the subscription database

The following steps walk you through the process of selecting the Subscriber and the subscription database to associate with your subscription:

1. If you haven't already done so, advance to the **Subscribers** page of the **New Subscription Wizard** (shown in Figure 7-5). On this page, you select the Subscriber and its associated subscription database.

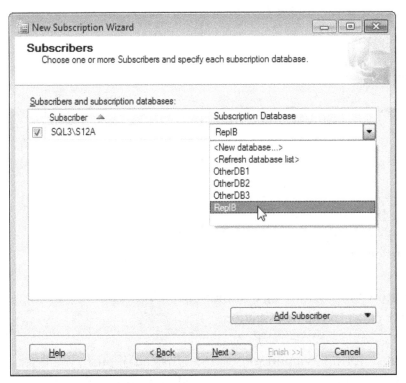

Figure 7-5:   Specifying the Subscriber and the subscription database.

2. The **Subscribers and subscription databases** grid already shows the Subscriber you connected to in the beginning – SQL3\S12A, in the example. However, you need to make sure the check box associated with the Subscriber is selected.

3. In the **Subscription Database** column of the row associated with your Subscriber, select the applicable subscription database. Or you can instead select the **New Database** option, which launches the **New Database Wizard** and lets you create a subscription database on the fly.

If you select an existing database, be careful to pick the correct one. The subscription initialization step drops and re-creates all objects in the subscription database that are part of the subscription.

Note

If you pick the wrong database and that database has objects with the same name as objects being replicated, those objects will be dropped. You will receive no warning messages to let you know that this is happening.

The **Subscribers** page of the **New Subscription Wizard** also lets you to associate more than one Subscriber with your publication. For this, you can click the **Add Subscriber** button to add as many Subscribers as necessary. However there are some limitations. For example, all Subscribers that are set up together in this way have to use the same subscription model (push or pull). Also, while it is possible to have a single Subscriber subscribe to a single publication more than once using distinct subscription databases, the wizard allows for each Subscriber to be included only once. It's generally advised that you run the wizard again for each new subscription. Therefore we won't be discussing this option further.

4. To complete this step, make sure that you've selected the correct subscription database and verified that the check box associated with your Subscriber is selected, and then click **Next** to advance to the security section of the wizard, which we cover in the following section.

Configuring security on the Distribution Agent

The main difference between setting up a push and a pull subscription can be found in the security setup. The Distribution Agent always uses Windows authentication to connect to the local instance where it is located.

In the case of a push subscription, the Distribution Agent runs on the Distributor. The connection to the distribution database is therefore made by impersonating the account the agent runs under.

For the connection to the subscription database, you can choose either to use impersonation or to provide a SQL Server login. If all machines are in the same domain, choosing impersonation is a best practice and SQL Server Books Online recommends always using it. However, if you are trying to replicate data between machines that are in separate domains, you might have to go with a SQL Server login in some situations.

In the case of a pull subscription, the Distribution Agent runs on the Subscriber. Here the connection to the subscription database is fixed to use process account impersonation; however, you can choose between impersonation and a SQL Server login for the connection to the distribution database.

The next step in configuring your subscription is to set up security for the Distribution Agent. This involves configuring the accounts used to connect to the Distributor and Subscriber and used to execute the agents. The following steps walk you through the process of setting up these accounts:

1. If you haven't already done so, advance to the **Distribution Agent Security** page of the **New Subscription Wizard** (shown in Figure 7-6). The **Subscription properties** grid displays one row per Subscriber. Any Subscribers listed here are those we selected earlier on the **Subscribers** page. In our case, we selected only one Subscriber: SQL3\S12A.

Figure 7-6:   Setting up security for the Distribution Agent.

2.   For each Subscriber, you have to select the necessary accounts by using the **Distribution Agent Security** dialog box. To launch the dialog box, click the ellipsis button at the end of the row associated with the specific Subscriber.

Figure 7-7 shows the **Distribution Agent Security** dialog box for our Subscriber (SQL3\S12A). The one shown here is specific to a push subscription. However, the dialog box that appears for a pull subscription is very similar. It differs only in the fact that it allows for a SQL Server login to be selected to connect to the Distributor, rather than the Subscriber.

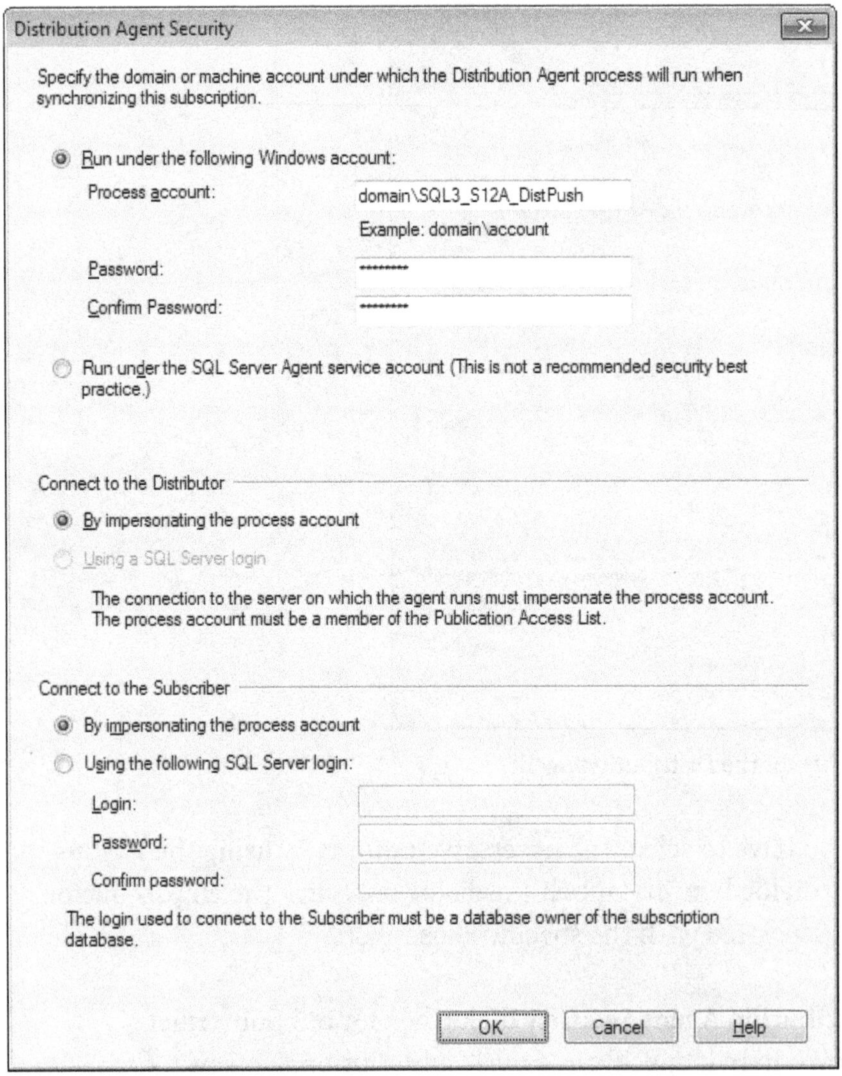

Figure 7-7: Assigning security accounts to the Distribution Agent.

The number of connections and accounts needed to set up replication can seem overwhelming at first. Refer back to Chapter 4 for more details about the replication agents. In addition, Chapter 8 will provide information about the SQL Server Agent jobs that drive the replication agents.

3. At the top of the **Distribution Agent Security** dialog box, provide a Windows account for the Distribution Agent to run under and the password associated with the account. For this you should create a new domain account without special access privileges and provide it together with its password here. This example uses the DOMAIN\SQL3_S12A_DistPush account.

You can instead choose to use the SQL Server Agent account, but as mentioned before, this is not a good idea from a security perspective.

4. For the connection to the Distributor and the connection to the Subscriber, select the option **By impersonating the process account**. Assuming your servers belong to the same domain and you are using a new domain account, there is no reason to specify a SQL login here.

5. Click **OK** to close the **Distribution Agent Security** dialog box. This brings you back to the **Distribution Agent Security** page of the **New Subscription Wizard**.

Account Permissions

Before we continue any further with the **New Subscription Wizard**, we should first grant the necessary permissions to the account(s) used to run the Distribution Agent, as described in the following guidelines:

*   The account running the Distribution Agent must have read access to the snapshot folder.

*   The account used by the Distribution Agent to connect to the subscription database must be a member of the db_owner fixed database role in that database.

*   The account used by the Distribution Agent to connect to the distribution database must be a member of the PAL and also a member of the db_owner fixed database role in the distribution database.

For these exercises, we're using the `DOMAIN\SQL3_S12A_DistPush` Windows account to run the Distribution Agent, and we're using impersonation to connect to the Distributor and the Subscriber. Therefore this is the only account we need to be concerned with for now. Providing the account with read access to the snapshot folder and making the account a member of the `db_owner` fixed database role should be straightforward. If you have any questions about how to do either, refer to the Windows and SQL Server documentation. And if you need help with adding the account to the PAL, refer back to Chapter 6.

Finalizing the Subscription

After granting the Distribution Agent account the appropriate permissions, we can continue with the New Subscription Wizard. You should still be on the **Distribution Agent Security** page, so follow these steps to finalize the subscription:

1. Click **OK** to advance to the **Synchronization Schedule** page, shown in Figure 7-8.

The **Synchronization Schedule** page lets you to select when the Distribution Agent should be executed. Your schedule options are listed in the **Agent Schedule** drop-down list associated with the Subscriber. The drop-down list supports three options:

-   **Run continuously** – This option is the default setting and is by far the most common choice. It causes the Distribution Agent to run at all times, in order to apply changes to the subscription database as soon as they're available.

-   **Run on demand only** – When this option is selected, you have to run the Distribution Agent manually every time you want the databases to synchronize. The agent does not start automatically. This option can be useful if another task, such as generating a nightly report, needs to finish running before synchronization can happen.

-   **Define schedule** – This option opens a standard SQL Server Agent **New Job Schedule** dialog box, where you can set up a schedule.

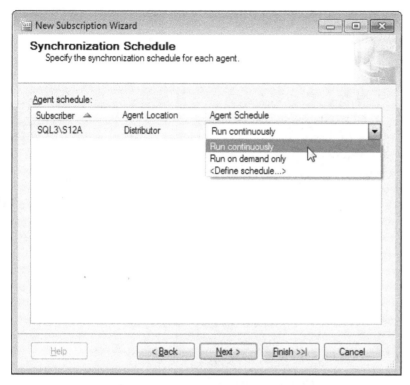

Figure 7-8: Configuring a synchronization schedule.

2. Ensure that **Run continuously** is selected, and then click **Next** to advance to the **Initialize Subscriptions** page, shown in Figure 7-9.

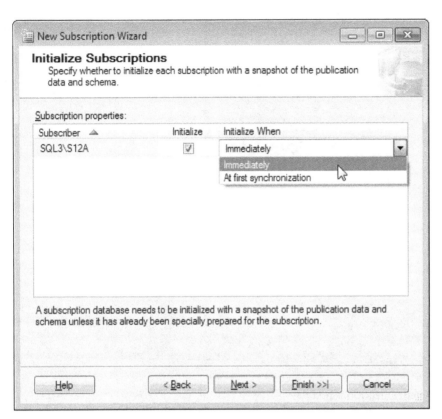

Figure 7-9: Initializing the subscription.

Here you can select when the subscription should be initialized. You have two options:
Immediately and **At first synchronization**. The latter holds off with the initialization
until the first synchronization is started. If you had selected anything but the default
on the previous page and if the first scheduled synchronization is far in the future, you
should delay the initialization here too.

The default is **Immediately** and in most cases this is the appropriate choice.

You can also choose not to initialize the subscription by deselecting the **Initialize** check
box. However, in that case you won't be able to use the subscription until it is initialized
by some other means.

For the initialization, a current snapshot must exist. If a long time (more than 24 hours) has passed since you created the snapshot, as outlined in Chapter 5, rerun the **Snapshot Agent** job manually now. You can find the Snapshot Agent job by looking in the **Job Activity Monitor** on the Distributor for a job in the REPL-Snapshot category that has your publication name as part of its name, as shown in Figure 7-10.

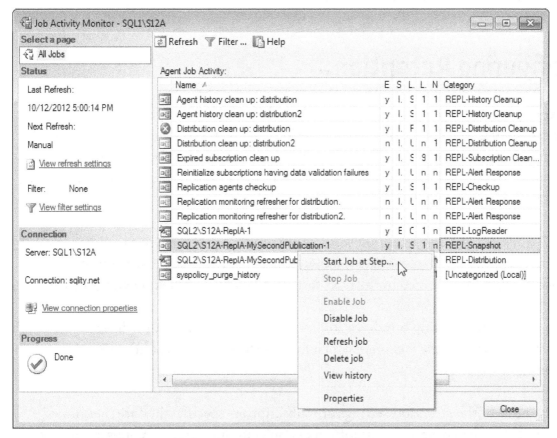

Figure 7-10: Manually starting the Snapshot Agent on the Distributor.

3.   On the **Initialize Subscriptions** page of the **New Subscription Wizard**, make sure both the **Initialize** check box and the **Immediately** option are selected, and then click **Next**.

4. On the next page that appears, the **Wizard Actions** page, you can choose whether the subscription is created upon completion of the wizard or whether a script is generated that you can run later to create the subscription. For this exercise, we'll go with the first option, so select **Create the subscription(s)**, and then click **Next**.

5. On the final page of the wizard, review your selections. If everything is to your liking, click **Finish** to create the subscription.

Configuring Retention

Once you've created your subscription, you should configure the settings that define replication's retention. Retention refers to the length of time vital publication data is kept before being deleted and how long a Subscriber can be offline before becoming invalid. SQL Server replication supports four retention settings. Three are defined on the Distributor and one on the Publisher.

The first three distribution retention settings are properties defined in the distribution database. Therefore, they are global for all Publishers using the same distribution database. All three are covered in the next section, *Configuring retention on the Distributor*.

The fourth retention setting is publication-specific and is covered in the later section, *Configuring retention on the Publisher*, which follows the section on configuring the Distributor.

Although none of the retention settings are subscription-specific, they are mentioned here because they can have a significant impact on your Subscribers. A Subscriber that does not request an update within the retention period will be deactivated or dropped. If that happens, a complete resynchronization of the Subscriber is required, making the data on the Subscriber unavailable during that time.

On the other hand, retention settings directly affect how much space you need to provide for the distribution database because data that has not yet been delivered to all Subscribers is held in that database for the specified time.

When selecting the replication retention settings, you need to provide your Subscribers with enough time to load the data from the Distributor. For this, you need to plan in time for accidental or scheduled outages. But you also need to keep the time short enough so that the distribution database does not run out of space.

Configuring retention on the Distributor

You configure the minimum and the maximum retention times on the Distributor. The maximum retention time specifies the time that the replication data is held in the distribution database if it has not been delivered to all Subscribers. The minimum retention time (also called transaction retention period) defines the minimum time the data is kept, even if it already was delivered to all Subscribers.

The minimum retention time is the maximum guaranteed time in which a snapshot can be used to initialize new or disabled Subscribers. However, if the option **Create a snapshot immediately and keep the snapshot available to initialize subscriptions** was selected during the creation of the publication, every snapshot is valid for at least the maximum retention time. During this time, the minimum retention time is effectively ignored. Therefore the distribution database might grow significantly, as the snapshot requires all the transaction data to be kept, too.

After the snapshot is expired, both the minimum and the maximum retention times are used again to determine the lifespan of replicated transactions.

The following steps explain how to set the retention times on the distribution database:

1. In SSMS, connect to the SQL Server instance that you've configured as the Distributor.

2. In **Object Explorer**, right-click the **Replication** folder for that instance, and then click **Distributor Properties**, as shown in Figure 7-11.

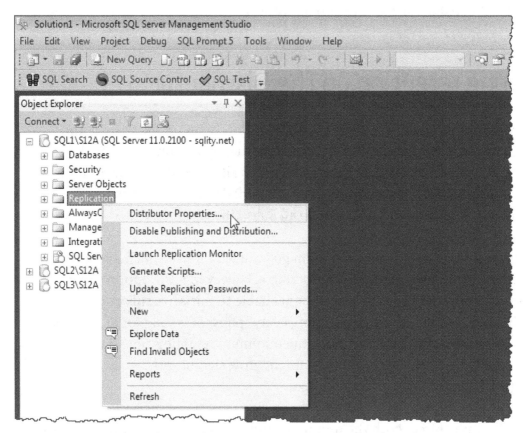

Figure 7-11:   Accessing the Distributor's properties.

When the **Distributor Properties** dialog box appears, it opens to the **General** page, as shown in Figure 7-12. The page displays a list of configured distribution databases and their retention values.

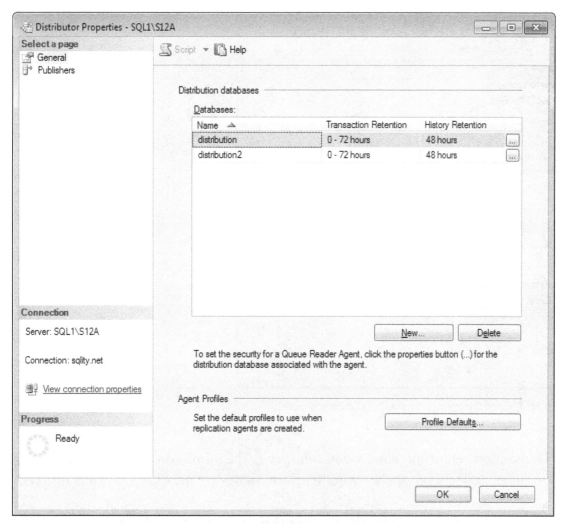

Figure 7-12: The **General** page of the **Distributor Properties** dialog box.

3. Click the browse (ellipsis) button at the end of the row that contains the distribution database whose settings you want to change. This launches the **Distribution Database Properties** dialog box, shown in Figure 7-13.

Figure 7-13: Configuring the transaction retention period.

In the **Transaction retention** section, you can specify the minimum and maximum retention times, and you can specify whether those values are measured in hours or days.

4. Set the times, click **OK** to close the **Distribution Database Properties** dialog box, and then click **OK** again to close the **Distributor Properties** dialog box.

As mentioned before, if there is transactional data in the distribution database that has not been synchronized with a Subscriber for more than the maximum retention time, the data will be purged, and the Subscriber will automatically be marked as inactive. To reactivate an inactive Subscriber, the subscription has to be reinitialized from a fresh snapshot.

If you have a Subscriber that becomes incapable of synchronizing from time to time, as can occur as the result of scheduled or unscheduled connection interruptions, you need to set the maximum retention time value high enough to guarantee that the Subscriber can reconnect before it is deactivated.

On the other hand, the longer the maximum retention time, the more data needs to be stored and kept in the distribution database. So the higher this value, the more storage you need for the distribution database. In addition to the distribution database taking up more hard-drive space, the replication throughput will also decrease.

So you need to find a happy medium between Subscriber availability and storage and performance requirements when setting this value. The default values for transaction retention are 0 hours for the minimum and 72 hours for the maximum.

Figure 7-13 also shows a **History retention** setting. This is the third setting referred to at the beginning of the discussion on retention. This setting defines how long information about the health of the replication setup is kept in the distribution database. The setting does not affect the Subscribers. However, the history data can be helpful in trouble-shooting issues that might arise. The default of 48 hours is usually a good choice.

The **Queue Reader Agent security** section at the bottom of the **Distribution Database Properties** dialog box is not used in a standard transactional replication installation and will not be covered in this book.

Configuring retention on the Publisher

Another important retention setting is defined on the publication: the publication retention period. The setting determines when a subscription is actually removed from the Distributor if data is not synchronized. The amount of time is usually a lot higher than the maximum retention setting in the distribution database.

For a push subscription, if a subscription lapses past the publication retention period, the subscription is removed completely from the Distributor and nothing remains. For a pull subscription, an orphan is left on the Subscriber that must be cleaned up manually. In either case, if you want to continue to use the instance as the Subscriber, you need to set it up again from scratch.

The default value for the publication retention period setting is two weeks (336 hours). The following steps explain how to modify the publication retention period:

1. In SSMS, connect to the SQL Server instance configured as the Publisher.

2. In **Object Explorer**, expand the **Replication** folder for that instance, and then expand the **Local Publications** subfolder.

3. Right-click the publication you want to change, and then click **Properties**.

4. When the **Publication Properties** dialog box appears, it opens to the **General** page, as shown in Figure 7-14. Here you can change the description of the publication as well as configure the retention period, which you do in the **Subscription Expiration** section. You can either specify a value (in hours) or set the retention period never to expire.

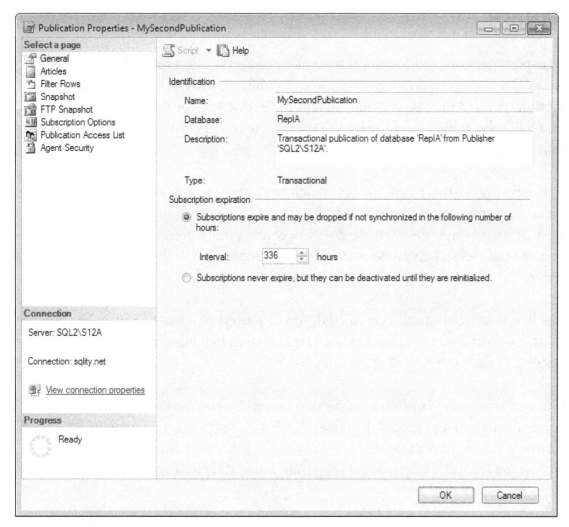

Figure 7-14: Configuring the retention settings on your publication.

5. Configure the retention setting, and then click **OK** to close the **Publication Properties** dialog box. All your retention settings should now be configured and your subscription is ready to go.

Summary

In this chapter, we worked through the final piece of a replication setup, the subscription. We discussed how to connect a subscription to a publication, as well as how to select the subscription type and the subscription database. We reviewed the differences between push and pull subscriptions and the importance of the retention periods. We also learned about the security requirements for a subscription.

By the time you get to this point, the first synchronization should be complete. If you connect to the subscription database, you should see that all the replicated objects have been created. However, if the database does not contain these objects yet, wait a little longer. It can take several minutes for the first synchronization to finish, even on a very small table.

After the first synchronization is completed, you can insert or update a row in the publication database. After your change has been replicated to the Subscriber, you'll be able to see it applied in the subscription database.

Transactional replication consists of many parts, including replication agents, SQL Server Agent jobs and special databases. We have already touched upon most of the parts. What we haven't yet discussed in detail are the SQL Server Agent jobs that process the replication agents and keep transactional replication running. Those, we dive into in Chapter 8.

Chapter 8: SQL Server Agent Jobs for Transactional Replication

In a standard replication installation, SQL Server creates a number of SQL Server Agent jobs to support the replication process. Many of those jobs are related specifically to the replication agents. By default, SQL Server creates one job per agent in order to run that agent. Additionally, SQL Server creates several other jobs to perform various maintenance tasks related to replication.

In this chapter, you'll learn about the SQL Server Agent jobs used to support replication. The chapter provides details about each job and shows you how to identify the tasks that they perform. The chapter also covers the different naming conventions used for the SQL Server Agent jobs, and discusses when in the setup process each job is created.

SQL Server Agent Jobs

During the replication setup process, SQL Server creates numerous SQL Server Agent jobs, some related to the replication agents, others related to maintenance tasks that need to be performed.

Snapshot Agent jobs

By default, SQL Server creates a SQL Server Agent job for each publication in order to execute the Snapshot Agent. These jobs are named according to the following pattern:

```
<Server>-<Publication Database>-<Publication>-<number>
```

If you need to generate a new snapshot for a publication, you can manually run the Snapshot Agent job associated with that publication, or you can schedule the job to run at a later time.

Log Reader Agent job

When you set up the first publication in a publication database, SQL Server creates a single SQL Server Agent job to execute the Log Reader Agent. The job is named according to the following pattern:

`<Publisher>-<Publication Database>-<number>`

Any subsequent publications you set up in that publication database will also use this job.

By default, the job is scheduled to start when the SQL Server service starts. That means the job is always running. Given how SQL Server reuses log space, this is the preferred setting, which means you should not change this behavior.

Distribution Agent jobs

By default, SQL Server creates a job for each subscription in order to execute the Distribution Agent. The job runs either on the Distributor (push subscription) or on the Subscriber (pull subscription). The push subscription distribution jobs are named according to the following convention:

`<Publisher>-<Publication Database>-<Publication>-<Subscriber>-<number>`

The pull subscription distribution jobs follow a slightly different naming pattern:

```
<Publisher>-<Publication Database>-<Publication>-<Subscriber>-
<Subscription Database>-<GUID>
```

Replication Maintenance jobs

In addition to the jobs that execute replication agents, SQL Server creates several jobs related to transactional replication maintenance. Those jobs are mainly tasked with cleanup and problem detection. Each of these jobs is discussed in more detail below.

Creating the SQL Server Agent Jobs

SQL Server creates the replication-related jobs automatically at various steps during replication setup. The following sections describe which job is created as part of which step. To illustrate when and where jobs are created, we've designated the SQL Server instance SQL1\S12A as the Distributor, SQL2\S12A as the Publisher, and SQL3\S12A as the Subscriber.

When you first enable SQL Server Agent on a SQL Server instance, the only job that exists is syspolicy_purge_history. Figure 8-1 shows how that job is listed in the SQL Server Agent **Job Activity Monitor** for all three SQL Server instances.

Figure 8-1: The default SQL Server jobs on the Distributor, Publisher, and Subscriber.

Local distribution

When you configure a SQL Server instance to be a Distributor, replication setup creates several SQL Server Agent jobs, as shown in Figure 8-2.

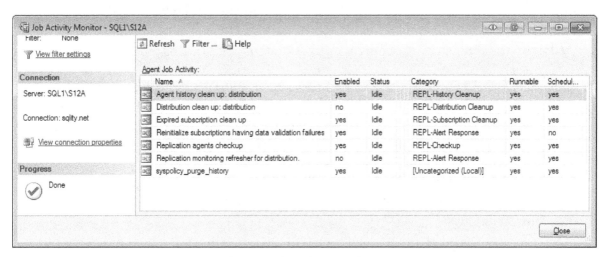

Figure 8-2: The SQL Server Agent jobs created on the Distributor.

As you can see, six SQL Server Agent jobs have been created on the Distributor:

- **Agent history clean up:** `<distribution database name>` – Removes from the distribution database all history records that keep track of the agents' performance. The job uses the **history retention** setting of the distribution database to determine which records to delete. SQL Server creates one job of this type for each distribution database on the Distributor.

- **Distribution clean up:** `<distribution database name>` – Removes old transaction information from the distribution database. The job also checks whether all Subscribers received each record. Based on the result of that check and the replication retention settings, the job then determines which records to delete from the distribution database. In addition, the job disables subscriptions that failed to read the transaction information in time. The job also regularly refreshes the statistics on the tables in the distribution database. SQL Server creates one job of this type for each distribution database on the Distributor.

- **Expired subscription clean up** – Removes subscriptions that fail to connect to the Subscriber within the publication retention period. This job runs on the Distributor as well as on the Publisher. SQL Server creates one instance of this job on each server.

- **Reinitialize subscriptions having data validation failures** – Identifies subscriptions with data validation errors and sets them up for re-initialization. You can use data validation to verify data consistency between the Publisher and Subscriber. For more information, see the topic, *Validating Replicated Data* in SQL Server Books Online.

- **Replication agents checkup** – Monitors the replication agents and creates an entry in the Windows Event Log if any replication agent fails to report its status in the distribution database.

- **Replication monitoring refresher for** `<distribution database name>` – Used by the replication monitor to refresh cached queries.

Remote distribution

When you configure remote distribution on a Publisher, replication setup creates one additional SQL Server Agent job to the Publisher, as shown in Figure 8-3.

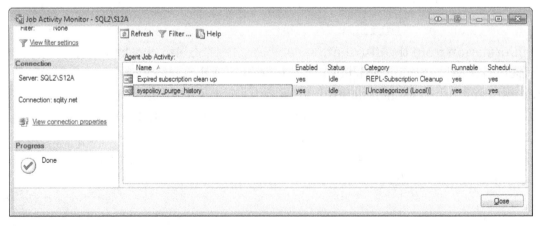

Figure 8-3: The SQL Server Agent job created for remote distribution.

The **Expired subscription clean up** job is responsible for removing the Publisher's metadata of expired subscriptions.

Publication

When you create a publication, SQL Server creates two jobs on the Distributor, but none on the Publisher, as you can see in Figure 8-4. Remember that SQL1\S12A is the Distributor and SQL2\S12A the Publisher.

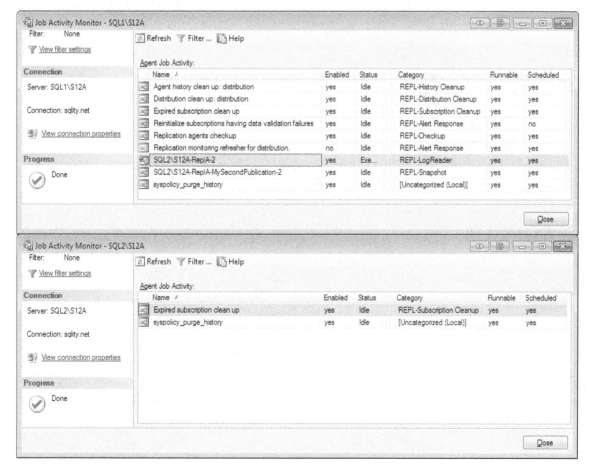

Figure 8-4:   Publication-related jobs located only on the Distributor.

The two publication-related jobs are SQL2\S12A-ReplA-2 and SQL2\S12A-ReplA-MySecondPublication-2. They run the Log Reader Agent and the Snapshot Agent, respectively.

You can tell which SQL Server Agent job runs which replication agent by referring to the **Category** column in the Job Activity Monitor.

Remember, the Snapshot Agent is used to prepare the first synchronization for each Subscriber. It copies all the schema information and all the data of the published objects into the snapshot folder. The Log Reader Agent is responsible to read the log file of the published database and copy all the data necessary to reproduce the object or data changes in the subscription database. It stores that information in the distribution database.

Push subscription

When you configure a push subscription, SQL Server creates a single SQL Server Agent job on the Distributor. The job runs the Distribution Agent. If you refer to Figure 8-5, you'll see that a new job, SQL2\S12A-ReplA-MyFirstPublication-SQL3\S12A-5, has been created on SQL1\S12A, which is our Distributor.

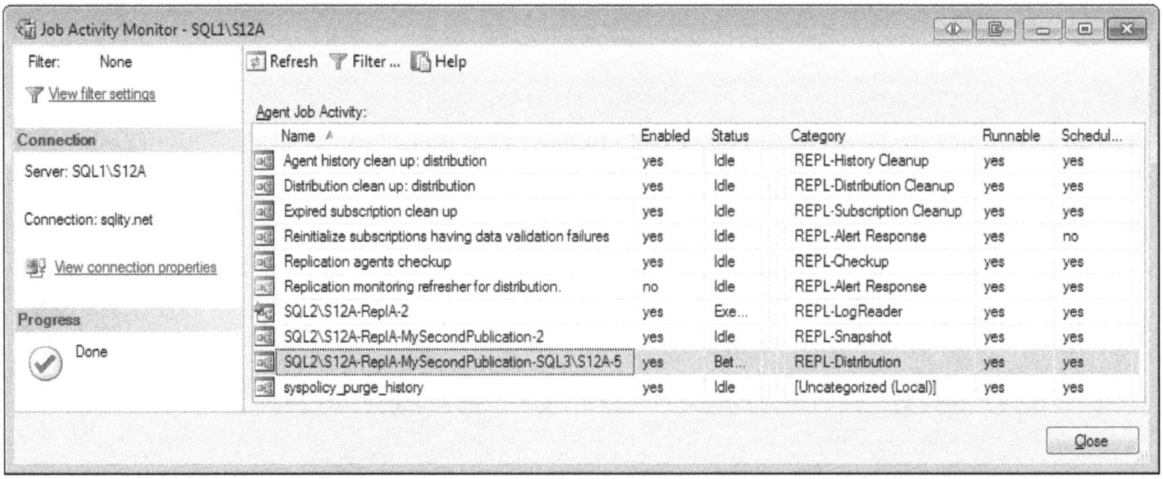

Figure 8-5: SQL Server Agent job on the Distributor to support a push subscription.

Figure 8-6 reveals that there are no additional jobs on either the Publisher or the Subscriber.

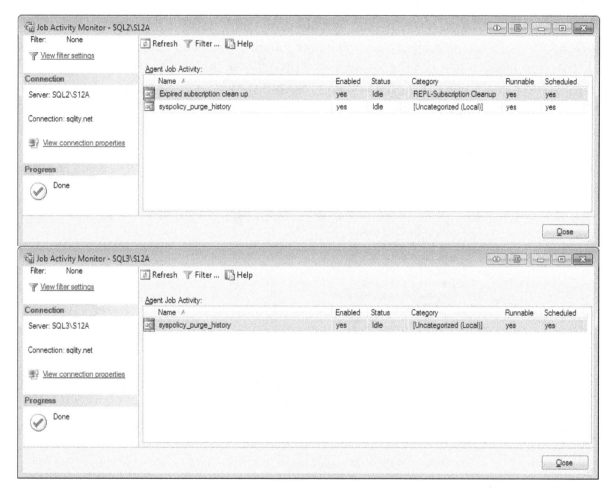

Figure 8-6: No subscription-related jobs on Publisher or Subscriber.

As you can see, in the push subscription model all three replication agents live on the Distributor.

Pull subscription

When you configure a pull subscription, SQL Server again creates only a single SQL Server Agent job to run the Distribution Agent, but this time it's located on the Subscriber. Figure 8-7 shows the Job Activity Monitor for the Distributor (SQL1\S12A) and the Subscriber (SQL3\S12A). In this case, the name of the job is rather long: SQL2\S12A-ReplA-MySecondPublication-SQL3\S12A-ReplB-CCEFBC29-C803-4A32-B743-FF86A59071BF.

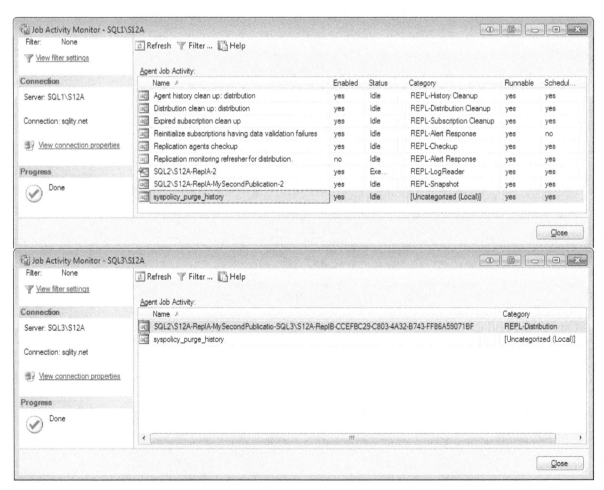

Figure 8-7:   SQL Server Agent job on the Subscriber to support a pull subscription.

Again, if you want to identify which SQL Server Agent job is associated with which replication agent, check the **Category** column.

Summary

In this chapter we discussed all the different SQL Server Agent jobs that are responsible for executing the replication agents as well as performing other maintenance tasks. We discovered when each job is created during the replication setup process and how to tell what each job's purpose is.

This chapter closes the section on transactional replication. The next few chapters will walk you through everything you need to know about merge replication.

Chapter 9: Merge Replication – the Replication Agents

Similar to the replication agents used in transactional replication, merge replication agents are external programs that facilitate data movement across the SQL Server instances participating in replication. However, in merge replication, the agents also utilize a special set of triggers, tables, and views implemented specifically to support merge replication. These components are unique to merge replication and are not used in transactional replication.

When you run the replication setup wizards, SQL Server automatically creates the necessary merge replication agents, the SQL Server Agent jobs that run those agents, and the set of triggers, tables, and views that the agents use.

In this chapter, you'll learn about the replication agents and the other components that support the merge replication process. The chapter explains what each component is, the role it plays, and how it interacts with other components to facilitate merge replication.

Merge Replication Components

In transactional replication, the Snapshot Agent creates the initial snapshot required to initialize the Subscribers. The Log Reader Agent and the Distribution Agent together facilitate the actual data movement from the Publisher to the Subscriber. For an in-depth explanation of the replication agents that support transactional replication, refer back to Chapter 4.

A merge replication setup looks a little different. It includes the following components:

- Snapshot Agent

- Triggers, tables, and views

- Merge Agent.

The Snapshot Agent used in merge replication plays the same role as in transactional replication: it creates a snapshot of the data in the publication database, which is required to initialize or reinitialize a Subscriber.

In merge replication, the role that the Log Reader Agent fills in transactional replication is taken by a set of triggers, tables, and views. These objects are added to each subscription database as well as to the publication database.

The Merge Agent is comparable to the Distribution Agent in transactional replication. It applies the collected changes to the Subscriber. Because merge replication is bi-directional, the Merge Agent also applies changes to the Publisher as required.

Figure 9-1 provides an overview of how these components work together.

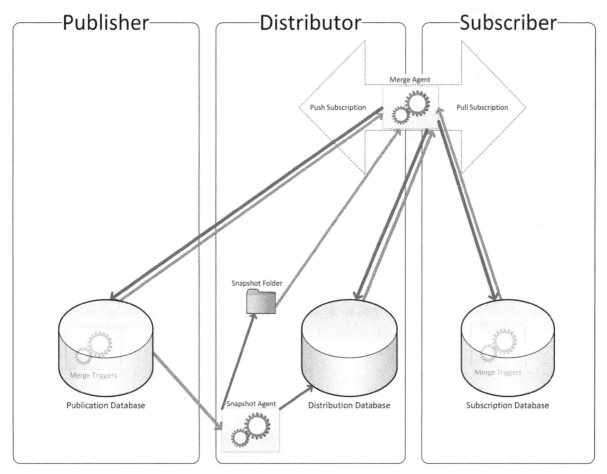

Figure 9-1:   **Merge replication agents and triggers.**

The arrows in Figure 9-1 show how the replication agents work with the data. The arrows reflect the direction of the data flow; the lighter-colored arrows indicate read access, whereas the black arrows indicate write access. The Merge Agent lives on either the Distributor or the Subscriber, depending on the subscription model.

Let's look a little closer at each of these components to better understand how they work.

Snapshot Agent

As in transactional replication, merge replication uses the Snapshot Agent to generate a snapshot of the data in the publication database. Merge replication then uses the snapshot to initialize the subscription database. As in transactional replication, there are other ways to execute the initial synchronization. However, using the Snapshot Agent is certainly the most convenient way.

Compared to transactional replication, there is one important difference in how merge replication uses the Snapshot Agent. In transactional replication, the Snapshot Agent uses concurrent processing, which means it doesn't take any extended locks on the published articles. This technique relies on markers written to the database log during the snapshot generation. The Log Reader Agent picks up these markers, and the Distribution Agent then uses the markers to figure out which changes still need to be applied to the Subscriber and which changes were already picked up by the Snapshot Agent. (See Chapter 4 for more details about how this technique works.)

Because merge replication does not use the Log Reader Agent, it cannot use these markers and concurrent snapshot processing is therefore not an option. As a result, the Snapshot Agent takes a lock on all published tables during a portion of the time it takes to generate the snapshot. This ensures transactional consistency between the publication and subscription databases.

This description is a stark oversimplification of what is actually going on during snapshot creation. Most of the locks are not actually taken on the published tables. Instead, they're taken on the metadata tables created by merge replication to hold the information about data changes. Even so, the locks still block other transactions trying to write to the published tables because those transactions would fire the merge replication triggers that write to the metadata tables. However, those locks do not interact with other reading transactions.

In addition, the length that each lock is taken has nothing to do with the amount of data in the published tables. Instead, it depends on the amount of data in the metadata tables, which is directly related to the amount of changes in the published tables since the last synchronization. Because of this, the Snapshot Agent is able to hold on to the locks for a shorter time in most cases. SQL Server Books Online gives a little more insight into this process, although it's not too detailed about it either.

The important point to take away is that the published tables cannot be updated during the time those locks are held. Processes attempting to update any of the published tables (or to change non-table articles) are therefore going to be blocked. Because of this locking behavior, you should try to schedule the snapshot generation to run during off-peak hours. Chapter 10 explains how to do this.

For each publication, SQL Server creates a SQL Server Agent job to execute the Snapshot Agent. Replication names these jobs based on the following pattern:

`<Server>-<Publication Database>-<Publication>-<number>`

If you need to generate a new snapshot, you can manually start the Snapshot Agent job for the publication, or you can schedule the job to run at a later time.

Triggers, tables, and views

When you configure merge replication, SQL Server adds a set of triggers, tables, and views to the publication database in order to monitor and record changes to the published articles. Because merge replication permits data to flow from the Publisher to the Subscriber as well as from the Subscriber to the Publisher, the same set of objects is also added to each subscription database.

Replication defines three triggers on every published table. The triggers conform to the following naming convention:

```
MSmerge_???_FA62745126C846858453EEF185F94618
```

The long hexadecimal number at the end of the name is the internal article identifier. The question marks (???) serve as a placeholder for one of the following three values:

- del (for delete trigger)
- ins (for insert trigger)
- upd (for update trigger).

These triggers are responsible for recording every change that is applied to the data in the published tables.

Replication also creates the following database triggers to capture any schema changes to the published articles:

- MSmerge_tr_alterschemaonly
- MSmerge_tr_altertable
- MSmerge_tr_altertrigger
- MSmerge_tr_alterview

The changes recorded by the triggers are not applied to the Subscribers right away. Instead, data that can be used to identify which records and columns changed is stored in replication metadata tables in the database in which the change happened. The names of all these tables begin with MSmerge_. Replication also creates several system views that follow the same naming pattern. These views are used by the internal merge replication processes. For more information about the triggers, tables, and views specific to merge replication, refer to SQL Server Books Online.

Merge Agent

The Merge Agent uses the information recorded by the database triggers to synchronize the changes between the Publisher and all its Subscribers. The Merge Agent, like the other replication agents, is an autonomous program separate from the SQL Server service.

By default, SQL Server creates a SQL Server Agent job for each subscription to execute the Merge Agent. The job runs either on the Distributor (for push subscriptions) or on the Subscriber (for pull subscriptions). The push subscription jobs conform to the following naming convention:

```
<Publisher>-<Publication Database>-<Publication>-<Subscriber>-
<number>
```

The naming convention for pull subscription jobs looks a little different:

```
<Publisher>-<Publication Database>-<Publication>-<Subscriber>-
<Subscription Database>-<number>
```

In both cases, the `<number>` placeholder represents a number, usually a small one, used to prevent name collisions.

Summary

This chapter introduced the different components that support the merge replication process and showed how those components interact to make merge replication work.

We talked about the Snapshot Agent and how it must take table locks to prevent changes to the underlying data while it generates the snapshot. As you've seen, there is a significant difference between the initialization of a merge replication setup and a transactional replication setup. We also talked about the Merge Agent and the different triggers that it relies on to record changes to the data in the replicated tables or changes to the replicated objects themselves.

In the chapters to follow, you'll learn how to set up merge replication so you can see for yourself the merge components in action.

Chapter 10: Merge Replication – the Publication

Merge replication, like transactional replication, involves a Distributor, a Publisher, and one or more Subscribers. On each Publisher, you can define one or more publications. Those publications can include merge publications, transactional publications, snapshot publications, or any combination of the three. As with transactional replication, merge replication requires that the articles in a publication reside in a single database. You can, however, define different publications on different databases or even multiple publications on the same database. You can also include the same article in more than one publication. But, as mentioned before, all publications on a single Publisher, regardless of their type, must use the same Distributor and distribution database.

Merge replication was designed to allow client systems (Subscribers) to work in a state disconnected from the main server system (Publisher). When the Subscribers reconnect to the Publisher, changes on the Publisher are copied to the Subscribers, and vice versa. This process allows for real asynchronous synchronization and therefore uninhibited work while disconnected. However, any form of bi-directional synchronization can result in conflicts, such as the same record being updated on the Publisher and a Subscriber at the same time, or on two Subscribers at the same time. To address such issues, merge replication includes a set of "conflict resolvers" that can automatically handle conflicts based on a set of rules.

As you'll recall from previous chapters, transactional replication makes use of the SQL Server transaction log to replicate data changes to the Subscribers. In contrast, merge replication does not keep a record of the changes but instead works with the data in the published tables when the synchronization is performed. This helps to reduce the storage requirements on each server while being disconnected from the rest of the replication setup. However, it does introduce some storage overhead and inflexibility, because there needs to be a way to identify records that changed between synchronizations. Chapter 9 explains how this process works.

In this chapter, you'll learn how to set up a merge publication and how to add articles to that publication. We'll also cover where you select the conflict resolver for each article and how to decide if that article is going to be synchronized bi-directionally or one way only.

To perform the exercises in this chapter, you need a database that contains objects you can replicate. We'll be using the ReplM database, which you can create by running the script in Listing 10-1.

```
USE MASTER;
GO
EXECUTE AS LOGIN = 'SA';
GO
CREATE DATABASE ReplM;
GO
USE ReplM;
GO
CREATE TABLE dbo.Tbl1(
  Id INT IDENTITY(1,1) PRIMARY KEY,
  Data INT CONSTRAINT Tbl1_Data_Dflt DEFAULT CHECKSUM(NEWID()),
  Data2 INT CONSTRAINT Tbl1_Data2_Dflt DEFAULT CHECKSUM(NEWID()),
  Data3 INT CONSTRAINT Tbl1_Data3_Dflt DEFAULT CHECKSUM(NEWID())
);

GO
INSERT INTO dbo.Tbl1 DEFAULT VALUES;
GO 1000
GO
CREATE TABLE dbo.Tbl2(
  Id INT IDENTITY(1,1) PRIMARY KEY,
  Data INT CONSTRAINT Tbl2_Data_Dflt DEFAULT CHECKSUM(NEWID()),
  Data2 INT CONSTRAINT Tbl2_Data2_Dflt DEFAULT CHECKSUM(NEWID()),
  Data3 INT CONSTRAINT Tbl2_Data3_Dflt DEFAULT CHECKSUM(NEWID())
);
```

```
GO
INSERT INTO dbo.Tbl2 DEFAULT VALUES;
GO 1000
GO
CREATE PROC dbo.Proc1
AS
BEGIN
  INSERT INTO dbo.Tbl1 DEFAULT VALUES;
END;
GO
CREATE VIEW dbo.View1
AS
  SELECT   Id, Data
  FROM     dbo.Tbl1
  WHERE    Id > 500;
GO
CREATE VIEW dbo.View2 WITH SCHEMABINDING
AS
  SELECT   Id, Data
  FROM     dbo.Tbl2
  WHERE    Id < 500;
GO
CREATE UNIQUE CLUSTERED INDEX [dob.View2(Id):CI] ON dbo.View2(Id);
GO
CREATE FUNCTION dbo.Func1()
RETURNS INT
AS
BEGIN
  DECLARE @r INT = (SELECT MAX(Id) FROM dbo.Tbl2);
  RETURN @r;
END;
GO
USE MASTER;
GO
REVERT;
GO
```

Listing 10-1:   Creating a test database for the merge publication.

Enabling a Database for Merge Replication

Similar to transactional publications, any member of a database's **db_owner** role can create a merge publication in that database. However, before that can happen, the database needs to be enabled for merge replication by a member of the **sysadmin** fixed server role.

Our first task, then, is to enable the **Repl M** database for merge replication. To perform this task, you need to be a member of the **sysadmin** fixed server role on the Publisher. In addition, you must have already set up the SQL Server instance hosting this database as a Publisher linked to your Distributor. Refer back to Chapter 3 for details on this second requirement.

Once your environment is ready, you can enable the **Repl M** database for merge replication. The following steps walk you through that process:

1. In SQL Server Management Studio (SSMS), connect to the SQL Server instance you have designated as your Publisher for this exercise. The examples in this chapter use the SQL Server instance **SQL2\S12A** as the Publisher.

2. In **Object Explorer**, right-click the **Replication** folder for that instance, and then click **Publisher Properties**, as shown in Figure 10-1.

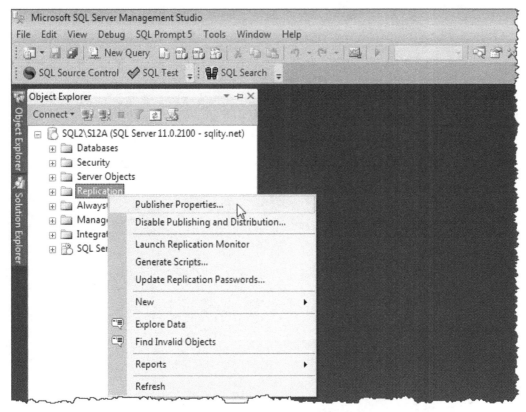

Figure 10-1: Accessing the Publisher Properties in Object Explorer.

3. In the **Publisher Properties** dialog box, go to the **Publication Databases** page, and select the **Merge** check box in the row associated with your database. Figure 10-2 shows the **Merge** check box selected for the Repl1M database, the database we created at the beginning of this chapter.

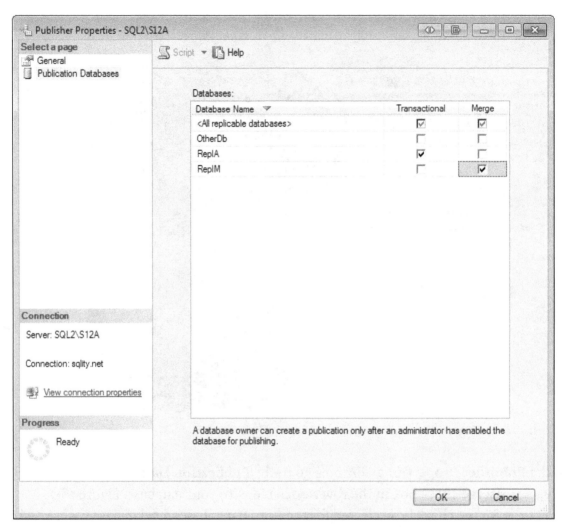

Figure 10-2: Enabling a database for merge replication.

4. After you have made your selection, click **OK** to close the **Publisher Properties** dialog box.

Now that you've enabled the database for merge replication, any member of the db_owner role associated with that database can define a publication on it.

Creating a Publication

You're now ready to create a merge publication. The rest of the chapter walks you through the steps necessary to add a publication to the `ReplM` database. For all these steps, we'll use the **New Publication Wizard**. The wizard is the simplest way to create a publication, although there are still a number of steps that must be performed. For that reason, we've grouped the steps into the following exercises: adding a publication to the publication database, adding articles to that publication, configuring the Snapshot Agent and its security, and finalizing your publication. After performing these exercises, you'll have a working publication that is ready to be subscribed to.

Adding a publication

After launching the **New Publication Wizard**, your first steps will be to create the initial publication in your publication database and then to select **Merge Replication** as its type. The following steps walk you through that process:

1. In **Object Explorer**, expand the **Replication** folder of the SQL Server instance that holds the database you want to publish. (This is the same database you enabled in the previous task.)

2. Right-click the **Local Publications** subfolder, and click **New Publication**, as shown in Figure 10-3.

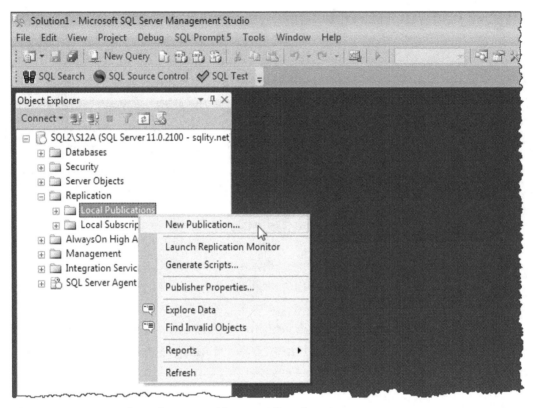

Figure 10-3: Launching the New Publication Wizard.

3. If the first page of the **New Publication Wizard** is the Welcome page, click **Next** to advance to the **Publication Database** page, shown in Figure 10-4. If you want, you can also select the option to disable the Welcome page so it doesn't appear when you use the wizard in the future.

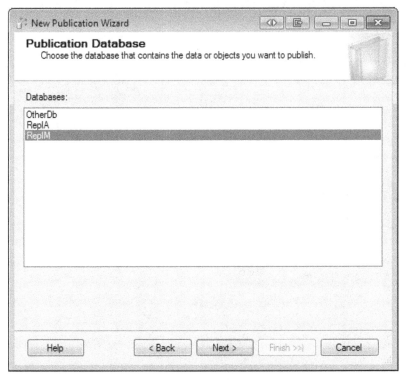

Figure 10-4:   Choosing the publication database.

4.   On the **Publication Database** page, select the database in which you want to define your publication. For the exercises in this chapter, we're using the Rep1M database, the same database we enabled for merge replication in the previous task.

5. Click **Next** to advance to the **Publication Type** page, shown in Figure 10-5. This is where we select the publication type.

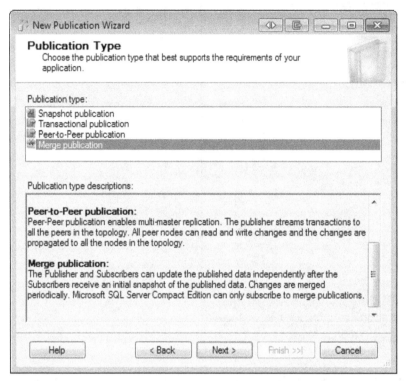

Figure 10-5: Selecting Merge publication as the publication type.

Up to this point, the steps for creating a merge publication have been very similar to those used to create a transactional publication. That, however, will change as we continue working through the wizard.

6. Select the **Merge publication** option on the **Publication Type** page, and then click **Next** to advance to the **Subscriber Types** page, shown in Figure 10-6.

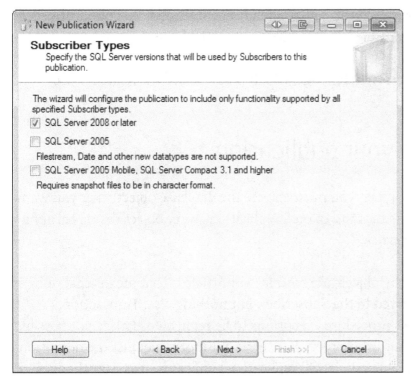

Figure 10-6: Selecting the Subscriber types that can use your publication.

On the **Subscriber Types** page, you select one or more SQL Server versions that the publication will support. Any Subscriber that connects to this publication must be running one of these versions. Note, however, that any selection other than SQL Server 2008 will cause the publication to run with reduced functionality. (SQL Server 2012 did not introduce any new functionality.) For details about these restrictions, refer to SQL Server Books Online.

7. Select one or more Subscriber types. For these exercises, we've selected only the **SQL Server 2008 or later** option. If possible, you should try to follow the same strategy so you can benefit from all the functionality now available to merge replication.

Note that, if your publication database already contains a merge publication, the **Subscriber Types** page might show a reduced number of options. That's because, with few exceptions, all merge publications in the same database need to use the same Subscriber types, and if a merge publication has already been defined, that publication's configuration settings will determine which options are available here.

8.   Click **Next** to advance to the **Articles** page, which is covered in the next section.

Adding articles to your publication

After you select the Subscriber types, you must choose the database objects that you want to include in the publication. As in transactional replication, every object that is part of a merge publication is called an *article*.

In merge replication, most of the objects are *schema-only* articles. That means that only the object's definition is replicated to the Subscriber, but nothing else. Transactional replication, for example, allows procedure executions to be replicated. This is not possible with merge replication. The only article type that allows for more than just the definition to be replicated is the table; a table article will replicate schema as well as data changes.

The main reason for this restriction is the way merge replication works. Transactional replication reads the transaction log and therefore has access to a detailed list of every action that happened in that database in chronological order.

Merge replication relies instead on a series of table triggers to capture data changes. It also uses object-level triggers that can capture schema changes of those objects but no other interaction with them, such as stored procedure executions. While this approach has limitations in some areas, as we have seen above, it is also more flexible in other places. For example, you can replicate tables that do not contain a primary key, something not possible with transactional replication. (For more details about the inner workings of merge replication, refer back to Chapter 9.)

To add articles to your publication, take the following steps:

1. If you have not already done so, advance to the `Articles` page in the **New Publication Wizard**. The **Articles** page should look similar to the one shown in Figure 10-7.

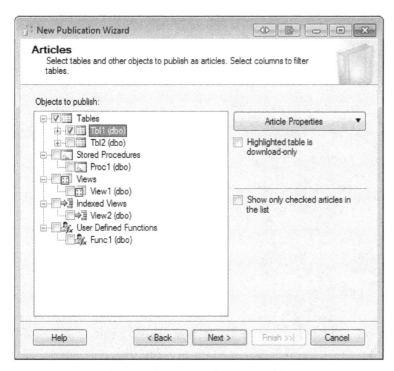

Figure 10-7: Selecting the articles for your publication.

On the **Articles** page, you can select tables, stored procedures, views, indexed views, and user-defined functions to be replicated to your Subscribers. For now, select only the `dbo.Tbl1` table.

2. As with transactional replication, you can replicate a table in its entirety or you can select individual columns to be replicated (vertical filter). For this exercise, we'll include a couple of columns from the `dbo.Tbl2` table, so expand the column list for that table by clicking the plus sign next to the table name. Then select columns `Id` and `Data2`. Figure 10-8 shows the selected columns on the **Articles** page.

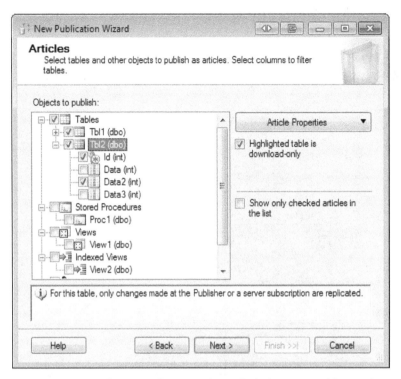

Figure 10-8: Selecting columns to be included in your table article.

When you highlight a table that is selected as an article, the **Highlighted table is download-only** option appears beneath the **Article Properties** button. If you select this option, changes to the table's data are not permitted on the Subscriber.

You should select this option for any table that contains data that should not be changed on the Subscriber(s). This selection causes significantly less data to be collected on the Publisher because there is no need to maintain data to help resolve conflicts. (A conflict occurs when a row is changed in more than one place at a time. If the Publisher is the only place where data changes can be made, conflicts cannot happen. See Chapter 12 for details on conflicts.) Not permitting changes to the replication data on the Subscriber side can therefore have a dramatic impact on performance and space requirements on the Publisher.

You can also set this option in the article's properties. To access the properties, ensure that the table article is selected in the **Objects to publish** list, click the **Article Properties** button, and then click **Set Properties of Highlighted Table Article**. This launches the **Article Properties** dialog box, shown in Figure 10-9.

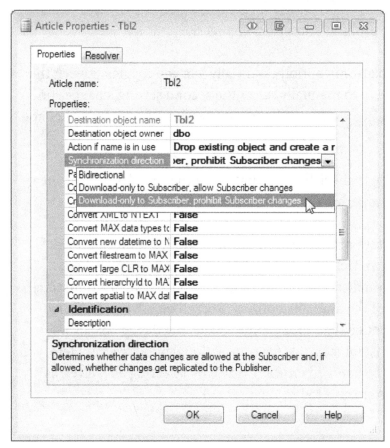

Figure 10-9:   Selecting a synchronization direction.

The article property that corresponds to the **Highlighted table is download-only** option is **Synchronization direction**. The property supports the following three settings:

- Bi-directional

- Download-only to Subscriber, allow Subscriber changes

- Download-only to Subscriber, prohibit Subscriber changes.

The **Highlighted table is download-only** option essentially lets you toggle between the first and the last setting. If you were to manually select the second setting, changes on the Subscriber would be allowed, but would not be transferred back to the Publisher and might be overwritten.

The fact that this option has a single check box alternative on the **Articles** page of the wizard shows the importance of selecting the appropriate setting for your articles.

Of course, there are other important properties you can also configure on an article. As you can see in Figure 10-9, the **Article Properties** dialog box includes numerous settings for an article in a merge publication, just as it does for an article in a transactional publication. (For a complete list of the available options for each object type, refer to SQL Server Books Online.) But notice that, for a merge article, the dialog box also includes the **Resolver** tab, which is not available for transactional publications. Here, you can specify how conflicts should be handled for each article by selecting a resolver, as shown in Figure 10-10. (Resolvers are covered in Chapter 12.)

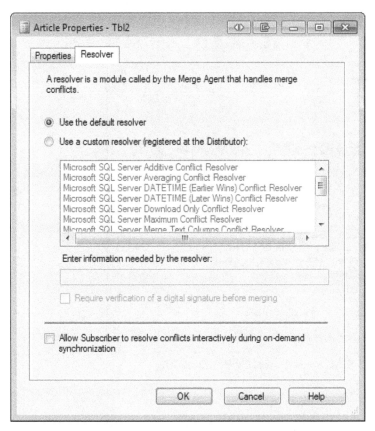

Figure 10-10: Determining how to handle merge conflicts.

3. Click the **Cancel** button to close the **Article Properties** dialog box and return to the **Articles** page of the **New Publication Wizard**. On the **Articles** page make sure that the **Highlighted table is download-only** option is checked for dbo.Tbl2, as shown in Figure 10-8, and then click **Next**.

4. The next page to appear in the **New Publication Wizard** is the **Article Issues** page, which provides you with any warnings that might apply to your publication. While there are several possible warnings that can be displayed here, you're most likely to see the one shown in Figure 10-11 when you're setting up a merge publication.

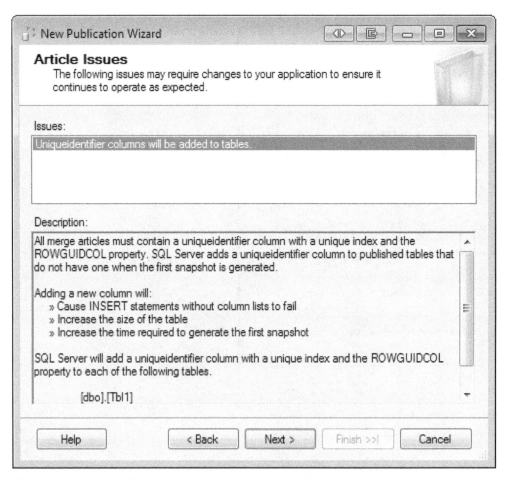

Figure 10-11: Receiving a uniqueidentifier warning.

The warning tells you that merge replication requires each replicated table to include a uniqueidentifier column configured with the ROWGUIDCOL property and a unique index. If such a column does not exist, SQL Server will automatically add it when the first snapshot is generated. That change can potentially break existing code accessing those tables. It will also increase the size of the table by at least 16 bytes per row.

*****

Warning

If you ever drop the merge publication, every `uniqueidentifier` *column that was automatically added to its articles will be removed automatically as well. This has the potential of breaking any code that was written after replication was established and that now relies on those columns being there. For that reason, it's a good practice to manually add those columns before you set up merge replication. That way, you have full control over the columns and if and when they get dropped.*

*****

5. For this exercise, we'll accept the default behavior and let SQL Server add the necessary columns. Click **Next** to advance to the **Filter Table Rows** page.

6. On the **Filter Table Rows** page (shown in Figure 10-12), you can add row level filters to your table articles. The page appears only if you've added at least one table article to the publication.

Figure 10-12: The Filter Table Rows page of the New Publication Wizard.

7. Click the **Add** button, and then click **Add Filter** to open the **Add Filter** dialog box.

8. In the **Add Filter** dialog box, select `Tbl2 (dbo)` from the **Select the table to filter** drop-down list. You can then add a row filter, in the **Filter statement** windows. A row filter, or *horizontal filter,* looks like a `SELECT` statement that includes a `WHERE` clause, as shown in Figure 10-13. However, you can edit only the code after the `WHERE` keyword.

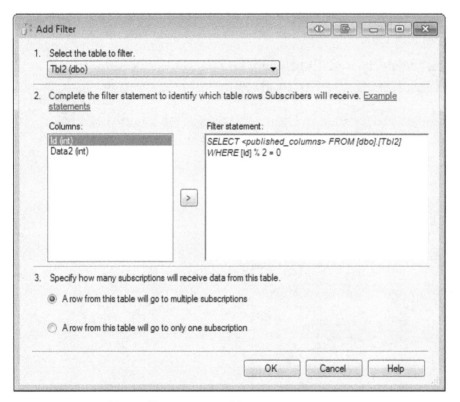

Figure 10-13:   Adding a filter to your publication.

9. The purpose of the column list on the left side of the **Add Filter** dialog box is to help you with remembering (and typing) the column names of the current article. The selected column does not affect the functionality of the filter.

10. Complete the query so it matches what is shown in Figure 10-13, and then click **OK**. This filter will cause only rows that have an even number value in the `Id` column to get replicated.

11. When you're returned to the **Filter Table Rows** page, it should now show that there is a filter defined for the table dbo.Tbl2, as shown in Figure 10-14.

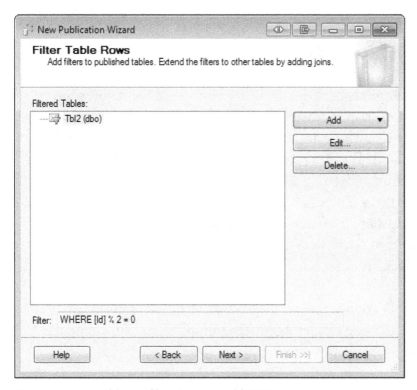

Figure 10-14: Adding a filter to your publication.

12. Click **Next** to advance to the Snapshot Agent section of the wizard, which we cover in the next section.

Configuring the Snapshot Agent

In the next part of the **New Publication Wizard**, you configure the Snapshot Agent. This process is almost identical to the steps you took to set up the agents for transactional replication. However, two differences stand out.

First, when you're setting up merge replication, the wizard by default configures the Snapshot Agent to create a snapshot immediately and to create a new one every 14 days, which is different from what you saw for transactional replication. Because merge replication is primarily meant for clients that are often disconnected from the Publisher, the likelihood that a resynchronization will be necessary is much higher than for always connected transactional Subscribers. Therefore, in merge replication, it's a good practice to regularly generate a new snapshot so a fresh one is available when needed. That way, you don't have to run the Snapshot Agent during high traffic times if the need for a snapshot arises. See the *Snapshot Agent* section in Chapter 9 for more information.

The second way that merge replication is different from transactional replication is that merge replication does not use the Log Reader Agent. Therefore, when you configure agent security, you'll find only the Snapshot Agent.

The Snapshot Agent used for merge replication requires the same access rights as the Snapshot Agent used for transactional replication. Any account you assign to the agent must be a member of the `db_owner` fixed database role in the publication and distribution databases. The account that the agent runs under must also have write access to the snapshot folder.

The following steps explain how to configure the Snapshot Agent:

1. If necessary, advance to the **Snapshot Agent** page of the **New Publication Wizard**.
    As you can see in Figure 10-15, you can select whether a snapshot should be created
    immediately, and you can schedule future snapshots. By default, both options
    are selected.

Figure 10-15: Configuring the Snapshot Agent.

2. Leave the default schedule settings (immediate, and every 14 days), and click **Next** to
    advance to the **Agent Security** page, shown in Figure 10-16.

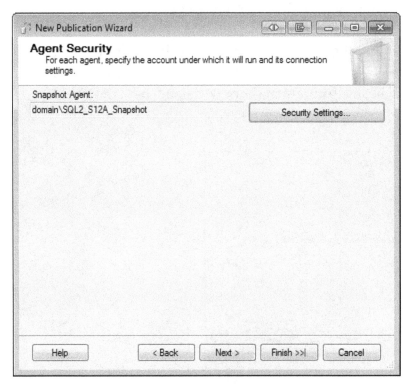

Figure 10-16: Configuring security for the Snapshot Agent.

3.   Click the **Security Settings** button to open the **Snapshot Agent Security** dialog box, shown in Figure 10-17.

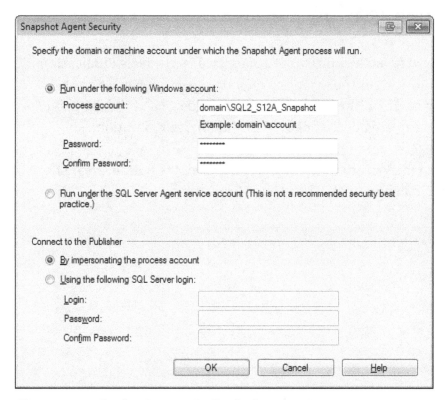

Figure 10-17: Configuring security for the Snapshot Agent.

4. Type the Windows account that the snapshot should run under. For these exercises, we're using the `domain\SQL2_S12A_Snapshot` account.

5. In the **Connect to the Publisher** section, select the option **By impersonating the process account**. Note that, as with transactional replication, instead of using impersonation you might have to specify a SQL Server login in some cases, such as when the Publisher and Distributor are in different domains.

6. Click **OK** to close the **Snapshot Agent Security** dialog box. You're returned to the **Agent Security** page of the **New Publication Wizard**.

7. Click **Next** to continue to the final section of the **New Publication Wizard**, which we cover in the following few paragraphs.

Finalizing your publication

The last few pages of the wizard are identical to the ones used by the **New Publication Wizard** when creating a transactional publication. You must specify what action the wizard should take when you are finished, and you must provide a name for the publication. The following steps explain how to finish setting up merge replication:

1. If necessary, advance to the **Wizard Actions** page, and select the option **Create the publication**, as shown in Figure 10-18. Then click **Next**.

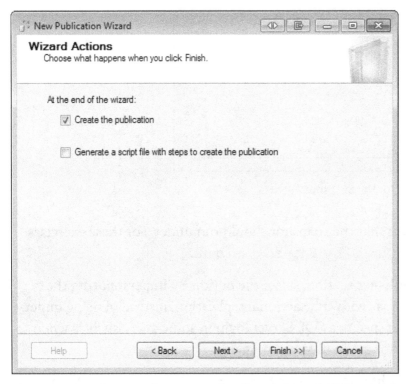

Figure 10-18: Choosing the action to be taken at the end of the wizard.

2. On the **Complete the Wizard** page, type a name for your publication. In this case, we've used `MyFirstMergePublication`, as shown in Figure 10-19.

Figure 10-19: Specifying a publication name and reviewing the options.

3. Review the actions listed on the **Complete the Wizard** page, and then click **Finish**. The **Creating Publication** page appears and provides details about the publication creation process, as shown in Figure 10-20.

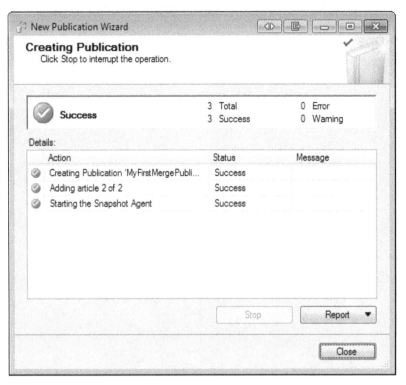

Figure 10-20: Creating the publication.

4. Before long, the **Creating Publication** page should show the steps executed and whether they were successful. If everything succeeded, click **Close** to close the wizard.

5. At this point, you have successfully created a merge publication. The next step is to create a subscription for this publication, which is the topic of Chapter 11.

Potential Problems

As with transactional replication, there are a lot of things that can go wrong when setting up merge replication. The most common problem to occur in merge replication, as well as in transactional replication, is that one of the specified accounts or logins does not have the appropriate permissions. (If you followed the example, you have specified only one account so far, the one used for the Snapshot Agent.)

If you run into problems, make sure all accounts used have the appropriate rights granted. For details on how to troubleshoot problems, review the *Potential Problems* section in Chapter 5, which covers problems you might run into when setting up a transactional publication. Most of the suggestions there can be helpful for merge replication as well. For more in-depth troubleshooting help, check out Chapter 14.

Summary

This chapter demonstrated how to create a publication for merge replication and how to add articles to that publication. The chapter listed the different types of articles and discussed their synchronization options. It also pointed out the differences from setting up a publication for transactional replication.

As with transactional replication, after doing all the work to set up a merge publication, there's not a lot to show for your efforts. To see something happening, you also need at least one subscription. In the next chapter, you'll learn how to set up a subscription to support merge replication.

Chapter 11: Merge Replication – the Subscription

In Chapter 10, we created a publication to support our merge replication setup. Our next step is to create a subscription, just like we did for transactional replication. To do this, we first need to designate a SQL Server instance to be the Subscriber. As with transactional replication, any instance on which a subscription is defined is considered a Subscriber, and the database that the published changes are applied to is called the subscription database.

Setting up a Subscription

To set up a subscription to support merge replication, we must perform a number of steps, such as selecting the Publisher, choosing the subscription type and subscription database, and configuring security. For most of these steps, we'll use the **New Subscription Wizard**, which walks us through the process of setting up the subscription. In addition to running the wizard, we'll need to take a few other steps to set up our subscription, such as setting up the Publication Access List (PAL) and configuring retention. After we've completed all these steps, we'll have a working merge replication setup with a single Subscriber and a single subscription.

The permissions you need to set up a merge subscription are very similar to the ones needed for a transactional subscription. In this chapter, we're going to create a pull subscription, as that is the more common scenario for merge replication. Therefore, we assume for the rest of the chapter that you have at least db_owner level permissions in the subscription database and that you are a member of the PAL for the publication we created in the previous chapter. For more details on how to add your account to the PAL, refer back to Chapter 6. For the permissions required to set up a push merge subscription, refer to SQL Server Books Online.

Selecting the Publisher

We'll start the process of setting up our subscription by opening the **New Subscription Wizard** and identifying the Publisher, publication database, and publication itself. The following steps walk you through this process:

1. In SQL Server Management Studio (SSMS), connect to the SQL Server instance you have designated as your Subscriber.

2. In **Object Explorer**, expand the instance folder and then the **Replication** folder. Right-click **Local Subscriptions** and then click **New Subscriptions**, as shown in Figure 11-1.

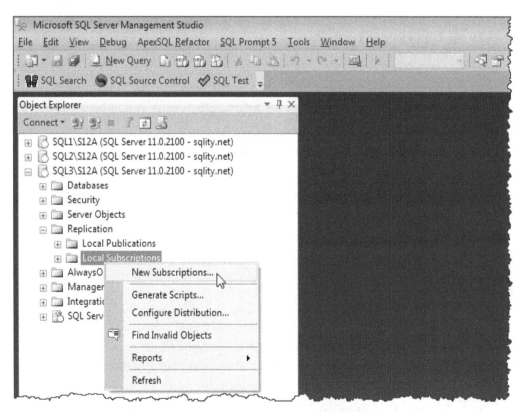

Figure 11-1:   Launching the New Subscription Wizard from Object Explorer.

3. When the **New Subscription Wizard** appears, advance to the **Publication** page, shown in Figure 11-2. This page is where you identify the Publisher, the publication database, and the publication.

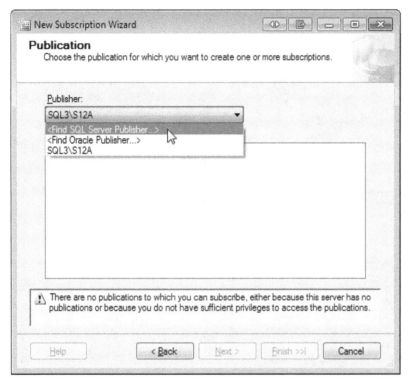

Figure 11-2:   Identifying the Publisher on the Publication page.

4. At the top of the **Publication** page is the **Publisher** drop-down list, where you select the Publisher. The list contains the name of the SQL Server instance you're currently connected to (the Subscriber), along with an option for finding a SQL Server Publisher and an option for finding an Oracle Publisher.

5. Note that the SQL Server instance shown in Figure 11-2, SQL3\S12A, is the instance that I've designated on my system as the Subscriber. You should see the instance you've set up as your Subscriber listed in the drop-down list.

6. From the **Publisher** drop-down list, click the **Find SQL Server Publisher** option. This opens a standard **Connect to Server** dialog box, where you can select your Publisher, as shown in Figure 11-3.

Figure 11-3:   Connecting to your subscription's Publisher.

7. Select your Publisher, provide the necessary authentication information, and then click **Connect**. You're returned to the **Publication** page of the **New Subscription Wizard**. The Publisher's publication database and any configured publications associated with that database now appear in the **Databases and publications** window, as shown in Figure 11-4.

Figure 11-4: Selecting your subscription's publication.

As you can see in Figure 11-4, the SQL Server instance that I've configured as my Publisher is SQL2\S12A. The publication database associated with that Publisher is ReplM, and the publication associated with that database is MyFirstMergePublication.

8. Expand the folder associated with your publication database, and then select the merge publication you created in Chapter 10. Click **Next** to advance to the **Merge Agent Location** page of the wizard, which we cover in the next section.

Selecting the Merge Agent location

As you'll recall from Chapter 7, you don't have to select the replication type when creating a subscription to a transactional publication because the type is defined by the publication. However, you do have to choose between the push and pull subscription models. The same is true for merge replication.

For transactional replication, the difference between a push subscription and a pull subscription is the location where the Distribution Agent runs. Merge replication does not use the Distribution Agent. Instead, every subscription has its own Merge Agent. Therefore, when you choose between a push or pull merge subscription, you're choosing where the Merge Agent runs. For a push subscription, the Merge Agent runs at the Distributor. For a pull subscription, the agent runs at its Subscriber.

Having each agent run at its own Subscriber gives the Subscriber full control over when the synchronizations occur, while reducing the stress on the Distributor. Because merge replication is designed primarily for the "work disconnected – synchronize when connected" model, a pull subscription is most often the preferred choice.

As it is the case with transactional replication, a single publication can support both push Subscribers and pull Subscribers.

For this exercise, we'll set up our subscription as a pull subscription so the Merge Agent runs on the Subscriber, as described in the following steps:

1. If you haven't already done so, advance to the **Merge Agent Location** page of the **New Subscription Wizard**, as shown in Figure 11-5. The page lets you choose between the push and the pull subscription models.

Figure 11-5: Specifying the Merge Agent location.

2. Select the option, **Run each agent at its Subscriber (pull subscriptions)**.

3. Note that the subscription type you select here will result in minor differences in some of the wizard pages that follow the **Merge Agent Location** page. However, because the differences are so minor, we won't be covering them here.

4. Click **Next** to advance to the **Subscribers** page of the wizard, which we cover in the following section.

Specifying the target database

In this section, we'll walk through the steps necessary to select the Subscriber and the subscription database. We'll make these selections on the **Subscribers** page of the **New Subscription Wizard**. The page lets you select multiple Subscribers and their subscription databases. However, we will cover only the "single Subscriber" scenario.

The following steps describe how to select your Subscriber and subscription database:

1. If you haven't already done so, advance to the **Subscribers** page of the **New Subscription Wizard**, shown in Figure 11-6.

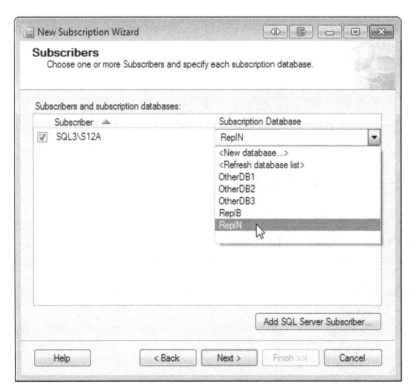

Figure 11-6:   Selecting the Subscriber and subscription database.

2. When the **Subscribers** page appears, the SQL Server instance from which you launched the **New Subscription Wizard** is listed in the **Subscribers and subscription databases** grid. On my system this is the SQL3\S12A instance. Ensure that the check box next to the Subscriber name is selected.

3. The **Subscription Database** drop-down list associated with the Subscriber lists all databases on the selected instance and allows you to select your subscription database. If you need to create a new database, you can do so by selecting the **New database** option. That option launches the **New Database Wizard**, which walks you through the process of creating the database.

4. When you pick an existing database, be careful to pick the correct one. Replication's initialization step drops and re-creates all objects that are part of the publication in the subscription database. If you pick the wrong database and that database contains objects with the same names as replicated objects, the objects in the target database are dropped. There is no warning about this anywhere in the process.

5. After selecting your subscription database, click **Next** to advance to the **Merge Agent Security** page. We cover security in the next section.

Configuring security

The next step in setting up our subscription is to configure Merge Agent security, which involves selecting the accounts and logins that replication will use to connect to the various databases participating in our replication setup. As always, it's a best practice to use different accounts for each Merge Agent and grant only the required permissions to each account.

To configure Merge Agent security, we'll use the **Merge Agent Security** page of the **New Subscription Wizard**. Each Subscriber that you selected in the previous step is listed on this page. For each Subscriber, you must select the accounts that the Merge Agent should use. In this case, because we selected only one Subscriber, we need to configure security for that one only.

The following steps walk you through the process of setting up Merge Agent security for your Subscriber:

1. If you haven't already done so, advance to the **Merge Agent Security** page of the **New Subscription Wizard**, shown in Figure 11-7. The page lets you to specify the account used to run the Merge Agent associated with each Subscriber and the accounts used by that agent to connect to the Publisher, Distributor, and Subscriber.

Figure 11-7: Specifying the accounts used by the Merge Agent.

2. In the **Subscription properties** grid you'll find the Subscriber you selected on the previous pages. (Again, my Subscriber is SQL3\S12A.)

3. Initially, no accounts are associated with the Subscriber's Merge Agent. To add the accounts, click the ellipsis button at the end of the row to launch the **Merge Agent Security** dialog box.

4. The **Merge Agent Security** dialog box lets you specify the accounts used to run the Merge Agent and connect to the various SQL Server instances, as shown in Figure 11-8. Note that the figure shows the dialog box as it appears for a pull subscription. The dialog box is slightly different for a push subscription. However, because the differences are minor, we'll stick with only the version shown here.

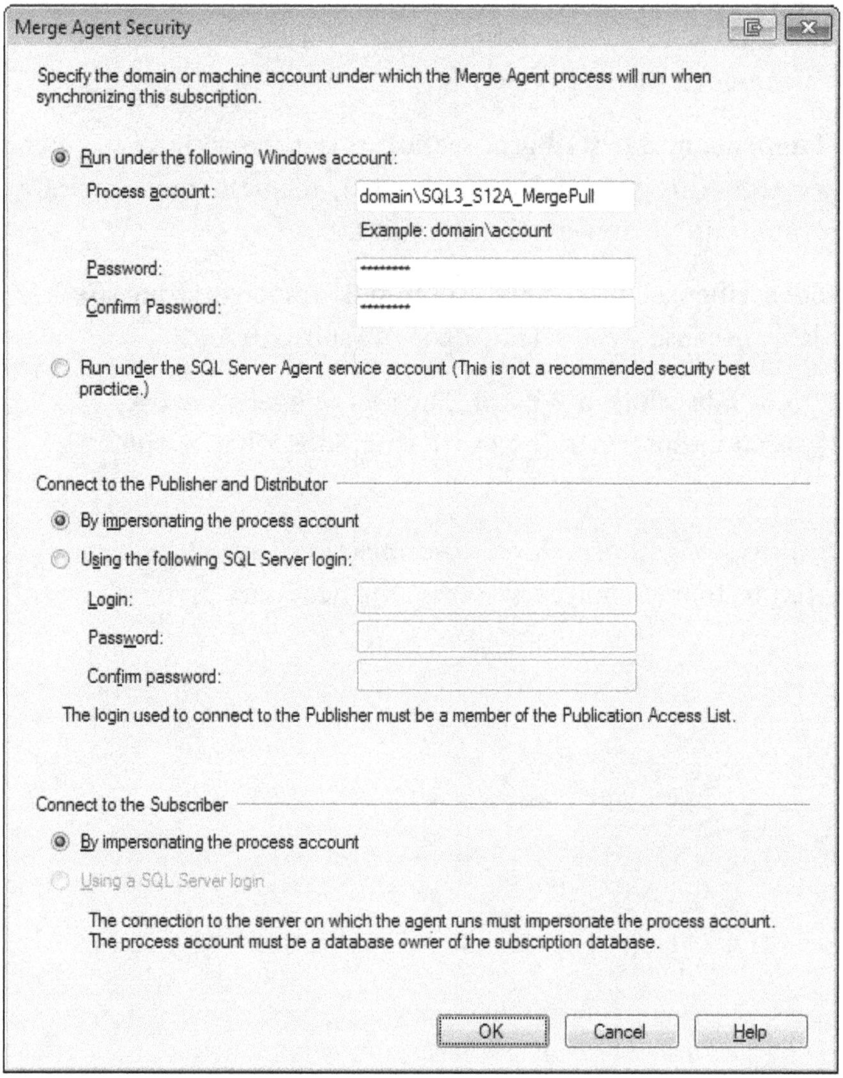

Figure 11-8: Selecting the Merge Agent security properties for a pull subscription.

5. Similar to transactional replication, there's an overwhelming amount of connection information needed to set up merge replication. Chapter 9 provides more details about the inner workings of merge replication and sheds light on the various connections. You can refer back to that chapter for more information.

6. Near the top of the **Merge Agent Security** dialog box, provide a Windows account for the Merge Agent to run under. Remember, in pull subscriptions the Merge Agent runs on the Subscriber, so this same Windows account will also be used to connect to the SQL Server instance designated as the Subscriber.

7. In the **Connect to the Publisher and Distributor** section, select the option **By impersonating the process account**. This is the default and usually the best choice. Using a SQL Server login here is appropriate only in rare circumstances.

8. In the **Connect to the Subscriber** section, only the option **By impersonating the process account** is available because we're setting up a pull subscription.

9. Click **OK** to return the **New Subscription Wizard**. The **Merge Agent Security** page should now display account information next to your Subscriber, as shown in Figure 11-9.

10. For now, we won't go any further with the **New Subscription Wizard**. But don't close or cancel it. We'll return to it as soon as we set up the necessary permissions on our accounts.

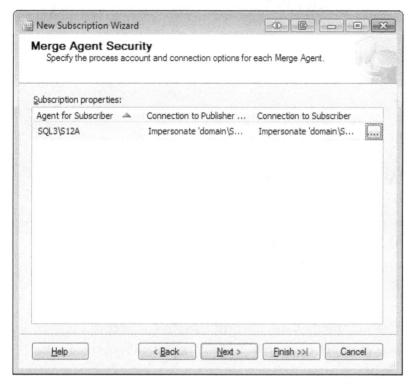

Figure 11-9: Selecting the Merge Agent security properties for a pull subscription.

Setting up permissions

The account you select to run the Merge Agent must be configured as follows:

- be a member of the **db_owner** fixed database role in the subscription database

- be a member of the PAL for the publication

- have read permissions to the snapshot share.

If you selected a SQL login to connect to the Publisher and Distributor during the previous step, that login must be added to the PAL instead of the Merge Agent account.

Remember, to be able to add an account to the PAL, the account must be configured as follows:

- be a login on the Publisher

- be a login on the Distributor

- have access to the publication database.

You access and configure the PAL through the publication's properties. Chapter 6 describes in more detail how to work with the PAL.

Once a login is added to the PAL, the user associated with it automatically becomes a member of several additional database roles in the publication database. Do not manually remove the user from those roles.

If you selected the push subscription topology, the account used to connect to the Distributor must additionally be a member of the **db_owner** fixed database role in the distribution database.

Setting up the schedule

The next step after setting up permissions is to return to the **New Subscription Wizard** to define the synchronization schedule. For each Subscriber, you can schedule the synchronization to occur continuously, on a fixed schedule, or on demand only.

By default, transactional replication is scheduled to run continuously, but this does not make a lot of sense if the connection between the Subscriber and the Publisher cannot be guaranteed. For a merge subscription, the default setting therefore is to start the synchronization by manual request only (on demand). The synchronization can then be triggered manually or by an external application, such as a virtual private network (VPN) establishing a connection. However, if your Subscriber will be connected at fixed times, say every day at midnight, you can also define a schedule for the synchronization.

For this exercise, we'll stick with on-demand synchronization. The following steps describe how to set up your subscription's synchronization to run on demand only:

1. If you haven't already done so, advance to the **Synchronization Schedule** page of the **New Subscription Wizard**, as shown in Figure 11-10.

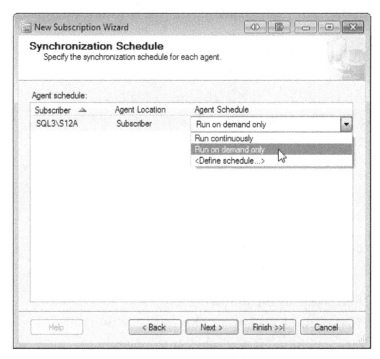

Figure 11-10: Setting up the synchronization schedule.

2. Select the **Run on demand only** option from the **Agent Schedule** drop-down list associated with your Subscriber.

3. Note that, if you want to schedule the synchronization, you should select the **Define schedule** option instead. This opens a standard SQL Server Agent **New Job Schedule** dialog box in which you can set up a schedule. We won't be going into this option any further.

4. Click **Next** to advance to the **Initialize Subscriptions** page of the **New Subscription Wizard**, which we cover in the next section.

Initializing the subscription database

After you set up your synchronization schedule, you can specify if and when the subscription should be initialized. During the initialization step, SQL Server creates the replicated objects in the subscription database and fills the tables with the data that is currently on the Publisher. Similar to transactional replication, merge replication requires in most cases that the subscription is initialized first. Check out SQL Server Books Online for details on scenarios that allow for the initialization step to be skipped.

If you have a lot of data that needs to be replicated, the initialization will take some time, so you should run the initialization when you can ensure that the connection between the Subscriber, the Publisher, and the Distributor will be uninterrupted for that entire timeframe.

The following steps describe how to initialize your subscription:

1. If you haven't already done so, advance to the **Initialize Subscription** page of the **New Subscription Wizard**, shown in Figure 11-11.

2. For each subscription, you can choose one of the following two options: **Immediately** or **At first synchronization**. The difference between the two is the time at which the synchronization is executed. If you select **Immediately**, the synchronization is started once you complete the **New Subscription Wizard**. If you select **At first synchronization**, the wizard will not start the initialization. Instead the initialization will automatically run the first time you start a manual or scheduled synchronization.

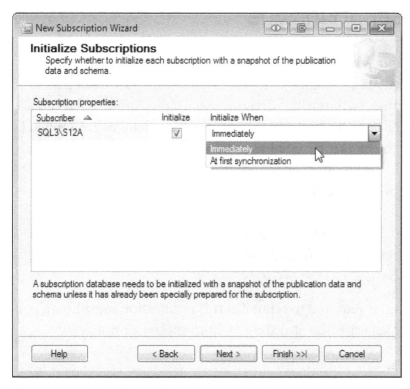

Figure 11-11:   Specifying when to initialize the subscriptions.

3.   For this exercise, we'll synchronize our subscription immediately. In the **Initialize When** column of the **Subscription properties** grid, select **Immediately** from the drop-down list associated with your Subscriber.

4.   Click **Next** to advance to the **Subscription Type** page of the **New Subscription Wizard**. We cover subscription types in the next section.

Selecting the subscription type

The next phase of setting up your subscription is to specify the subscription type and subscription priority. These settings are unique to merge replication and are not part of transactional replication. Together, both settings determine if a subscription itself can act as a publication to additional Subscribers, and the priority in which changes are applied if there is a conflict anywhere in the hierarchy of Subscribers and Sub-subscribers.

You can set up a merge subscription to be either a client or server:

- **Client**: This is the default setting. A Subscriber marked as client cannot republish the articles to additional Subscribers. All conflicts between different "clients" are handled on a first-come-first-served basis.

- **Server:** Each subscription that is required to republish this publication must be set as a server subscription. A server subscription also allows you to specify a priority for changes.

You can assign a priority value between 0 and 99.99 to a server Subscriber. The value determines how Subscribers are prioritized in the event of a conflict. In general, higher values win over lower values. Note, however, that these priority-based conflict resolution rules apply only to articles for which the default conflict resolver is selected.

The process involved in conflict resolution is much too complex to describe in a single paragraph. In Chapter 12, we'll dig into the details on how the priorities are handled and how client and server subscriptions interact with each other.

For our example, we'll set up the subscription as a client because we won't be creating a hierarchy of Subscribers. The following steps walk you through the process of specifying the subscription type:

1. If you haven't already done so, advance to the **Subscription Type** page of the **New Subscription Wizard**, as shown in Figure 11-12.

Figure 11-12: Specifying the subscription type and conflict priorities.

2. Select **Client** from the **Subscription Type** drop-down list associated with your Subscriber. Because you cannot specify a priority for a client, the **Priority for Conflict Resolution** text box is read only. If you had selected **Server**, you would be able to specify the priority for this subscription here.

3. Click **Next** to advance to the **Wizard Actions** page of the **New Subscription Wizard**.

Finishing up your subscription

The last three pages of the wizard should be familiar to you by now. On the **Wizard Actions** page, you can select whether you want the wizard to create the subscription or create a script that you can use later to create the subscription. For this exercise, we'll let the wizard create the subscription, as described in the following steps:

1. If you haven't already done so, advance to the **Wizard Actions** page of the **New Subscription Wizard**, shown in Figure 11-13.

Figure 11-13: Choosing what happens when you finish running the wizard.

2. Select the **Create the subscription(s)** option, and then click **Next**.

3. On the **Complete the Wizard** page you get a chance to review all your settings, as shown in Figure 11-14.

Figure 11-14: Reviewing the options for creating the subscription.

4. Once you're satisfied that the settings look correct, click **Finish**.

5. The **Creating Subscription(s)** page, shown in Figure 11-15, appears and informs us of the wizard's progress as it creates the subscription.

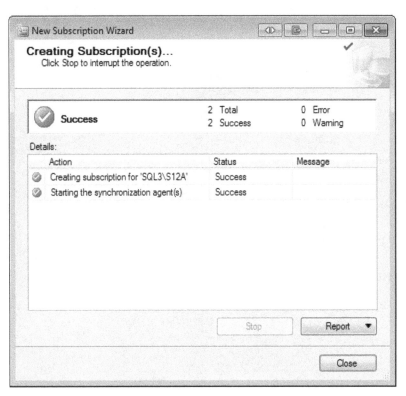

Figure 11-15: Generating the subscription.

6. If everything succeeds, click **Close** to close the **New Subscription Wizard**.

Your subscription should now be created and about ready to go. However, before you start synchronizing your subscription, there's one more step you need to take: configuring the subscription's retention settings.

Setting Up Your Subscription's Retention

The retention settings determine how long to maintain the data necessary to synchronize a Subscriber. The settings directly affect the space required on the Publisher and the Subscribers, as well as how long a Subscriber can be offline. You need to balance these two sides of the medal and pick the shortest interval possible before a subscription expires and can no longer be synchronized.

You configure retention in the publication's properties. However, because the retention settings affect Subscribers directly, we cover them here.

The retention settings for merge replication are a lot simpler than the ones for transactional replication. While transactional replication has three separate retention settings, merge replication has only a single setting that defines how long a Subscriber can be offline. If the Subscriber exceeds that time limit without a successful synchronization, you have to reinitialize that Subscriber. In such cases, changes that happened on the Subscriber since the last synchronization will be lost. In addition, if the Subscriber has not been reinitialized within a timeframe of twice the retention period, the subscription is dropped completely.

For example, the default retention period for merge replication is 14 days. That means, by default, the Subscriber will be disabled if it has not been synchronized within 14 days. Then, if the Subscriber is not reinitialized within the 14 days after that, the subscription is removed completely from the Publisher. In the case of a push subscription, its Merge Agent is automatically removed too. In either case, the data in the tables on the Subscriber remains unchanged.

For a Subscriber that is republishing, you can select a different retention setting, as long as it is smaller than the retention setting on its Publisher. However, it is strongly recommended that you use the same retention setting on all republishing Subscribers in a single merge replication hierarchy.

The following steps describe how to set up the retention period on your subscription:

1. In SSMS, connect to the SQL Server instance that you've set up as your Publisher.

2. In **Object Explorer**, expand the **Replication** folder for that instance and then expand the **Local Publications** subfolder.

3. Right-click your publication and select **Properties**. This launches the **Publication Properties** dialog box. The dialog box opens to the **General** page, as shown in Figure 11-16. The page contains the **Subscription expiration** section, which is where you can select the length of the retention period. You can also select a unit of time, such as minutes, hours, or days. The default is 14 days.

4. For this exercise, we'll stick with the default setting, so click **Cancel** to close the **Publication Properties** dialog box.

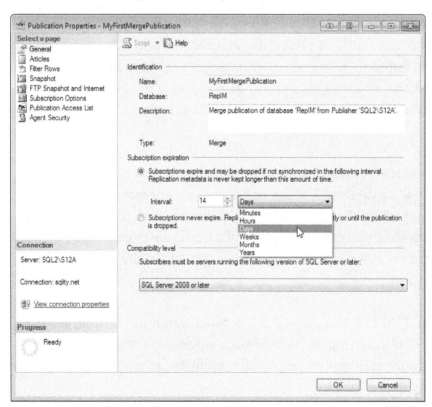

Figure 11-16: The publication's subscription expiration setting.

Synchronizing Your Subscription Manually

During the subscription setup process, we selected the **Run on demand only** option on the **Synchronization Schedule** page of the **New Subscription Wizard**. One way we can run an on-demand synchronization is to execute a manual synchronization from SSMS. This section describes how to do that.

Manual synchronization is an easy way to synchronize a single Subscriber with its Publisher. However, if there are multiple Subscribers or even multiple levels of republishing Subscribers in your topology, manual synchronization becomes very cumbersome. For example, to get changes from Subscriber A to Subscriber B on the same Publisher, you have to first synchronize Subscriber A with the Publisher and then Subscriber B with the Publisher. After that, you have to synchronize Subscriber A with the Publisher again to pick up the changes that happened on Subscriber B. In a multi-level hierarchy, this process very quickly becomes complex. That's why it's recommended to use manual synchronization only for the simplest replication setups.

However, even if you have synchronization scheduled or otherwise automated, you can still execute an additional manual synchronization at any time. This can be helpful, for example, if you have a synchronization scheduled nightly, but your Subscriber was not connected at the scheduled time. The next time it's connected, you can simply execute a manual synchronization to get the latest data.

Follow these steps to start the synchronization of a single subscription:

1. In SSMS, connect to the SQL Server instance that you've set up as the Subscriber.

2. In **Object Explorer**, expand the **Replication** folder for that instance, and then expand the **Local Subscriptions** subfolder. Right-click the subscription you want to synchronize and click **View Synchronization Status**, as shown in Figure 11-17.

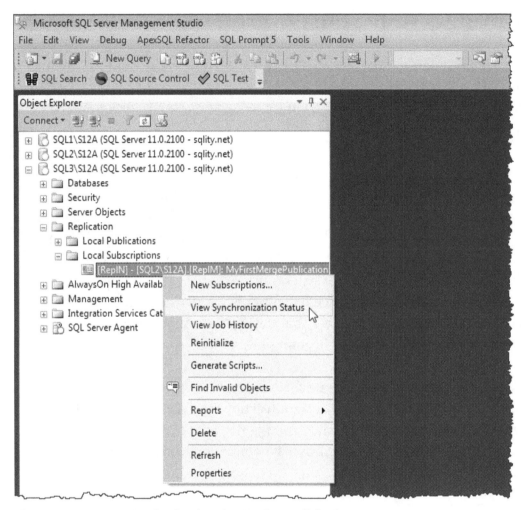

Figure 11-17: Accessing the Synchronization Status dialog box.

3.   When you click the **View Synchronization Status** option, the **View Synchronization Status** dialog box appears. The dialog box should appear similar to the one in Figure 11-18, except that it will show the SQL Server instances and databases you've configured in your own replication setup.

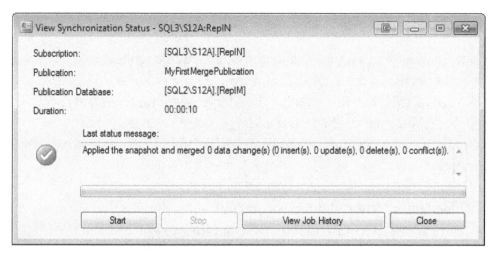

Figure 11-18:   Launching the View Synchronization Status dialog box.

The **View Synchronization Status** dialog box includes several options related to synchronizations:

- **Start**: run the Merge Agent job that performs the synchronization.

- **Stop**: stop a Merge Agent job that's currently synchronizing a subscription.

- **View Job History**: view the history of the most recent Merge Agent job executions.

- **Close**: close the **View Synchronization Status** dialog box.

4.   Click **Start** to execute the synchronization of your subscription. The dialog box will show progress information.

5.   You can click **Close** at any time to close the dialog box. You don't have to wait for the synchronization to finish, as it will continue in the background.

Summary

In this chapter, you learned how to set up a subscription on a merge replication Subscriber. First, you connected to the Publisher and selected the publication that the subscription would connect to. Next, you selected the Merge Agent location and specified the subscription database. You then configured the Merge Agent security. Finally, you learned how to set up the synchronization schedule, initialize the subscription database, and select the subscription type.

The chapter also included information about push and pull subscriptions. Plus, you learned how to configure your subscription's retention and how to synchronize the subscription manually.

If you followed the steps in this chapter's exercises, you should have a working merge replication setup. You can test that setup by changing data on the Publisher as well as the Subscriber and see how those changes are replicated with each synchronization. Keep in mind that you need to synchronize manually before you can see the data changes on the other side of your replication setup because we did not create a schedule on the **Synchronization Schedule** page.

In Chapter 12 you'll be introduced to conflict resolvers and you'll learn how they automatically handle conflicts in merge replication.

Chapter 12: Merge Replication – Conflicts

Merge replication allows data changes to be synchronized between the Publisher and one or more Subscribers. If a row in a published table at a Subscriber changes, the change will be replicated to the Publisher during the next synchronization with that Subscriber. From there, the change will be propagated to the other Subscribers during their next synchronizations.

Such a system opens up the possibility for conflicts. For example, suppose someone changes a customer's phone number on Subscriber A, and then someone else changes the same phone number on Subscriber B, but to a value different from the one on Subscriber A. If Subscriber A is synchronized before Subscriber B, the Publisher will accept the change from Subscriber A. Afterwards, when Subscriber B is synchronized, the Publisher will detect a conflict.

This chapter introduces the conflict resolvers that are used to automatically handle conflicting updates in replication. First, we define in detail what types of updates are considered a conflict. Afterwards, we look at how to select a conflict resolver and how that choice affects our data. We also cover some of the resolvers that come pre-installed with SQL Server, such as the default resolver and the interactive resolver. In addition, the chapter covers ways in which you can develop your own resolvers. The chapter closes with a section on how to review, or even change, the outcome of an automatic conflict resolution.

Conflict Types

The most common cause for a conflict is that a row is changed on one node (Publisher or Subscriber) and then changed on another node, as in the example above. This type of conflict is called an *update-update conflict*.

However, if a row is updated on one node, but deleted on another node, the resulting conflict is called an *update-delete conflict*.

A conflict can also occur if a change that is applied to one node cannot be applied to another node. For example, a successful update on one Subscriber might result in a constraint violation on another Subscriber. This type of conflict is called a *failed-change conflict*.

Failed-change conflicts can occur due to a number of reasons, such as mismatched constraint definitions or mismatched triggers or identity columns being used without automated identity management. For a complete list of reasons why failed-change conflicts can occur, refer to SQL Server Books Online.

Now let's look at how to configure merge replication to handle various types of conflicts.

Configuring the Tracking Level

When setting up merge replication, you can choose between two tracking options that determine how the Merge Agent compares concurrent changes in order to identify conflicts:

- row-level tracking
- column-level tracking.

The two options are available through the **Tracking level** property associated with each table article. You can access the property through the **Article Properties** dialog box for that article, as shown in Figure 12-1.

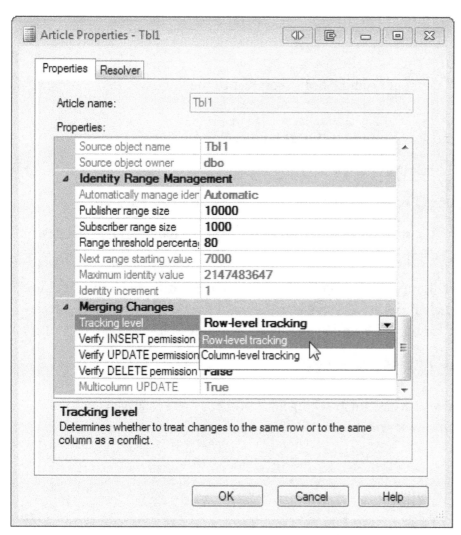

Figure 12-1: Selecting a value for the **Tracking level** property.

While creating the publication, you can access the **Article Properties** dialog box from the **Articles** page of the **New Publication Wizard**. This is the same dialog we used in Chapter 10 to change the **Synchronization direction** setting.

The following steps describe how to change the property or check its current value in an existing publication:

1. In SQL Server Management Studio (SSMS), connect to the Publisher in **Object Explorer**.

2. Expand the **Replication** folder and its **Local Publications** subfolder.

3. Right-click your publication and select **Properties**.

4. When the **Publication Properties** dialog box appears, go to the **Articles** page.

5. From the list of articles, select the table article you want to change, and then click the **Article Properties** button.

6. When a drop-down list appears, select **Set Properties of Highlighted Table Article**. This opens the **Article Properties** dialog box shown in Figure 12-1. Here you can view the current setting for the tracking-level property or change its value.

7. Click **OK** twice to close both dialog boxes.

Now that you know how to access the tracking level property, let's take a closer look at the differences between row-level and column-level tracking.

Row-level tracking

By default, merge replication uses row-level tracking because it requires the least amount of resources. If a row gets updated, the merge triggers record the value from the row's UNIQUEIDENTIFIER column. The UNIQUEIDENTIFIER column identifies a row across the Publisher and all Subscribers, even if all other column values have changed.

During the synchronization of two nodes, the Merge Agent checks if the same row has been changed on both sides. If that has occurred, the Merge Agent records that the row has a conflict and resolves the conflict according to the conflict resolution rules that were set for the article. How to influence those rules and how to review conflicts are described in the *Conflict Resolvers* and *Reviewing Conflicts* sections, below.

Row-level tracking requires only the UNIQUEIDENTIFIER value for each changed row to be stored in the change log. Therefore, row-level tracking uses only a minimal amount of storage space. However, this process potentially marks non-conflicting changes as conflicts. For example, assume Person A updates a customer's phone number on the Publisher and Person B updates the email address of that same customer on the Subscriber. Those two changes are not in conflict with each other. However, if both values are stored in the same row of the Customer table, row-level tracking will mark those changes as a conflict because both changes affected the same row.

Column-level tracking

Column-level tracking does not consider changes to two different columns in the same row as a conflict. However, to be able to make the distinction, this form of tracking requires more resources. In addition to recording the UNIQUEIDENTIFIER value for each changed row, column-level tracking also tracks the specific columns that have changed.

Consider again the scenario described above, in which one person updates the customer's phone number and another person updates that customer's email address. Because column-level tracking tracks the column information, the Merge Agent can correctly identify this situation as a non-conflict.

Only if the same column in the same row changes at different sites, does the Merge Agent record a conflict and handle it according to the conflict resolution rules.

Conflict Resolvers

When a conflict is detected, the Merge Agent employs a conflict resolver to determine which version of the changes is kept. You can think of a conflict resolver as a Merge Agent plug-in whose specific purpose is to deal with conflicts.

When setting up merge replication, you can choose which conflict resolver is used on a per article basis. Chapter 10 briefly describes how to select a resolver in the **Article Properties** dialog box, which you can open from within the **New Publication Wizard**. As you saw in the previous section, you can also open the dialog box from within SSMS for an existing publication. Figure 12-2 shows the dialog box, opened to the **Resolver** tab.

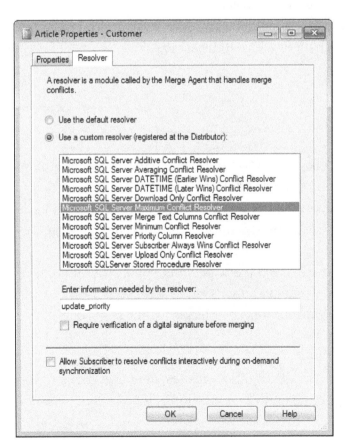

Figure 12-2: Selecting a conflict resolver.

In the **Article Properties** dialog box, you can choose to use either the default resolver or any other resolver that has been registered with the Distributor. Figure 12-2 shows all the conflict resolvers that come pre-installed with SQL Server.

A resolver decides which version of the conflicting data wins; that is, which version of the changes will be used on both nodes. For example, the resolver selected in Figure 12-2, **Maximum Conflict Resolver**, bases its decision on the value of a single column. You can specify which column it uses by providing a column name in the **Enter information needed by the resolver** text box under the list of resolvers.

In a conflict situation, the side that has the larger value in this column wins the conflict. This can be useful in a situation where updates can have different priorities. Suppose that Person A updates the phone number of a customer on one subscriber. Because the phone number is rarely used to contact customers, Person A sets the value in the update_priority column of that same row to 1. At the same time Person B changes the email of the same customer. Email is the main communication channel for the company, so Person B marks this change as important by setting the value in the priority column to 3. If merge replication is set up to resolve conflicts based on the value in the update_priority column and also set up to use the **Maximum Conflict Resolver**, the change to the email will win this conflict situation, while the change to the phone number will be lost. The phone number change however will be copied into a conflict table so you can review it at a later time. (In the *Reviewing Conflicts* section, below, we discuss the conflict table in more detail.)

The resolver that is selected by default is aptly named the *default resolver*. It follows a fairly complex set of rules that are described in the following section.

The default resolver

Chapter 11 briefly mentions a subscription's *priority* and *subscription type*. The default resolver uses the priority in conjunction with the subscription type to decide which version of the data survives a conflict. You can designate each subscription as either a client type or a server type. For a server type subscription, you can pick a priority value between 0 and 99.99. (Note that the subscription's priority is not the value in the `update_priority` column from the previous example, but rather a setting for the entire subscription. Refer back to Chapter 11 for details on how to set this value.)

The first publication always has a priority of 100. A client type subscription does not have a priority itself. Instead, all changes made at a Subscriber with a client type subscription assume the priority of the publication at the time of synchronization. All changes originating from a Subscriber with a server type subscription assume the priority of that subscription. Also keep in mind that on a Subscriber you can create a publication that republishes articles of a subscription only if these articles were created by a server type subscription.

Once a change has been synchronized the first time and therefore has a priority assigned to it, that priority does not change again throughout subsequent synchronizations.

Let's look at an example, to better understand how this works. Figure 12-3 contains eight nodes in a merge replication hierarchy. Node A is the Publisher that contains the main publication. It has a priority of 100. Node C is a Subscriber with a server type subscription subscribing to Node A. That subscription has a priority of 50. Node C republishes to three of its own Subscribers. Node B and Node H are Subscribers that each have a client type subscription. Remember, client type subscriptions don't have their own priority value. All other nodes are Subscribers that each have a server type subscription. Those subscriptions each have their own priority, as shown in Figure 12-3.

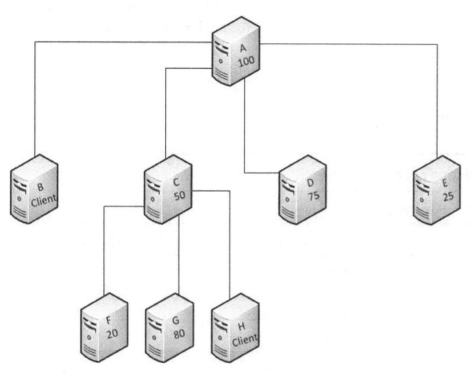

Figure 12-3: Example of a merge replication setup.

In a topology like this, you have to run several synchronization steps to get every change to every node. For example, suppose a user modifies data on Node F. To distribute this change, Node F must first sync with Node C. Then Node C must sync with Nodes A, G and H. Finally Node A must sync to Nodes B, D and E.

If at that time a conflict is detected between a change at Node D and the original change at Node F, D's change will win because of the higher priority. As a result, Node A now must sync again with B, C and E. After that, C must sync with all of its Subscribers. In this scenario, five synchronization steps are required to fully synchronize this change. Keep this in mind when you design a complicated layout of merge replication participants. The greater the number of nodes involved, the more steps it takes to fully synchronize each one.

For the rest of this section, we'll use the term *full synchronization* to mean a complete synchronization that includes all the steps necessary to get all nodes in sync.

Table 12-1 shows which change survives a full synchronization if conflicting changes occur on two nodes. The information in the table assumes that all articles use the default resolver and both changes occur before the first synchronization step.

Nodes with conflicting change		Result of a full synchronization
A	Any other node	A wins
B	D	The first node that synchronizes with A wins
D	E	D wins
D	G	G wins
F	E	E wins
H	E	The first node that synchronizes with C wins
H	B	The first node that synchronizes with A wins

Table 12-1:   Synchronization priorities for the topology shown in Figure 12-3.

In short, the default resolver in merge replication adheres to the following synchronization rules:

- A change on the main Publisher always wins any conflict.

- A change on a node with a client type subscription loses if a conflicting change occurred on its direct Publisher before the synchronization. It's immaterial whether the conflicting change to the Publisher was applied directly or through synchronization with another node.

- A change on a node with a client type subscription that was successfully synchronized with its direct Publisher without a conflict will, at successive synchronization steps, be treated exactly as if the change had originated at that Publisher.

- If two conflicting changes originate at two nodes with server type subscriptions, the change applied to the node with the higher priority wins, independent of the type, number, and priority of nodes between them, and independent of the order of the synchronization steps.

Other resolvers

Several predefined resolvers are installed when you set up SQL Server, as you have seen in Figure 12-2. They range from date-dependent resolvers, to resolvers that use the maximum or minimum value of the conflicting values, to those that build an average of the conflicting values. See SQL Server Books Online for details on how to use these resolvers.

There is also one special type of resolver in this list, the **Stored Procedure Resolver**. It allows you to supply a stored procedure that contains the necessary logic to determine which version wins. This is probably the easiest way to implement a customized resolver. For details on how to implement this type of resolver, I again have to refer you to SQL Server Books Online.

Custom resolvers

Above, I mentioned that resolvers can be thought of as plug-ins. The plug-in interface for resolvers is actually published, so you can write your own conflict resolvers using C++. This way, you can really customize how merge replication conflicts should be treated.

After creating your own custom resolver, you must register it with the Distributor before it can be used. For details on how to create a custom resolver that uses the plug-in interface and how to register the resolver with a Distributor, check out SQL Server Books Online.

Business logic handlers

Another way to influence the outcome of conflicts is to use business logic handlers (BLHs), which are assemblies written in managed code using the Common Language Runtime (CLR). You install BLHs the same way you install custom resolvers. However, BLHs are a lot more flexible. They can be executed at the Subscriber or at the Distributor and can respond to a long list of events, including data changes with no conflict. A BLH that tracks updates is executed for every row that's updated. During its execution, a BLH can reject changes, resolve conflicts, and even modify values. You can find more details about BLHs in SQL Server Books Online.

Interactive conflict resolution

Another way to resolve conflicts is to use the Windows Synchronization Manager to resolve them interactively. Getting Windows Synchronization Manager to work with SQL Server merge subscriptions is beyond the scope of this book. However, you should keep in mind several important points:

- you must run the Windows Synchronization Manager on the Subscriber

- the subscription must be a pull subscription

- you must configure a series of properties on the subscription as well as on the publication.

The Windows Synchronization Manager is not part of SQL Server; instead it comes pre-installed on Windows desktop operating systems and can be installed on server operating systems. For details on how to make all this work, check out your Windows documentation and SQL Server Books Online.

Reviewing Conflicts

The Merge Agent records all automatically resolved conflicts. You can review them later and even change their outcome. The following steps describe how to review automatically resolved conflicts:

1. First, we need a conflict to work with. Execute an update statement against the same two rows in both the subscription and the publication databases. If you used the examples provided when setting up merge replication, you can use the following statement:

```
UPDATE dbo.Tbl1 SET Data2 = CHECKSUM(NEWID()) WHERE Id IN (13,42);
```

2. After executing the update in both databases, connect to the Subscriber in **Object Explorer** and expand the **Replication** folder and its **Local Subscriptions** subfolder. Right-click your subscription and then click **View Subscription Status**, as shown in Figure 12-4.

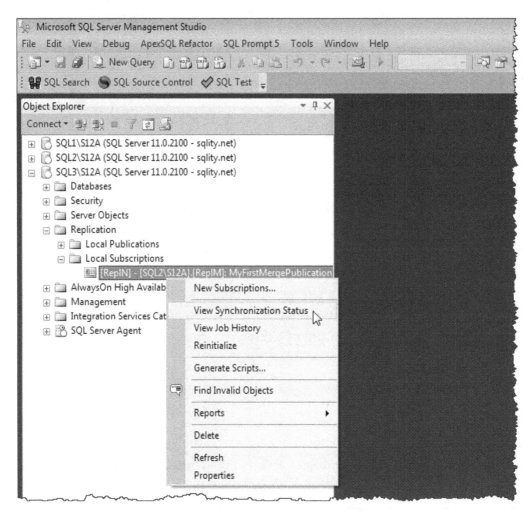

Figure 12-4:   Accessing the **Synchronization Status** dialog box.

3.   In the **Synchronization Status** dialog box, click **Start** to synchronize the tables. This should result in two conflicts, as shown in Figure 12-5.

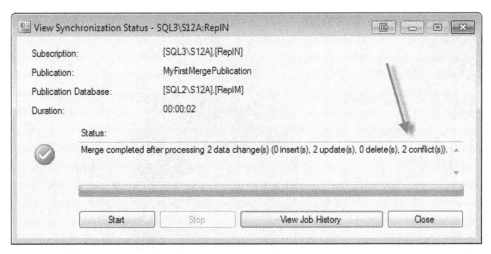

Figure 12-5:   Synchronization resulting in conflicts.

4.   Click **Close** to dismiss the **Synchronization Status** dialog box.

5.   In SSMS, open a new query window connected to the publication database and run the following query:

```
SELECT * FROM dbo.Tbl1 WHERE Id IN (13,42);
```

Leave the query results open for later review.

6.   Use **Object Explorer** to connect to the **Publisher**, expand the **Replication** folder, and the **Local Publications** subfolder.

7.   Right-click the publication and then click **View Conflicts**, as shown in Figure 12-6.

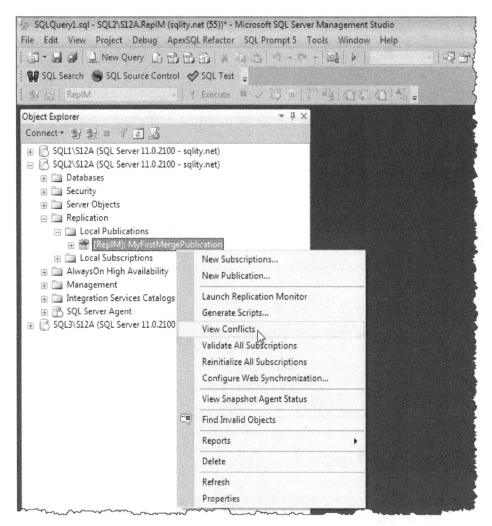

Figure 12-6: Viewing conflicts recorded on the Publisher.

8. When the **Select Conflict Table** dialog box appears, you can select the table for which you want to review the conflicts. Only tables that encountered conflicts are shown, together with the number of conflicts for each of them. Because we created our two conflicts in a single table, the dialog box will list only that table, as shown in Figure 12-7.

Figure 12-7:   Selecting a table with conflicts.

9.   Select **Tbl1** and click **OK**. This opens the **Replication Conflict Viewer** dialog box, shown in Figure 12-8.

The **Replication Conflict Viewer** dialog box is split into an upper pane and lower pane. The upper pane contains the list of all conflicts that occurred on the selected table. The list specifies the conflict loser, the type of conflict, and when the conflict was detected. When you select one of the conflicts in this list, the bottom pane shows details about the column values of the conflicting rows. It includes the values of the winner as well as the loser.

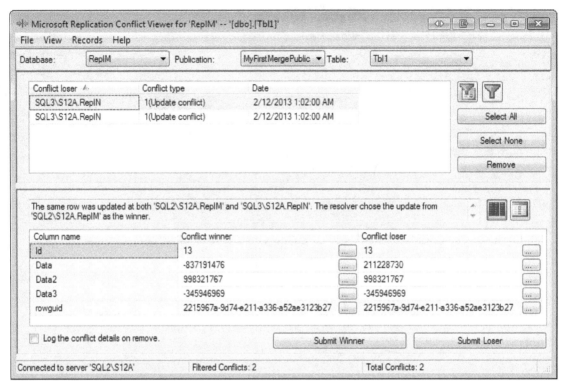

Figure 12-8: Viewing conflicts in the Conflict Viewer.

10. Select the conflict whose Id value equals 42 (probably be the second conflict listed in the upper pane), and then click the **Remove** button. This will remove the conflict from the list. Removing an entry like this will not change any data in the replicated tables. It just tells SQL Server that you accept the change.

11. In the upper pane, select the remaining conflict, the one whose Id value equals 13, and then click the **Submit Loser** button at the bottom of the dialog box. This will tell SQL Server that you do not accept the automatic conflict resolution and that you're submitting the prior loser of the conflict as new winner.

Submitting a new winner for a conflict will remove the entry from the conflict list and will update the Publisher to reflect the new values. From there, the changes will be distributed to the other nodes during their next synchronization.

12. Close the **Replication Conflict Viewer** dialog box.

13. Run the SELECT statement in Step 5 again, but in a new query window, also connected to the publication database. Compare the result to the results you received in Step 5. For Row 42, they should match. However for Row 13, you should see that the value in the Data2 column changed because we changed the outcome of that particular conflict.

At this point, you can close the query windows in Management Studio or even close Management Studio itself if you're finished with merge replication for now.

Summary

This chapter explained how merge replication handles synchronization conflicts. We talked about the different types of conflicts and conflict resolvers. We also discussed different options for providing your own logic for conflict resolution. In addition, we provided an in-depth look at how the default resolver works in a multi-tiered merge replication setup. Finally, we examined the capabilities of the merge replication conflict viewer.

This closes out the part of the book about merge replication. In the next two chapters, we will look at the Replication Monitor and learn a few ways to troubleshoot replication.

Chapter 13: Replication Monitor

Replication Monitor is a tool that lets you see the health of the components in a replication setup in one convenient place. The tool provides information on several levels so you can quickly see whether your Publishers and Subscribers are working as they should. If there are problems, you can use Replication Monitor to drill down through the Publisher, its publications, and their subscriptions to determine where the problems lie.

In this chapter, we'll walk you through the process of accessing Replication Monitor and viewing information about various replication components. The chapter assumes that you have followed the exercises in the earlier chapters and have set up both transactional and merge publications. We'll be using those publications to demonstrate how to use Replication Monitor.

Starting Replication Monitor

Replication Monitor is not part of SQL Server Management Studio; it is a separate executable named SqlMonitor.exe. However, in a standard SQL Server installation, you will not find Replication Monitor listed in the **Start** menu. The easiest way to launch Replication Monitor is from SQL Server Management Studio, as described in the following steps:

1. In SSMS, connect to the SQL Server instance you've set up as your Publisher.

2. In **Object Explorer**, navigate to the **Replication** folder for that instance, right-click the folder, and then click **Launch Replication Monitor**, as shown in Figure 13-1.

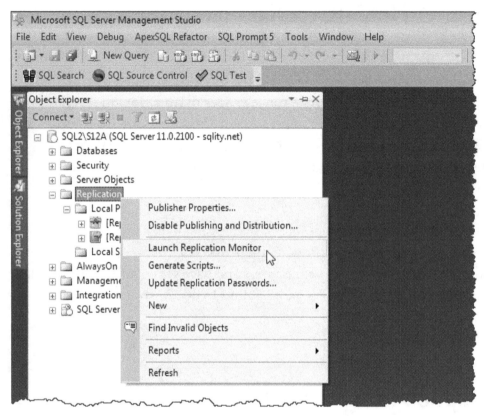

Figure 13-1: Launching Replication Monitor.

When Replication Monitor opens, you'll see that the main screen is divided into two windows, as shown in Figure 13-2. The left window provides a hierarchical view of the publications associated with each Publisher currently being monitored. By default, the only Publisher listed is the one from which you launched Replication Monitor. On my system, that Publisher instance is SQL2\S12A.

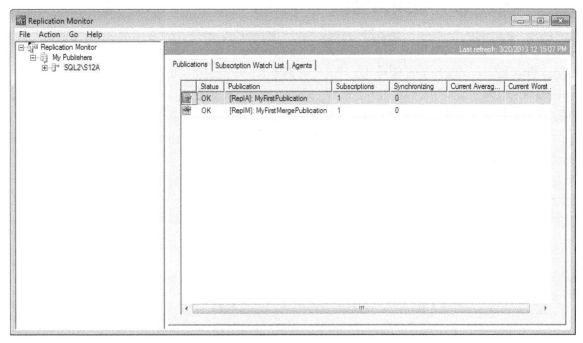

Figure 13-2: Viewing Publisher information in Replication Monitor.

The information in the right-hand window shows details about the item selected in the left-hand window. For example, in Figure 13-2, because the Publisher is selected, the right-hand window shows details about the publications associated with that Publisher.

3. Click the **My Publishers** node or the **Replication Monitor** node in the left-hand window. The right-hand pane will display links to additional information about monitoring replication. You'll also find a link for adding a Publisher to Replication Monitor.

You do not need to take any other steps for this exercise. Leave Replication Monitor open, because we will start from here in the next exercise.

Removing a Publisher

In the left window of Replication Monitor, you can remove individual Publishers from the list. This does not change any data on the Publisher itself; it just stops showing information about this Publisher in Replication Monitor. You probably won't have to remove a Publisher very often, but I've included it here to demonstrate how it works and to set the stage for the next exercise. The following steps describe how to remove a Publisher from Replication Monitor:

1. Right-click the Publisher you want to remove, and then click **Remove**, as shown in Figure 13-3.

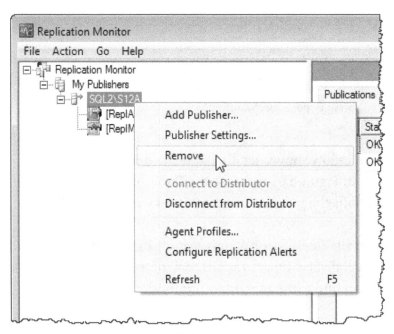

Figure 13-3:   Removing a Publisher from Replication Monitor.

2. Click **Yes** when prompted to confirm whether you want to remove the selected Publisher.

3. Repeat the same steps for the **My Publishers** node. This is possible only if there are no more Publishers listed under this node. Note that the node is referred to as a *group* and is used to organize your Publishers. In the next exercise, you'll learn how to create a group.

4. After removing the Publisher and the **My Publishers** node, the Replication Monitor window will just show the **Replication Monitor** node on the left-hand window, and the information on the right-hand window, as shown in Figure 13-4.

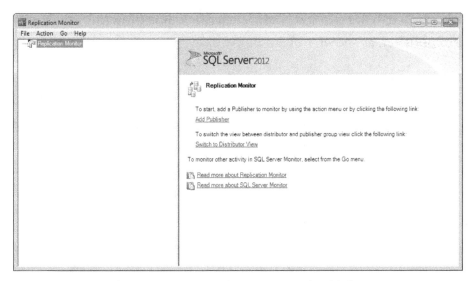

Figure 13-4: Replication Monitor without connected Publishers.

5. Leave the window open for the next exercise.

Connecting to a Publisher

If you started Replication Monitor by using the context menu of a Publisher in SSMS, the Publisher is listed automatically. However, you can connect to additional Publishers within Replication Monitor or reconnect to one that you removed before. In this exercise, we'll add back to the list the Publisher we deleted in the previous exercise, as described in the following steps:

1. In Replication Monitor's left-hand window, right-click the **Replication Monitor** node, and then click **Add Publisher**, as shown in Figure 13-5.

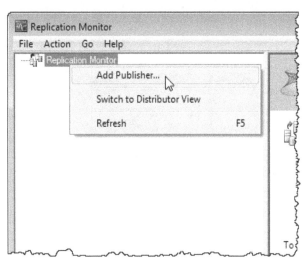

Figure 13-5:   Adding a Publisher to Replication Monitor.

2. When the **Add Publisher** dialog box appears, click the **Add** button, and then click **Add SQL Server Publisher**, as shown in Figure 13-6.

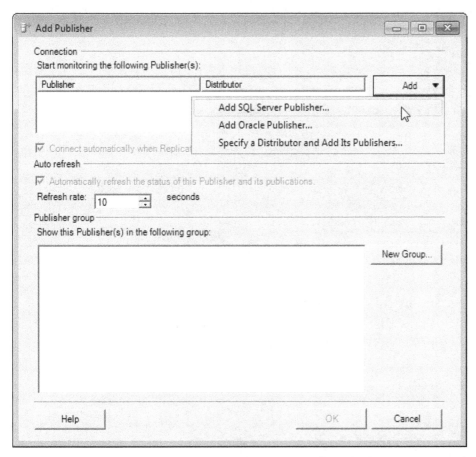

Figure 13-6:   Using the Add Publisher dialog box to add a Publisher.

3.   When the **Connect to Server** dialog box appears, provide the necessary connection information. On my system, I'm connecting to the instance SQL2\S12A, as shown in Figure 13-7. Once you've entered the necessary information, click **Connect**.

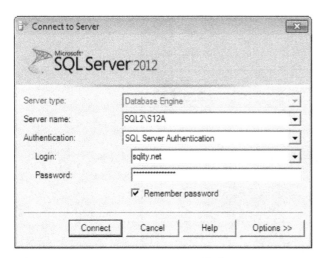

Figure 13-7: Connecting to a Publisher.

4. If the connection is successful, a message box appears, similar to the one shown in Figure 13-8. It lets us know that, in order to monitor a Publisher, Replication Monitor needs to connect, not only to that Publisher, but also to the Distributor.

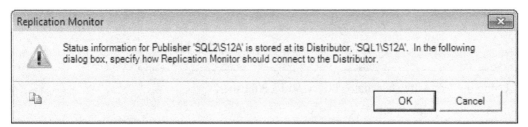

Figure 13-8: A connection to a Publisher also requires a connection to the Distributor.

5. When you click **OK** to close the message box, another **Connect to Server** dialog box appears, with your publication's Distributor preselected. Provide the necessary credentials and click **Connect**.

6. You will be returned to the **Add Publisher** dialog box. It should now list your Publisher and Distributor in the **Start monitoring the following Publisher(s)** section. You can connect to additional Publishers by clicking the **Add** button and repeating the steps above.

7. Next, you must provide a group under which the Publisher will be listed in Replication Monitor. The bottom half of the **Add Publisher** dialog box lists all groups that are currently defined. Because we removed the only group in the previous exercise, this list is empty. Click **New Group** to create a one. This launches the **New Group** dialog box, as shown in Figure 13-9.

Figure 13-9:   Creating a new Publishers group.

8. Type **My Publications** in the **Group Name** text box, and then click **OK**. This will add the new group to the list of groups and automatically select it. If you have multiple groups listed here, make sure the new one is selected.

9. The last thing you need to set is the refresh interval. It determines how often information about the Publisher is collected from the Publisher as well as the Distributor. The default value of 10 seconds is usually a good choice, so we'll leave that value unchanged. Your **Add Publisher** dialog should now look similar to the one shown in Figure 13-10.

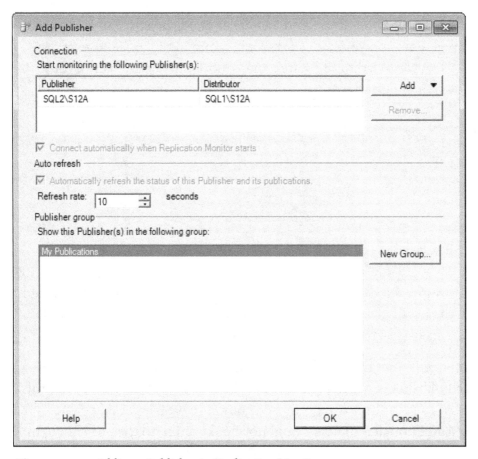

Figure 13-10: Adding a Publisher to Replication Monitor.

10. Click **OK** again to close the **Add Publisher** dialog box. Replication Monitor's left-hand window should again list the Publisher, as shown in Figure 13-11.

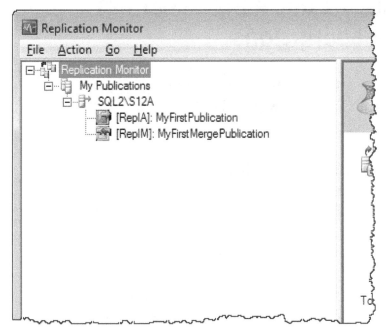

Figure 13-11: The newly added Publisher.

Note that you cannot create a group inside of another group, nor can you create more than one connection to a Publisher at a time. That means each Publisher can be in only a single group at any given time. If you try to connect to a publisher a second time, Replication Monitor will display a friendly message box telling you it won't tolerate such an attempt.

11. Leave Replication Monitor open for the remainder of the chapter.

Viewing Information About a Publisher, Its Publications and Subscriptions

Throughout the rest of the chapter, we focus on where to find information about specific components in your replication setup. Although Replication Monitor is well structured, information is not always easy to find.

To help demonstrate where to find what, we start with the information available about your Publishers. From there, we go to the information available for each publication. After covering the differences in this information between transactional and merge replication, we look at where to find information about each subscription. We then follow this with a discussion on how to set up alerts to notify you about problems in your replication setup.

Although we try to cover many of the features in Replication Monitor, the most we can hope to provide is an overview of the variety of information and functionality available in Replication Monitor. Describing everything in detail would fill an entire book. For that reason, the rest of this chapter does not follow the step-by-step approach we've used up to this point. Instead, we present the information in a way that will help you know where to look when you need to find specific information.

Viewing information about a Publisher

In Replication Monitor, when you select a Publisher in the list on the left, the right-hand window displays details about that Publisher. The information is displayed in what I refer to as the *Publisher module,* which is separated into three tabs: **Publications**, **Subscription Watch List**, and **Agents**. Figure 13-12 shows the **Publications** tab for the Publisher SQL2\S12A.

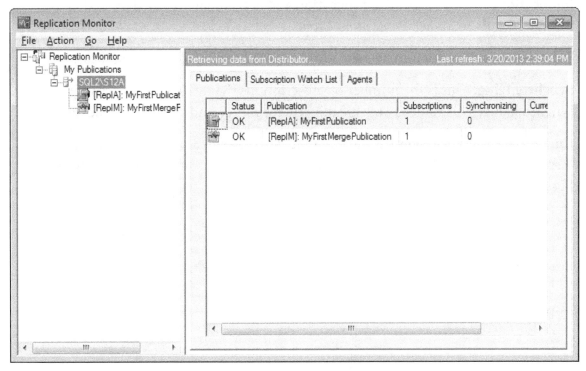

Figure 13-12: Viewing the Publishers and publications in Replication Monitor.

The **Publications** tab displays information about all publications defined on the selected Publisher. The information is divided into the following columns:

- **Status**: This column gives information about the general health of this publication and its subscriptions. There are four possible values:

  - Error

  - Performance Critical

  - Retrying failed command

  - OK.

285

- **Publication:** The names of the publication and database it's defined in, in this format: *[Database Name]: Publication Name*.

- **Subscriptions**: This column lists the number of Subscribers for each publication.

- **Synchronizing**: This is the number of subscriptions that are currently actively synchronizing. This value is only meaningful for merge and snapshot replication.

- **Current Average Performance** and **Current Worst Performance**: These columns display information about the current performance of all subscriptions combined. Possible values are:

  - Excellent

  - Good

  - Fair

  - Poor

  - Critical.

The performance measurement for the last two columns is based on the performance of all subscribers. Performance for transactional subscriptions is measured only if the performance thresholds have been enabled in the **Warnings** tab (described in the next section). Merge publication performance is displayed only after at least five synchronizations.

The second tab of the Publisher module is the **Subscriptions Watch List** tab, shown in Figure 13-13. The tab displays a list of subscriptions associated with the selected Publisher, based on subscription type.

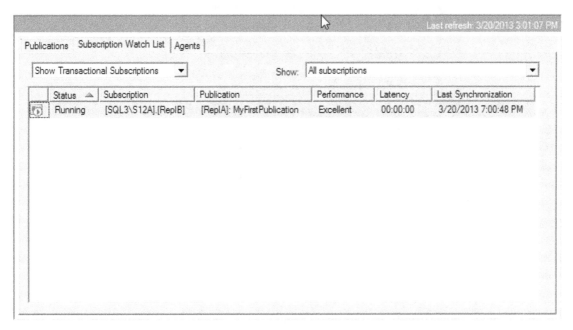

Figure 13-13: Viewing subscriptions on the **Subscription Watch List** tab.

You select the subscription type from the drop-down list near the top-left corner of the **Subscription Watch List** tab. You can view information about transactional, merge, or snapshot subscriptions. The list of columns is different for each type. (The sections that follow provide more details about what information is displayed.)

The drop-down list near the top-right corner of the tab allows you to filter your list of subscriptions based on problem areas. Figure 13-14 shows the list of available options in the drop-down list.

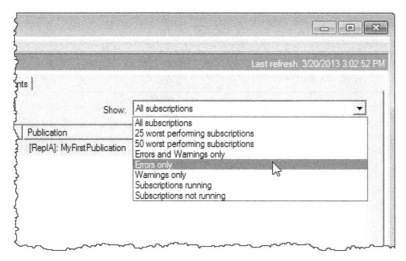

Figure 13-14: Filtering the list of subscriptions based on a problem area.

If you select one of these filters, only subscriptions that match the filter are included in the list. This can be a great help if you are dealing with a lot of subscriptions.

The third tab of the Publisher module, **Agents**, displays information about the replication agents, as shown in Figure 13-15.

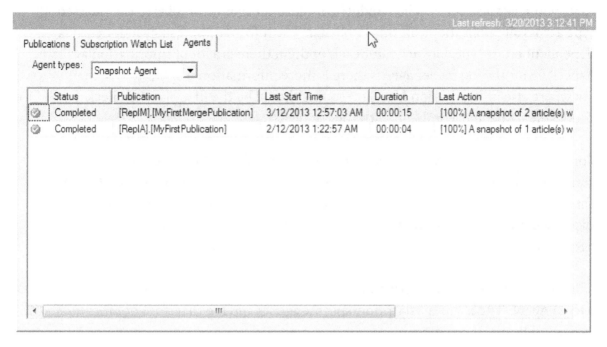

Figure 13-15: Viewing information about the replication agents.

In the **Agent types** drop-down list, you can select which types of agents you want to display. The available types include the following:

- Snapshot Agent

- Log Reader Agent

- Queue Reader Agent

- Maintenance Jobs.

In reality, the last entry in this list is not an agent. Instead, it covers all the additional maintenance jobs that are created by replication.

After you make a selection, the window will show all agents (or jobs) of the selected type across all publications on this Publisher. The information displayed for each is dependent on its type. However, for each of them there is a lot of information available. Especially for the log reader agents there is more information displayed here than anywhere else in Replication Monitor, so this should be the first place to check if you think you are having a problem with the log reader.

For all agent types, you will find at least information about the current status, the last start time, the duration, and the last action performed. In addition, for all selections of the **Agent types** drop-down list, with the exception of **Maintenance Jobs**, the tab also displays performance information for the most recent run, as well as counts for transactions and commands processed during the most recent run.

The **Agent types** drop-down list contains neither the Distribution Agent nor the Merge Agent. Those are subscription-specific agents and are therefore not included in the Publication's **Agents** tab.

Viewing information about transactional publications

If you select a transactional publication in Replication Monitor's left-hand window, the right-hand window displays information about that publication. This publication module includes four tabs. The first is the **All Subscriptions** tab. It shows a list of all subscriptions associated with the selected publication. For each subscription, you can find information about its status and performance. Figure 13-16 shows this **All Subscriptions** tab for the MyFirstPublication publication, which includes only one subscription.

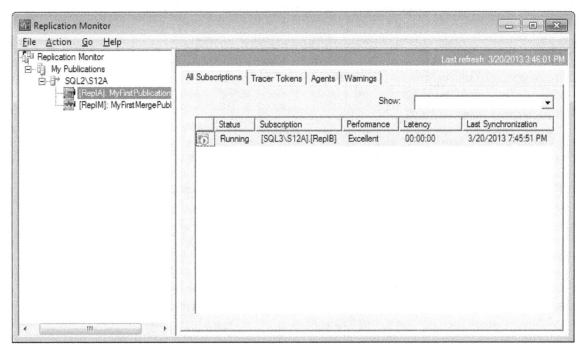

Figure 13-16: The subscription associated with a transactional publication.

The **Status** column indicates the health of the Distribution Agent for this subscription. The column supports the following values:

- Error

- Retrying failed command

- Not Running

- Running.

There are also three possible warnings that can be included in addition to the status:

- Performance critical

- Expiring soon / Expired

- Uninitialized subscription.

For example, you might see a status of **Running, Performance critical**.

The **Performance** column provides a rough overview of the speed of the Subscriber. You can find the same values here that are used for the Publisher performance. The **Latency** column specifies the time that it takes for a change to replicate from the Publisher to this Subscriber.

The second tab of the publication module is the **Tracer Tokens** tab. It displays latency measurements from the Publisher to the Distributor, the Distributor to the Subscriber, and the total latency, as shown in Figure 13-17.

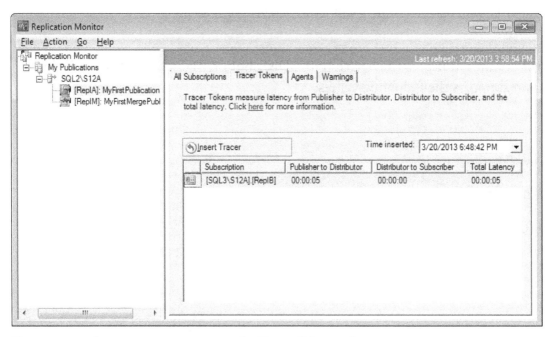

Figure 13-17:   Latency measurements on the **Tracer Tokens** tab.

A tracer token is a special mark that gets inserted into the log file of the publication database. A tracer token does not change the data in the replicated tables on the Publisher or any Subscriber. However, to the replication agents, this mark looks like a normal transaction. That means it moves through all the standard replication steps, allowing SQL Server to measure the latency between Publisher and Distributor as well as between the Distributor and each Subscriber. You can insert a new tracer token into the log by pressing the **Insert Tracer** button on the **Tracer Tokens** tab.

The **Tracer Tokens** grid displays a single row per Subscriber. You can retrieve previous latency measurements by selecting the date and time from the **Time inserted** drop-down list. The date and time in this list represent when the token was inserted into the log.

The next tab in the publication module is the **Agents** tab. It displays information about the SQL Server Agent jobs that run the Snapshot Agent and the Log Reader Agent, as shown in Figure 13-18.

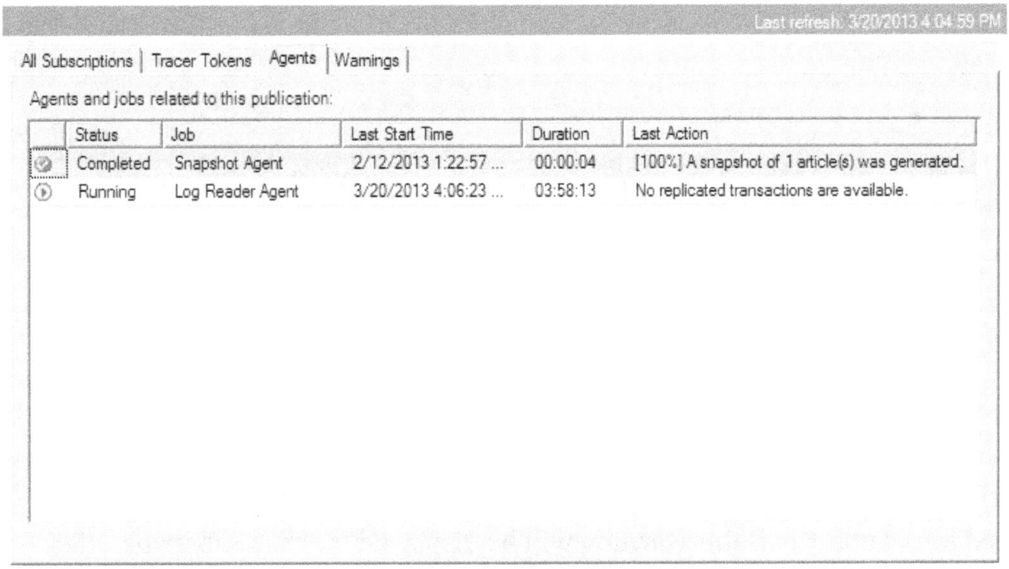
Last refresh: 3/20/2013 4:04:59 PM
All Subscriptions
Tracer Tokens
Agents
Warnings
Agents and jobs related to this publication:
Status
Job
Last Start Time
Duration
Last Action
Completed
Snapshot Agent
2/12/2013 1:22:57 ...
00:00:04
[100%] A snapshot of 1 article(s) was generated.
Running
Log Reader Agent
3/20/2013 4:06:23 ...
03:58:13
No replicated transactions are available.

Figure 13-18: The transactional replication agents associated with a publication.

The information includes the job status, the last start time, and the duration of the last execution (which can still be running). The **Agents** tab also displays information about the last action that was taken by each agent.

Information about the Distribution Agents is not included in this tab. Later in the chapter, you'll see where to find this information.

The last tab of the publication module is the **Warnings** tab, shown in Figure 13-19. The tab lets you enable warnings and configure their thresholds.

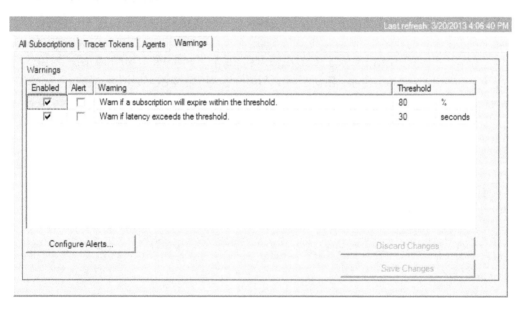

Figure 13-19: Warning messages related to transactional replication.

For transactional replication, you can specify the thresholds for two warnings. The first is an expiration warning. If more than the specified percentage of the maximum retention time has passed for a Subscriber, this warning will be displayed for that Subscriber. (See Chapter 7 for information about maximum retention times.)

The second threshold is related to a latency warning. You'll receive a warning when the latency exceeds the specified time limit (in seconds, minutes, or hours). You can disable either warning by deselecting the **Enabled** check box associated with the specific warning.

The actual warnings are displayed in the **Status** column on the **All Subscriptions** tab. A yellow triangle is also tagged onto each level of the Publisher hierarchy in the left-hand window. Figure 13-20 provides an example of what the warning tags look like.

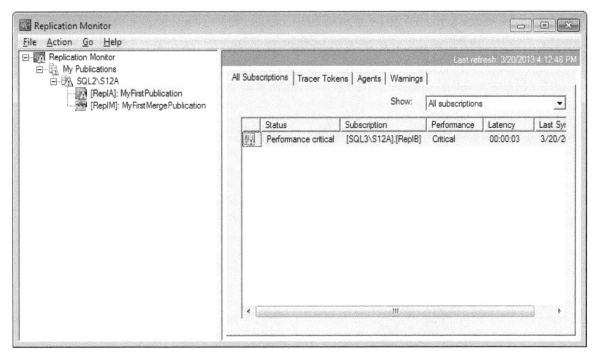

Figure 13-20: Warning tags associated with a subscription.

Viewing information about merge publications

If you select a merge publication in Replication Monitor's left-hand window, the right-hand window displays information about that publication, similar to what you saw with transactional publications. However the publication module displayed for merge publications includes only three tabs. (There's no **Tracer Tokens** tab because merge replication doesn't use the transaction log and therefore cannot accommodate tracer tokens.)

The first of the three tabs, **All Subscriptions**, shows a list of subscriptions associated with the selected publication. For each subscription, you can see information about its status and performance. Figure 13-21 shows the **All Subscriptions** tab for `MyFirstMergePublication`, the publication we created in Chapter 10.

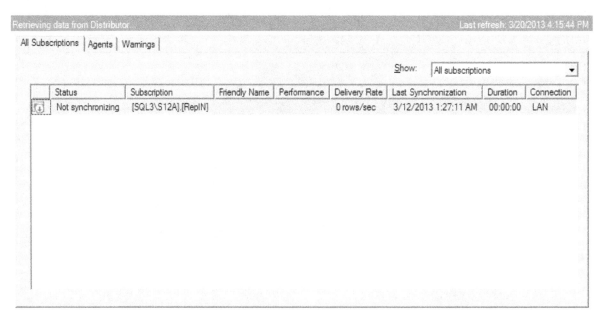

Figure 13-21: Viewing the subscriptions associated with a merge publication.

The **All Subscriptions** tab contains a row for each subscription associated with the selected merge publication. For each row, you can see the current status, connection type, time and duration of the last synchronization, performance-related information, and the delivery rate.

The **Status** column can contain any of the following values:

- Error
- Retrying failed command
- Not synchronizing
- Synchronizing.

There are also four possible warnings that can be included in addition to the status:

- Performance critical
- Long-running merge
- Expiring soon / Expired
- Uninitialized subscription.

For example, you might see a status of **Synchronizing, Performance critical**.

The **Performance** column can contain any of the following four values:

- Excellent
- Good
- Fair
- Poor.

There are some additional columns shown in Figure 13-21. They are mostly self-explanatory. Check out SQL Server Books Online for more details about those columns.

The second tab of the publication module associated with merge publications is the **Agents** tab. It's similar to the one used for transactional publications (shown in Figure 13-18), except that, for merge publications, it displays information only about the Snapshot Agent.

The third tab, **Warnings**, lets you configure warning thresholds, as shown in Figure 13-22.

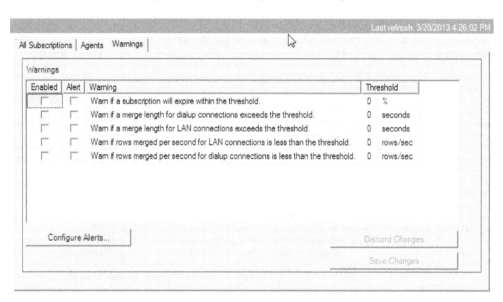

Figure 13-22:   Warning messages related to a merge publication.

The **Warnings** tab includes five warnings that you can enable and configure for merge replication. The first warning is displayed when a subscription is about to expire. The second and third warnings are displayed when a length of a single synchronization exceeds this threshold. The first of these is specific to dialup connections, and the second is specific to LAN connections; only one of the two is active for any given synchronization, based on the current connection type. The last two warnings are displayed when the rate of rows merged per second drops below the threshold set here. In this case, the first of these is specific to LAN connections, and the second to dialup connections.

The warnings themselves are displayed in the same way as they are for transactional subscriptions. Refer back to Figure 13-20 for an example of how warnings are displayed.

Viewing information about snapshot publications

Although we don't cover snapshot replication to any great degree in this book, you can use Replication Monitor to view information about your snapshot publications and their subscriptions as well. If you select a snapshot publication on the left, the right-hand side displays details about that publication. Figure 13-23 shows the **All Subscriptions** tab for an example snapshot publication.

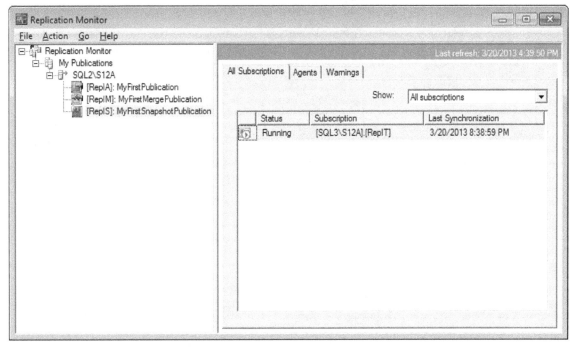

Figure 13-23:   Viewing details about a snapshot publication.

The information shown in the three tabs for snapshot publications is similar to the information available for merge publications. However, because of the simpler architecture of snapshot replication, the amount of information available is significantly reduced. For example, the publication module includes no performance information on the **All Subscriptions** tab, and the only warning available on the **Warnings** tab is the expiration warning.

Subscription Information

Throughout this chapter, you've seen several examples of how Replication Monitor lists subscriptions in the right-hand window. Everywhere you have a subscription list, you can access more options available to each subscription by right-clicking the subscription. This opens a context menu, as shown in Figure 13-24.

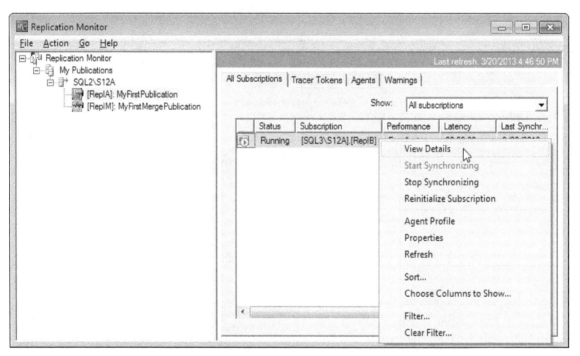

Figure 13-24: Accessing details about your subscription.

In this case, the subscription is a transactional subscription associated with the MyFirstPublication publication. Notice that, from the context menu, you can start or stop the synchronization process, reinitialize the subscription, or access the subscription's properties or agent profile. In addition, you can click the **View Details** option to open the **Subscription** dialog box, shown in Figure 13-25.

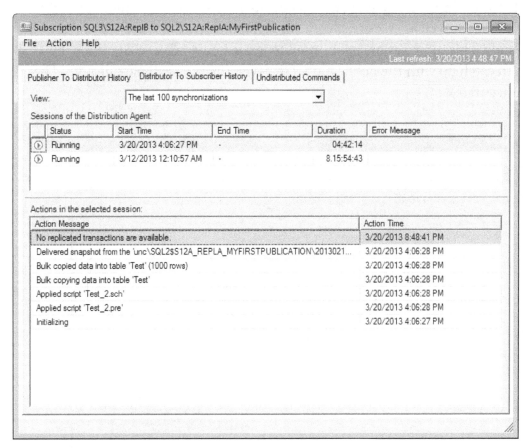

Figure 13-25: Viewing details about your transactional subscription.

The **Subscription** dialog box for a transactional subscription includes three tabs:
Publisher To Distributor History, **Distributor To Subscriber History**, and **Undistributed Commands**. The first two tabs contain information about the last synchronizations.
The first shows information about the synchronizations between the Publisher and
Distributor, and the second tab shows information about the synchronizations between
the Distributor and the selected Subscriber. In the bottom half of each tab, you'll find
a list of the last actions that were performed, such as **Bulk copied data into table 'Test'
(1000 rows)**. This information can sometimes be helpful when troubleshooting as it can
provide insight into when the problem started.

The third tab, shown in Figure 13-26, contains information about the number of undistributed commands as well as an estimate for the remaining runtime needed to distribute those commands. This information can be used to judge how long it will take for the subscription to catch up with the publication. However, the time estimate displayed here is not always accurate.

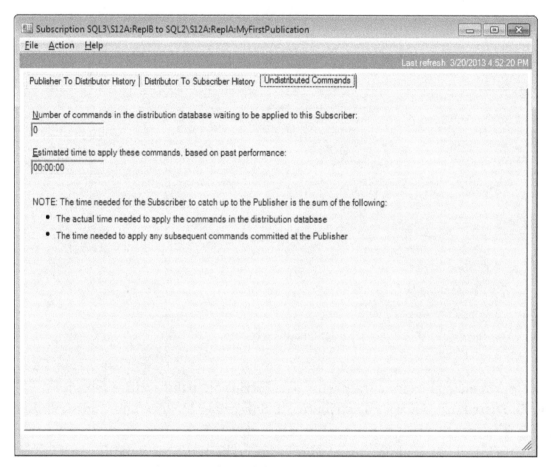

Figure 13-26: Viewing information about undistributed commands.

For a merge subscription, the **Subscription** dialog box contains only a single tab, **Synchronization History**, which displays information about the last synchronizations, as shown in Figure 13-27.

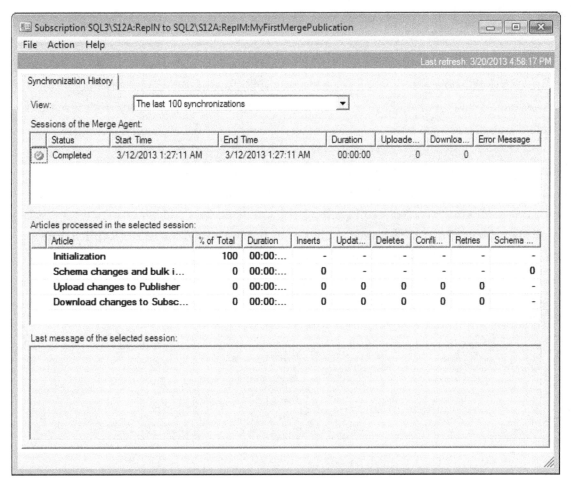

Figure 13-27: Viewing additional details about a merge subscription.

For each merge synchronization, you can display detailed statistical information in the bottom half of the dialog box by selecting that synchronization in the list. If you have a lot of synchronizations, the drop-down list at the top of the window can help narrow down the list of synchronizations. The default is to show the last 100 synchronizations.

For a snapshot subscription, the **Subscription** dialog box also contains only a single tab, the **Distributor To Subscriber History** tab. It is similar to the one displayed in Figure 13-25 for transactional subscriptions.

Alerts

When you enable a warning on a publication's **Warnings** tab, a yellow triangle is displayed when one of the Subscribers exceeds the set threshold. By default, no additional action is taken. However, you can also set up a SQL Server alert so that SQL Server notifies you if that threshold has been exceeded.

Replication supports several predefined alerts that you can utilize. You can set up the alerts directly in SSMS or on the **Warnings** tab of Replication Monitor, which is a much simpler process. If you refer back to Figure 13-19, you'll see that the **Warnings** tab includes the **Configure Alerts** button. When you click that button, the **Configure Replication Alerts** dialog box appears, as shown in Figure 13-28.

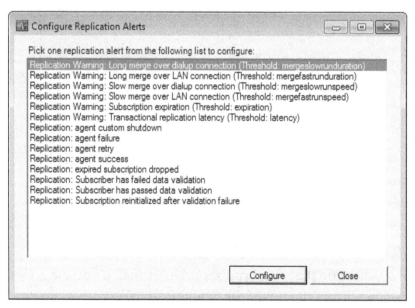

Figure 13-28: Configuring replication alerts.

To configure an alert, select it from the list and then click the **Configure** button. This launches a standard **alert properties** dialog box, prefilled with the information needed for the selected alert. An example is shown in Figure 13-29.

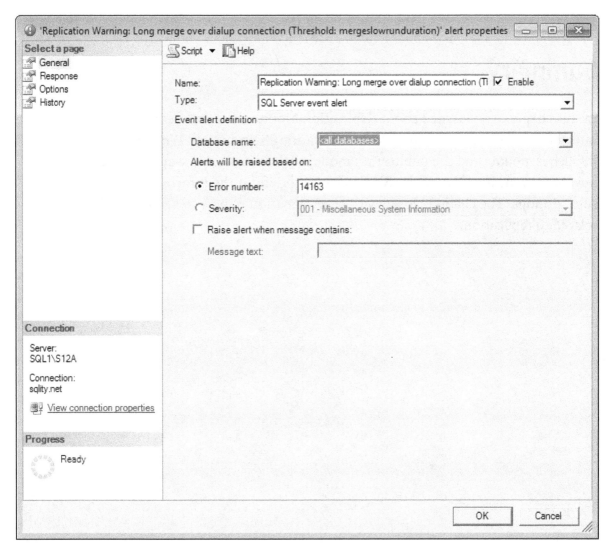

Figure 13-29: Creating a replication alert.

You can use this form to specify what SQL Server should do, and who should be notified when the alert fires. For details on how to use alerts, check out the article, *Stairway to SQL Server Agent, Level 3: Agent Alerts and Operators* at HTTP://WWW.SQLSERVERCENTRAL.COM/STAIRWAY/72403/.[1]

Summary

In this chapter, you learned about Replication Monitor and the vast amount of information it can provide about your replication environment. We examined the Publisher module and the publication module. We investigated warnings and learned how to set warning thresholds. We also looked briefly at the information provided for subscriptions. The chapter closed with an explanation of how to set up SQL Server alerts related to replication.

---

[1]

Chapter 14: Troubleshooting

Troubleshooting replication can be a daunting task. Any replication setup has a lot of moving parts, and the tools available do not always make it easy to identify a problem.

As you'll recall from Chapter 13, Replication Monitor provides a single interface that lets you view information about the components in your replication setup. Replication Monitor also lets you enable and configure a number of warnings that are triggered when certain events occur. Therefore it seems to be a good place to start a troubleshooting process.

However, the warnings provided by Replication Monitor often do little more than tell you that something isn't right, without providing any specific details. Even if you manage to find an actual error message, it is often inconclusive or even points in the wrong direction.

To help you find the answers you need, this chapter explains how to troubleshoot some of the more common issues you might run into during the setup of replication, including issues that could arise with a publication or subscription.

The examples in this chapter are based on a transactional replication setup. The setup includes a publication named `ProblemPublication`, which has one subscriber. For this scenario, assume that the person who performed the setup forgot to grant permissions to the relevant Windows accounts and did not create their associated SQL Server logins. While it is unlikely you'll encounter exactly this situation in real life, walking through its resolution we will help you address smaller problems you might encounter. Once you understand how to investigate the causes of these diverse situations, you'll be better prepared to handle your own replication issues.

Troubleshooting the Publication

When you open Replication Monitor after a publication has generated an error, you will see red error symbols associated with that publication as well as its Publisher, as shown in Figure 14-1.

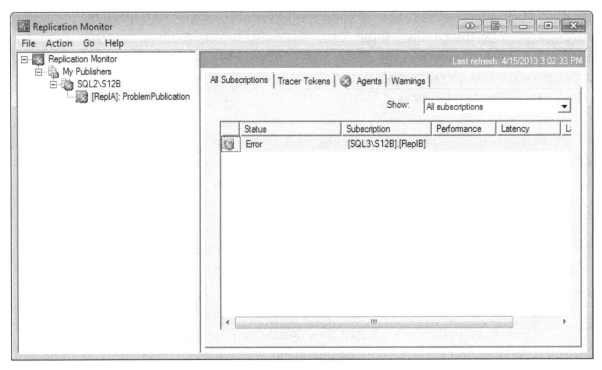

Figure 14-1: Replication Monitor showing that `ProblemPublication` has a problem.

The Log Reader Agent

If the error is related to one or more of the publication's replication agents, as is the case in our example, you will also see the red error symbol on the **Agents** tab, next to each agent that is having a problem, as shown in Figure 14-2.

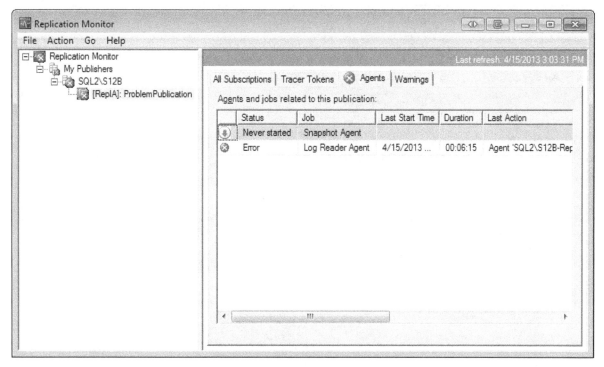

Figure 14-2: Errors associated with a publication's replication agents.

You can see in Figure 14-2 that the Log Reader Agent has generated errors. You can find more information about an agent and its errors by double-clicking the agent in this listing. If you do this with the Log Reader Agent, the **Log Reader Agent** dialog box appears, as shown in Figure 14-3.

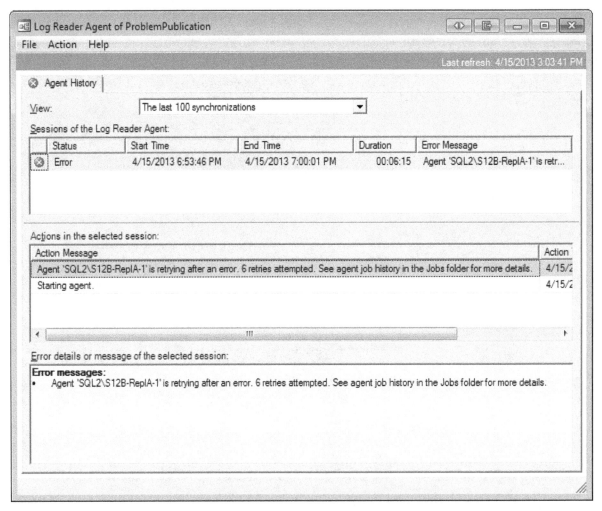

Figure 14-3: Details about the Log Reader Agent.

As you can see, there is not much information available here. However, the error message recommends checking out the agent job history in the Jobs folder. This refers to the job history for the SQL Server Agent job that runs the Log Reader Agent. Remember, the Log Reader Agent runs on the Distributor. So, to get to the job history, connect to the Distributor in **Object Explorer** (SQL1\S12B, in my case), open the **SQL Server Agent** folder, and double-click **Job Activity Monitor**, as shown in Figure 14-4.

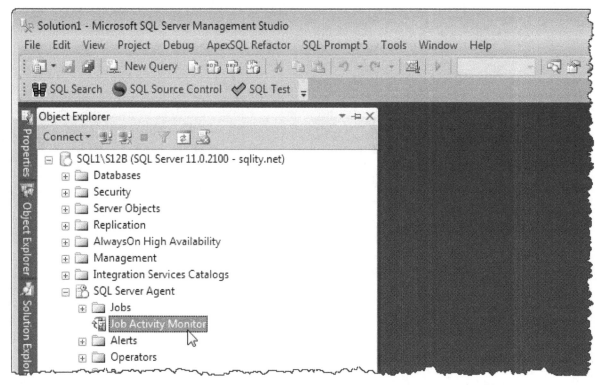

Figure 14-4: Starting the Distributor's Job Activity Monitor.

When the **Job Activity Monitor** dialog box appears, find the Log Reader Agent's job. The easiest way to identify this job is to look at the **Category** column. The category of the Log Reader Agent's job is `REPL-LogReader`. Right-click the job and then click **View History**, as shown in Figure 14-5.

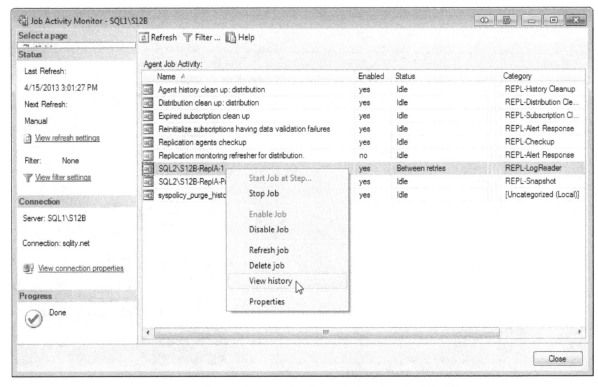

Figure 14-5: Opening the history for the Log Reader Agent in Job Activity Monitor.

This opens the **Log File Viewer** dialog box. On the right-hand side it shows one row per job execution, with the latest job on top. If you click the plus sign at the left end of a row, you can view details about the individual steps that have run as part of the job. Figure 14-6 shows details about the steps in one of those executions.

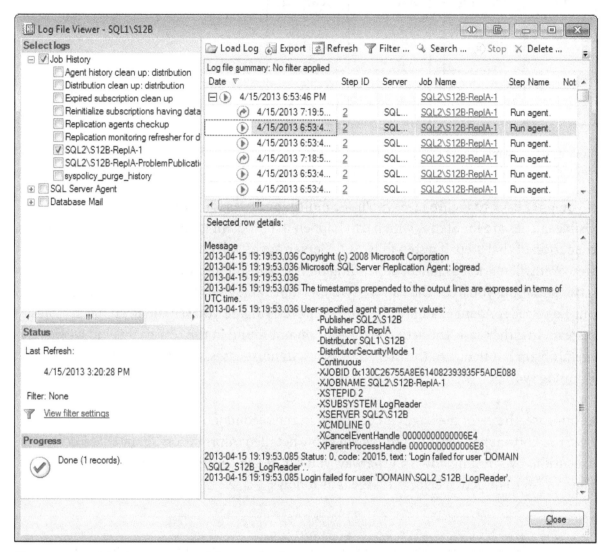

Figure 14-6: SQL Server Agent job history for the Log Reader Agent.

With each execution and execution step in the job history, you'll find one of the four symbols listed in Table 14-1.

Symbol	Meaning	Symbol	Meaning
⊗	Failure	⊙	Running
✔	Success	⟳	Retrying

Table 14-1:   Symbols that indicate execution status.

If you refer back to Figure 14-6, you'll see multiple entries for Step 2. In fact, all visible entries are for Step 2, which can happen if a problem is encountered during the execution of that step. If a step fails, SQL Server Agent will either try to re-execute that step or it will mark it as failed, depending on how the job step was configured. In the latter situation, you'll see the Failure symbol from Table 1 next to that step. However, in our Log Reader Agent example, the step keeps retrying, so you see the Retrying symbol instead. In either case, the actual error is often not found in the row that is indicating the problem but in one of the preceding rows. In most cases, that row will still show the Running symbol.

In our case, the error message can be found in the second job step row. If you click that row, the bottom half of the window will show detailed information about that job step execution. By scrolling down all the way, you can see the error message. (Refer back to Figure 14-6.) The actual error message is as follows:

```
Login failed for user 'DOMAIN\SQL2_S12B_LogReader'.
```

This looks helpful at first glance, but it really isn't. It is telling us that the login failed. However, at no point does the job step output reveal what it was trying to log on to. Usually a SQL Server error has a telling "Msg" in front, such as the one shown in the following error message:

```
Msg 18456, Level 14, State 1, Server SQL1\S12B, Line 1
Login failed for user 'SomeUser'.
```

However, since that information is stripped out of our job step message, we can't even be sure that it's a SQL Server error instead of, for example, a Windows error.

In this case, however, I know that the attempt to connect to the Distributor SQL Server instance failed. The reason I know this is that errors occurring while connecting to the Distributor are the only ones where no instance name is included. The error here is caused by DOMAIN\SQL2_S12B_LogReader not being a known SQL login on the Distributor. To correct this situation, we're going to use a short T-SQL script (rather than using a wizard) to create the login:

```
CREATE LOGIN [DOMAIN\SQL2_S12B_LogReader] FROM WINDOWS WITH DEFAULT_
DATABASE=[tempdb]
```

The default database does not really matter in this case. I usually set it to tempdb for all my logins because that is the place where the least amount of damage can be caused if one forgets to explicitly select a database after logging in.

After running the above T-SQL snippet on the Distributor, go back to the Log File Viewer and click **Refresh**. You should now see a new job step execution, although you might have to wait a minute for this to show up. As it turns out, this new job step execution still ends in a retry. The new error is shown in Figure 14-7.

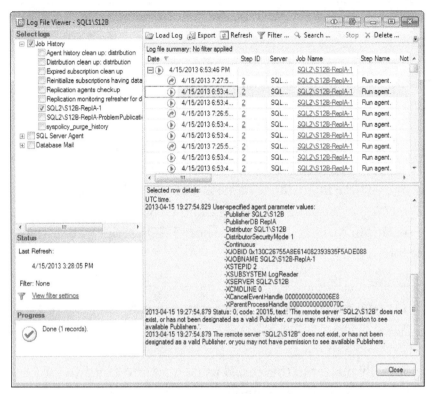

Figure 14-7: Log Reader Agent still failing to connect to Distributor.

This message is another example of why troubleshooting replication can be difficult. It states that SQL2\S12B does not exist or is not a valid Publisher. It looks as though it's indicating that the agent cannot connect to the Publisher. However, this error is actually still caused on the Distributor. The last part of the error, "...you may not have permission to see available Publishers," is pointing to the actual problem. While the Log Reader Agent can now successfully connect to the Distributor, the login has not yet been mapped to a user in the distribution database. Therefore, it cannot access the list of valid Publishers. To fix this, we need to run more T-SQL on the Distributor:

```
USE [distribution]
GO
CREATE USER [DOMAIN\SQL2_S12B_LogReader] FOR LOGIN [DOMAIN\SQL2_S12B_LogReader]
ALTER ROLE [db_owner] ADD MEMBER [DOMAIN\SQL2_S12B_LogReader]
```

The T-SQL creates the user account and adds it to the db_owner role (which is required, as you will recall from Chapter 5).

Creating the user and granting the missing permissions, however, still does not solve the problem. After another refresh, the job history of the Log Reader Agent still shows continuous retries. Checking the latest execution in the log reveals that there is now a different problem: the agent cannot connect to the Publisher. This information is again all the way at the bottom of the step output, as shown in Figure 14-8.

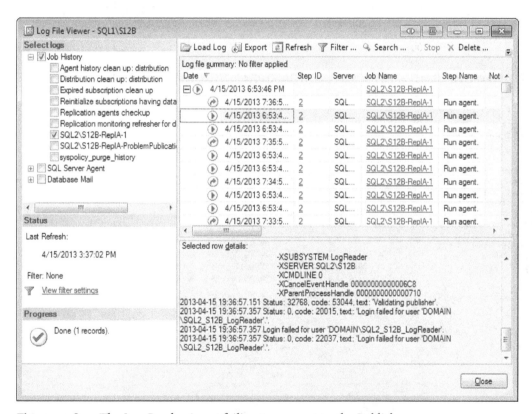

Figure 14-8: The Log Reader Agent failing to connect to the Publisher.

The error you will find there sounds strangely familiar:

```
Login failed for user 'DOMAIN\SQL2_S12B_LogReader'.
```

This is exactly the same error that we had before. However, this time, if you go up a few lines in the output, you will see the helpful remark "Validating publisher." So while the error doesn't seem much more helpful than the first time we saw it, this additional piece of information at least tells us what the Log Reader Agent was trying to do when the error occurred.

So this time, we'll connect to the Publisher and run the same T-SQL snippet as before, in order to resolve this problem:

```
CREATE LOGIN [DOMAIN\SQL2_S12B_LogReader] FROM WINDOWS WITH DEFAULT_
DATABASE=[tempdb]
```

Unfortunately, this only leads us to the next problem, as shown in Figure 14-9.

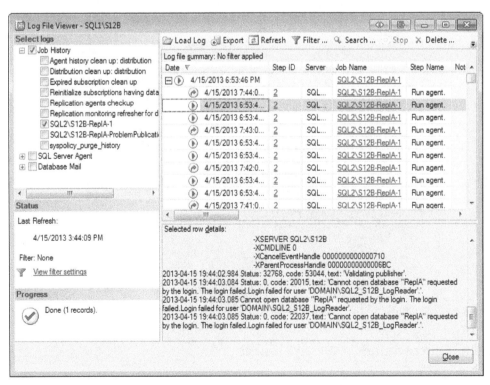

Figure 14-9: Message indicating that the publication database cannot be opened.

This error message is actually surprisingly helpful. To resolve the issue raised, we need to grant the newly created login **db_owner** rights in the publication database (**ReplA**, in my case):

```
USE [ReplA]
GO
CREATE USER [DOMAIN\SQL2_S12B_LogReader] FOR LOGIN [DOMAIN\SQL2_S12B_LogReader]
ALTER ROLE [db_owner] ADD MEMBER [DOMAIN\SQL2_S12B_LogReader]
```

After we grant this last bit of access to the publication database, the Log Reader Agent gets to work successfully. As you can see in Figure 14-10, the message associated with the most recent execution indicates that the replication has been successfully started.

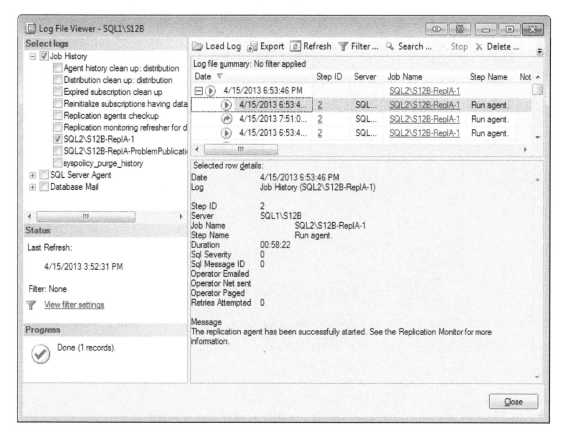

Figure 14-10: Message indicating that the Log Reader Agent started successfully.

The Snapshot Agent

Let's return our attention to Replication Monitor. Usually, Replication Monitor informs us of a problem by placing an issue-related icon in the left hierarchy section on the node where the problem originates, as well as each level above that node. Figure 14-2 showed an example of this process. However, for an uninitialized subscription, the warning icon is displayed only on the subscription itself. Figure 14-11 shows an example of this. The left-side hierarchy indicates that everything is up and running, but on the right-hand side, you can see that this is not the case.

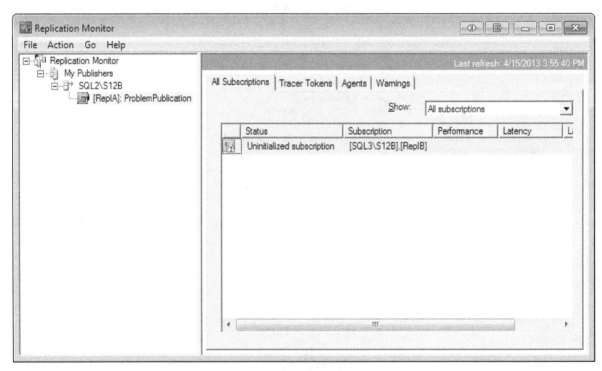

Figure 14-11: Hidden problem: an uninitialized subscription.

We can quickly discover why our subscription is not yet initialized. The **Agents** tab, shown in Figure 14-12, tells us that the Snapshot Agent was never executed.

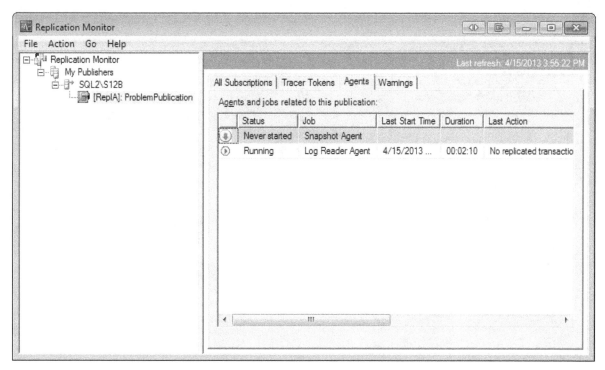

Figure 14-12:   Failure of the Snapshot Agent to start.

This is quickly fixed. Right-click the **Snapshot Agent** listing on the **Agents** tab, and then click **Start Agent**, as shown in Figure 14-13.

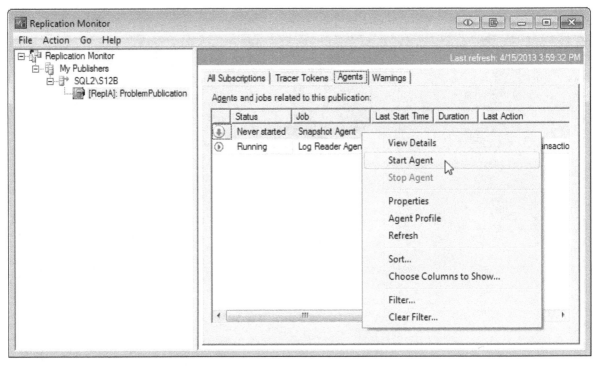

Figure 14-13: Starting the Snapshot Agent.

After starting the Snapshot Agent, everything appears to be running great, as you can see in Figure 14-14.

The Snapshot Agent usually starts, does its thing, and stops right away. Given that our database is so small, this process should finish in a few seconds. So let's wait. After a few minutes of staring at this screen you probably start wondering why we still show a status of **Running**. This makes no sense if everything really is running as smoothly as the Replication Monitor leads us to believe.

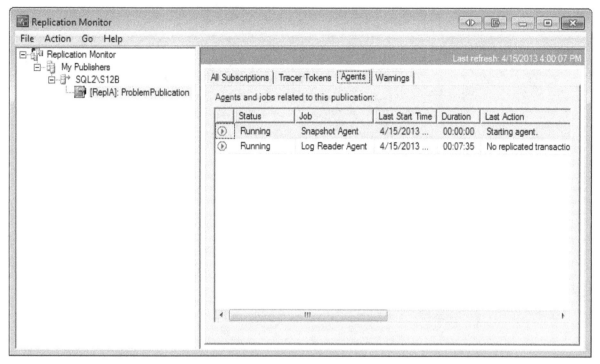

Figure 14-14: Everything is running fine – or is it?

In reality, the Snapshot Agent failed right away. However, Replication Monitor relies on the Snapshot Agent to regularly report status information. Only if that report is not sent for about 10 minutes does Replication Monitor report a problem. You can see this in Figure 14-15. Notice the reported execution duration.

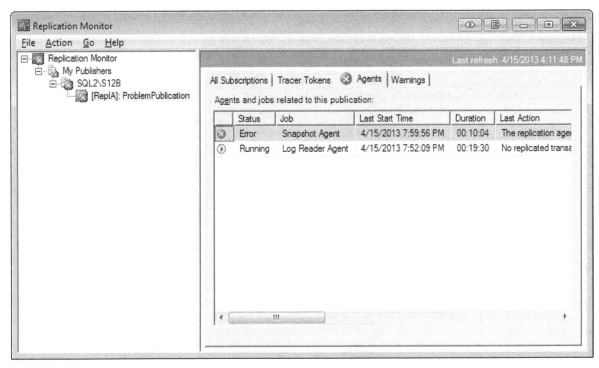

Figure 14-15: The Snapshot Agent showing a problem after 10 minutes.

Unfortunately, double-clicking the listing for the failed Snapshot Agent doesn't provide us with any more details, as Figure 14-16 shows.

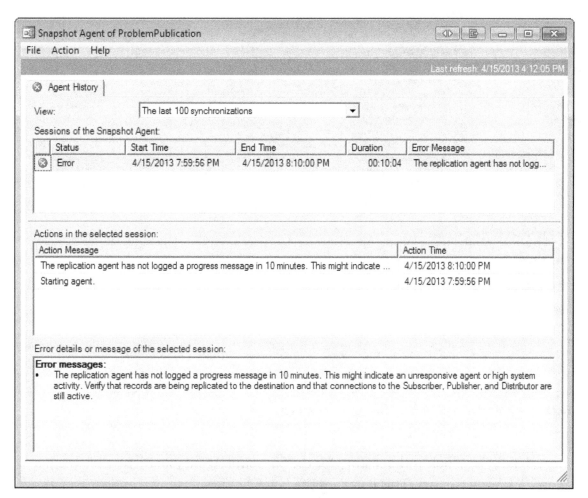

Figure 14-16: No more information available here, either.

The only hint we're given is to make sure everything is still working. However, we know already that's not the case, so let's check out the next tool of choice, the Job Activity Monitor.

The Snapshot Agent also runs on the Distributor, so we need to go to the same place we went to earlier for the Log Reader Agent. As before, you can identify the Snapshot Agent job by looking at the job category column. Figure 14-17 shows that a problem was indeed encountered during the last execution of the Snapshot Agent.

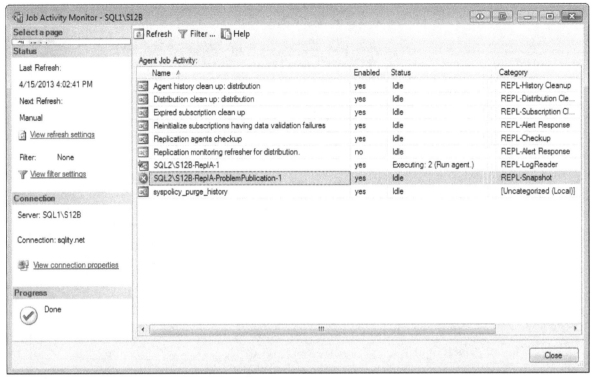

Figure 14-17:   Failure of the last Snapshot Agent execution.

For more details, let's look at the history for the Snapshot Agent job. Right-click the job and then click **View History**. This launches the Log File Viewer, shown in Figure 14-18.

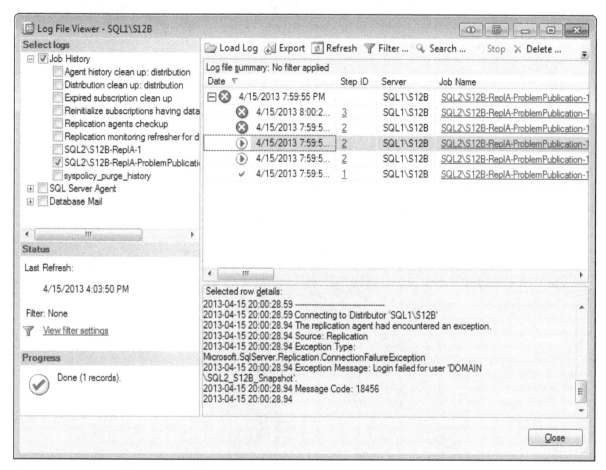

Figure 14-18: Snapshot Agent job history.

Figure 14-18 shows the history for my setup. Step 1 succeeded and Step 2 failed during the last execution. Again, the actual error is not in the entries that have the error symbol, but in the last one that does not. In this case, the error is one we've seen before:

```
Login failed for user 'DOMAIN\SQL2_S12B_Snapshot'.
```

A few lines up, we can see that the agent was trying to connect to the Distributor when the error happened. By now, we know what we have to do to fix this. Execute the following T-SQL snippet on the Distributor:

```
CREATE LOGIN [DOMAIN\SQL2_S12B_Snapshot] FROM WINDOWS WITH DEFAULT_
DATABASE=[tempdb]
```

To see if this change helped, we have to manually start the Snapshot Agent again, as it is not configured to run continuously like the Log Reader Agent. You can use the Replication Monitor to start the Snapshot Agent, as shown in Figure 14-19.

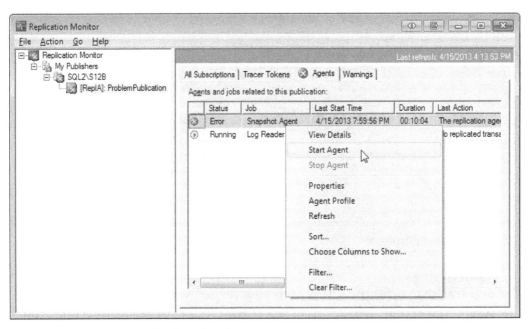

Figure 14-19: Restarting the Snapshot Agent.

Because we already know that the above change was not sufficient, we do not wait for the Replication Monitor to get to the same realization but head over to the job's history right away. You might have to refresh the history by clicking the **Refresh** icon in the top row. As expected, Figure 14-20 shows that there is another problem to fix.

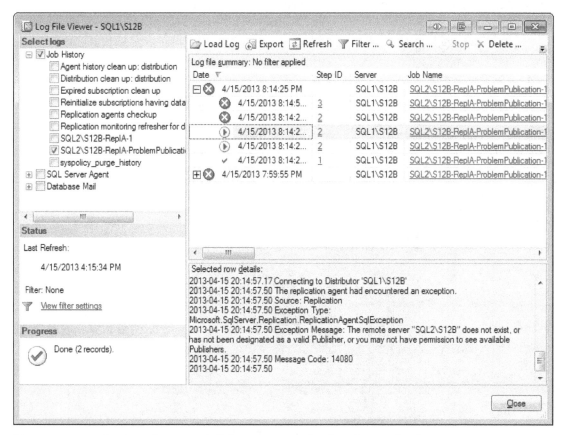

Figure 14-20: The Snapshot Agent's failure to access the distribution database.

The error sounds again very familiar. As before, it seems to tell us that we lost the Publisher in the depth of our network. However, it really means that the Snapshot Agent cannot access the distribution database. The Snapshot Agent also needs db_owner level permissions in this database, so we must run the following T-SQL snippet against the Distributor:

```
USE [distribution]
GO
CREATE USER [DOMAIN\SQL2_S12B_Snapshot] FOR LOGIN [DOMAIN\SQL2_S12B_Snapshot]
ALTER ROLE [db_owner] ADD MEMBER [DOMAIN\SQL2_S12B_Snapshot]
```

As before, to see if this had the desired effect, we must restart the Snapshot Agent. This, however, leads to our next error, which occurs when validating the Publisher. Figure 14-21 shows the latest error message.

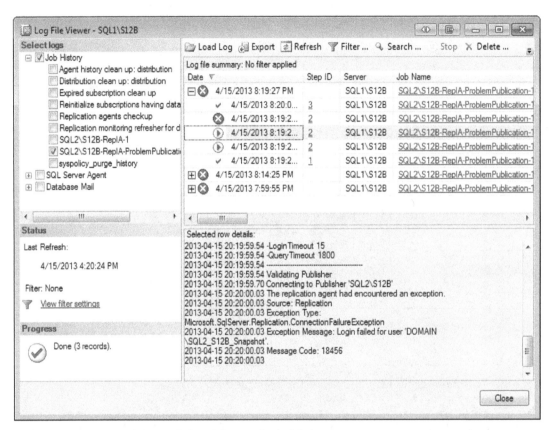

Figure 14-21: Login failure while validating the Publisher.

To fix our latest problem, we need to create the missing login on the Publisher:

```
CREATE LOGIN [DOMAIN\SQL2_S12B_Snapshot] FROM WINDOWS WITH DEFAULT_
DATABASE=[tempdb]
```

After running this statement, we can again use Replication Monitor to restart the Snapshot Agent. And then we return to Snapshot Agent's job history. Figure 14-22 shows our latest error.

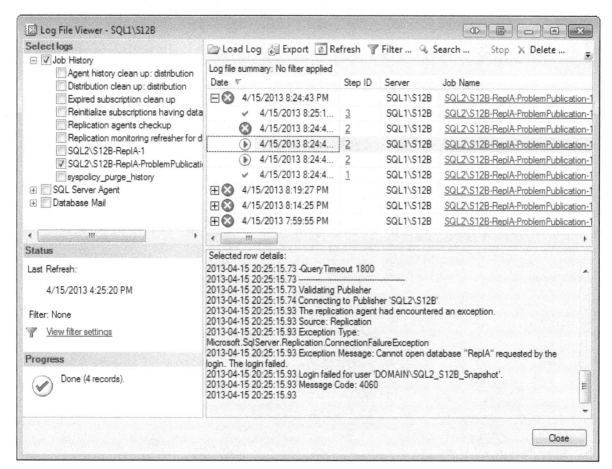

Figure 14-22: The Snapshot Agent's failure to access the publication database.

Again the fix is easy. We need only to grant the login **db_owner** permissions in the publication database by running the following T-SQL snippet on the Publisher:

```
USE [ReplA]
GO
CREATE USER [DOMAIN\SQL2_S12B_Snapshot] FOR LOGIN [DOMAIN\SQL2_S12B_Snapshot]
ALTER ROLE [db_owner] ADD MEMBER [DOMAIN\SQL2_S12B_Snapshot]
```

After restarting the Snapshot Agent and refreshing the history in the SQL Server Agent Log File Viewer, we will be confronted with the last problem we need to fix for the Snapshot Agent. The error message that points to the problem is shown in Figure 14-23.

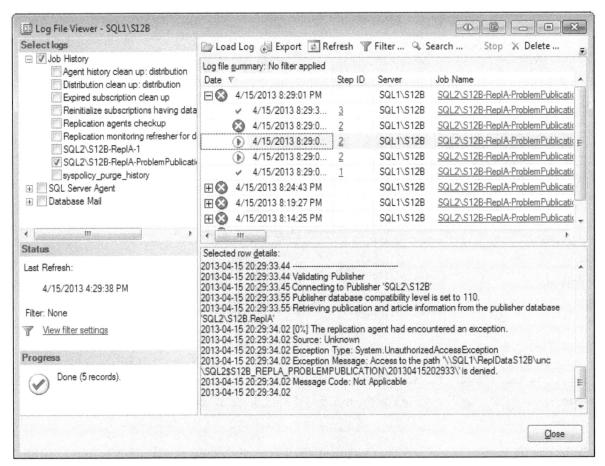

Figure 14-23: The Snapshot Agent's failure to access the snapshot folder.

The error indicates denied access to a lengthy network path. If you get an error like this, the most likely reason is that the Snapshot Agent does not have the required permissions on the snapshot folder. Remember, the account that is used to execute the Snapshot Agent needs to have write access to this folder.

To grant the required permission, log on to the server that hosts the Distributor (using Remote Desktop, if necessary), and navigate to the snapshot folder in Windows Explorer. Right-click the folder and click **Properties**. Go to the **Sharing** tab and click the **Advanced Sharing** button. In the **Advanced Sharing** dialog box, click the **Permissions** button to open the **Permissions** dialog box, shown in Figure 14-24.

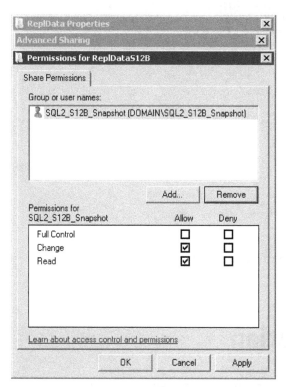

Figure 14-24: Setting the required permissions for the snapshot folder.

Add the required permissions and close all dialog boxes by clicking the **OK** button of each one.

After we've addressed the share-access problem, the publication should be up and running. The **Agents** tab for our publication in Replication Monitor should inform us that the Snapshot Agent completed successfully after creating a snapshot. The Log Reader Agent, on the other hand, is still running but was able to successfully complete at least one action. Figure 14-25 shows the status of both replication agents.

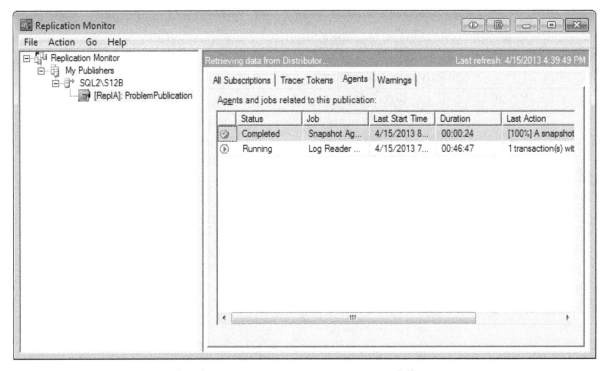

Figure 14-25: Publication and replication agents now running successfully.

Troubleshooting a Subscription

Although we've addressed the issues with the replication agents associated with our publication, the subscription in our example is still not working. We need to return to Replication Monitor and view our publication's **All Subscriptions** tab. At first, it appears that our subscription is running as expected, as shown in Figure 14-26. However, our subscription is still uninitialized.

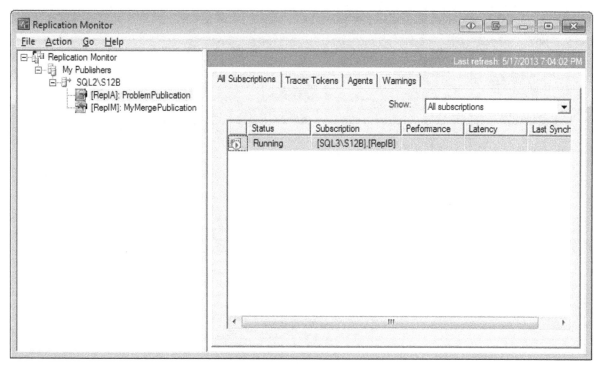

Figure 14-26: A still uninitialized subscription.

The fact that no **Performance** or **Latency** value is displayed is a strong indication that something is seriously wrong. To get more information, you can double-click the uninitialized subscription. This opens a dialog box that displays detail information about the current state of the subscription. The **Distributor to Subscriber History** tab gives us information about the past data movement between the Distributor and the Subscriber. As you can see in Figure 14-27, there is no sign that anything is wrong.

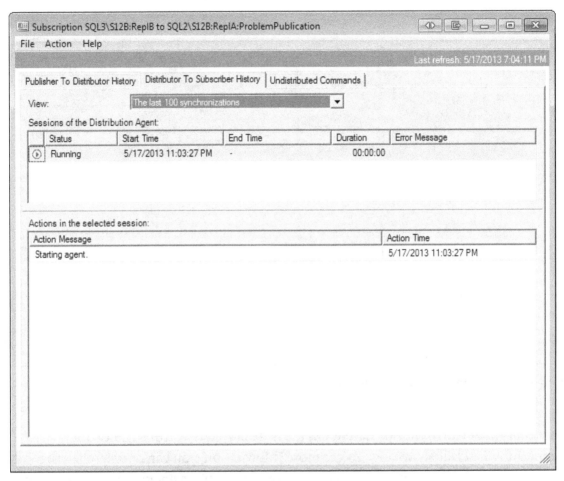

Figure 14-27: History of past data movement between the Distributor and the Subscriber.

So we have to go somewhere else to find the cause of our problem. The data movement between Distributor and Subscriber is handled by the Distribution Agent. The next thing to check, therefore, is whether the Distribution Agent's job is reporting any problems. Where you find that job is dependent on the subscription model. In the case of a pull subscription, the Distribution Agent runs on the Subscriber. However, our example is set up as a push subscription, so we need to connect to the Distributor. Once connected, open the **Job Activity Monitor** and find the Distribution Agent's job. As before, you can use the job category to identify this job, which is highlighted in Figure 14-28.

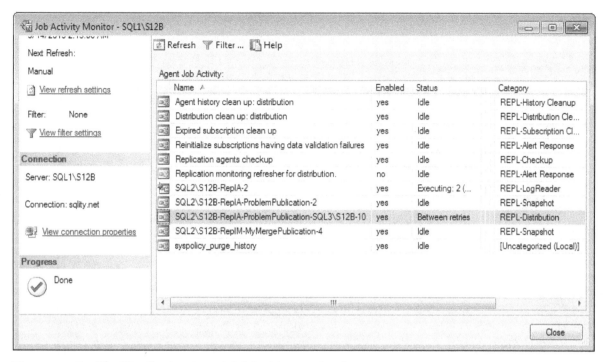

Figure 14-28: The Distribution Agent's job looking good – almost.

On first glance, everything seems fine here too. However, note the **Status** column, which says: "Between retries."

This means that, during the execution of the previous job step, a problem was encountered, and now the SQL Server Agent is waiting a minute before retrying that same step. Right-click the job and select **View history** to get to the root of this problem. Figure 14-29 shows the history with its many rerun attempts of Step 2.

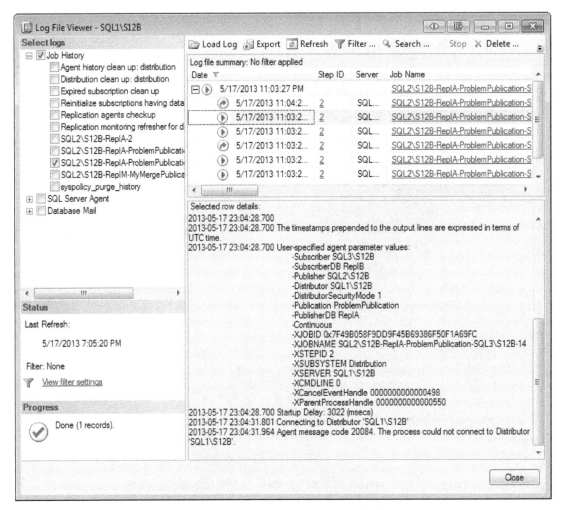

Figure 14-29: The Distribution Agent's job history showing multiple attempts to run.

Figure 14-29 also shows the error that is causing the continuous retries: the connection to the Distributor keeps failing. To address this issue, we must create the missing login by executing the following T-SQL snippet on the Distributor:

```
CREATE LOGIN [DOMAIN\SQL3_S12B_DistPush] FROM WINDOWS WITH DEFAULT_
DATABASE=[tempdb]
```

Not surprisingly, the step continues to fail despite the new login. That's because the login doesn't yet have access to the subscription database. You can see the new error in Figure 14-30.

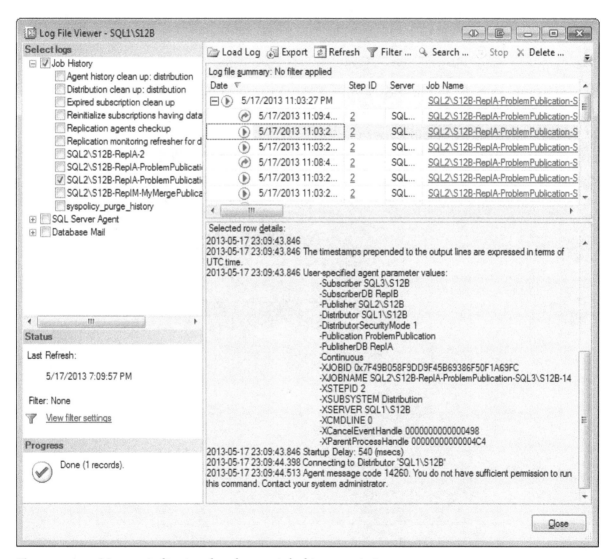

Figure 14-30: Message indicating that the user is lacking permissions.

To resolve this issue, we must create the user in the distribution database and add it to the db_owner role:

```
USE [distribution]
GO
CREATE USER [DOMAIN\SQL3_S12B_DistPush] FOR LOGIN [DOMAIN\SQL3_S12B_DistPush]
ALTER ROLE [db_owner] ADD MEMBER [DOMAIN\SQL3_S12B_DistPush]
```

So far, it looks as if the Replication monitor is not useful at all. However, if you wait long enough after a problem occurs, Replication Monitor will eventually show that there is a problem too. Usually you will have to wait less than 10 minutes for an error to show up. Figure 14-31 shows an example telling us that our subscription still has a problem.

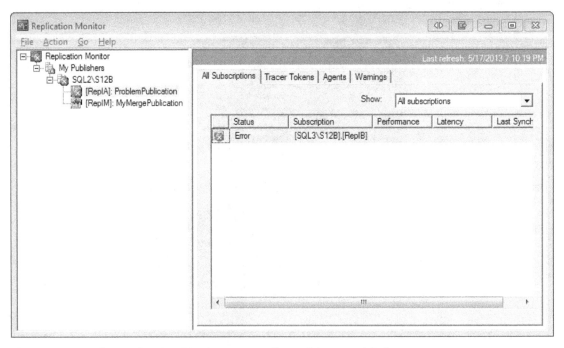

Figure 14-31: The Replication Monitor eventually catching up with the error.

Double-clicking the error opens the **Subscription** dialog box. In this case, it even shows a useful error message, as you can see in Figure 14-32.

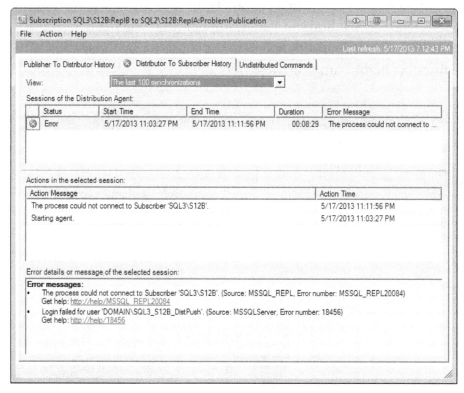

Figure 14-32: The Replication Monitor showing the connector error.

Despite the information provided by Replication Monitor in this example, I tend to concentrate on the job history for replication troubleshooting, at least during the setup phase of replication, because the information there is usually more comprehensive and up to date. However, after replication has been running for a while, you might encounter problems about which you can get good details only by using Replication Monitor. For an example, see the section, *Data problems*, later in this chapter.

Let's get back to our current error. It tells us that the process cannot connect to the Subscriber. So, let's create the missing login by running this snippet on the Subscriber:

```
CREATE LOGIN [DOMAIN\SQL3_S12B_DistPush] FROM WINDOWS WITH DEFAULT_
DATABASE=[tempdb]
```

The next two errors, shown in Figures 14-33 and 14-34 are by now neither surprising nor hard to fix. Following each figure, you'll find the T-SQL snippets that you need to run to fix the problems. Because both errors deal with access to the subscription database, you must connect to the Subscriber before running these statements.

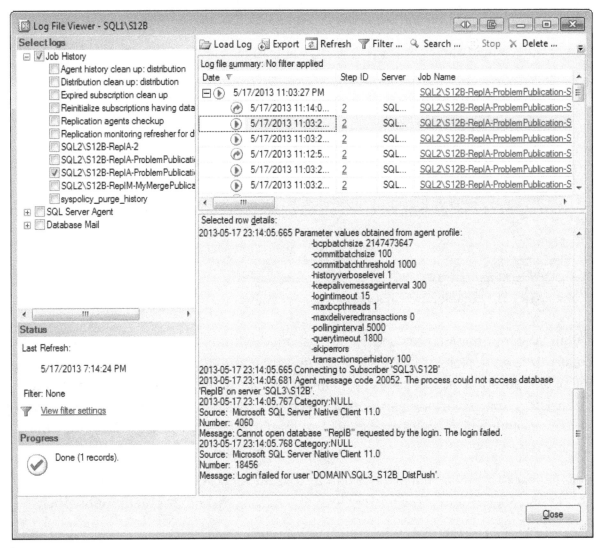

Figure 14-33: Failure to open the subscription database.

To address the error shown in Figure 14-33, run the following T-SQL snippet on the Subscriber:

```
USE [ReplB]
GO
CREATE USER [DOMAIN\SQL3_S12B_DistPush] FOR LOGIN [DOMAIN\SQL3_S12B_DistPush]
```

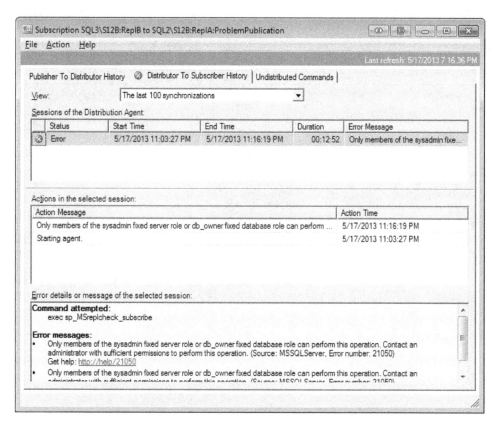

Figure 14-34: Membership required in the db_owner fixed database role.

To address the error shown in Figure 14-34, run the following T-SQL snippet on the Subscriber:

```
USE [ReplB]
GO
ALTER ROLE [db_owner] ADD MEMBER [DOMAIN\SQL3_S12B_DistPush]
```

The last error that we have to deal with is shown in Figure 14-35.

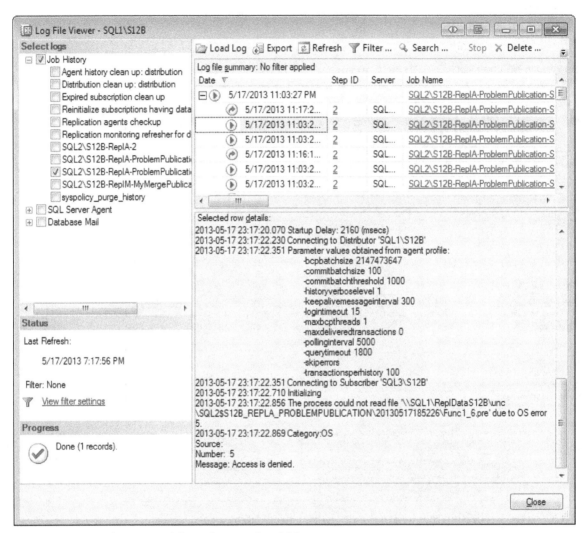

Figure 14-35: Failure to read from the snapshot folder.

This is, again, not surprising. To fix this problem, you need to log on to the Distributor and grant the account executing the Distribution Agent read access to the snapshot folder share. Figure 14-36 shows what the **Permissions** dialog box looks like after adding the new permission. This is the same dialog box that is shown in Figure 14-24. Just before that figure, you can also find details on how to access the dialog box.

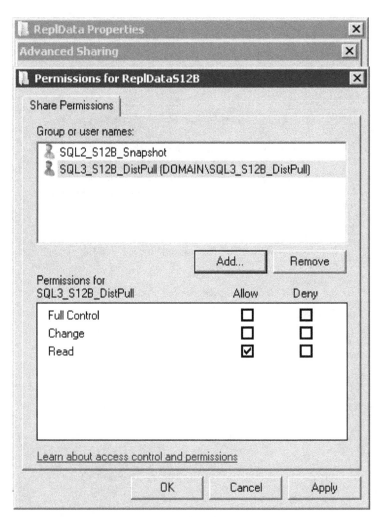

Figure 14-36: Granting read access to the snapshot folder.

After performing the last step, the Distribution Agent should now run successfully, as shown in Figure 14-37.

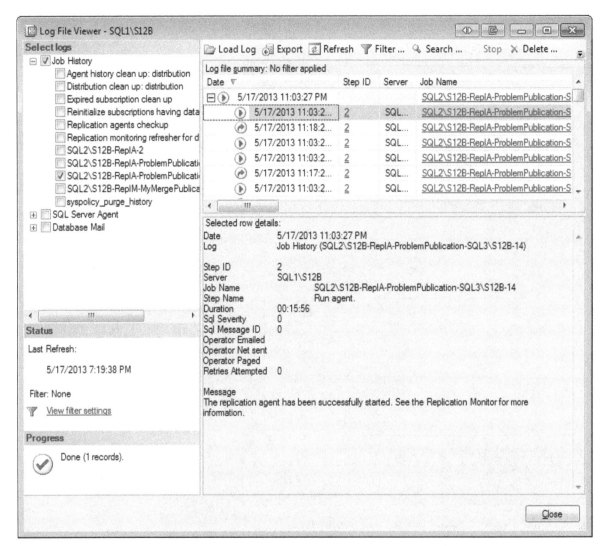

Figure 14-37: The Distribution Agent running as expected.

If you now go back to Replication Monitor, you should see a happy subscription with a status of **Running** and performance displayed as **Excellent**. However, in the first few minutes after setting up a subscription or fixing a subscription problem, Replication Monitor often reports the performance as critical, as shown in Figure 14-38. That usually goes away after a few moments, so don't be too alarmed if performance is off at first.

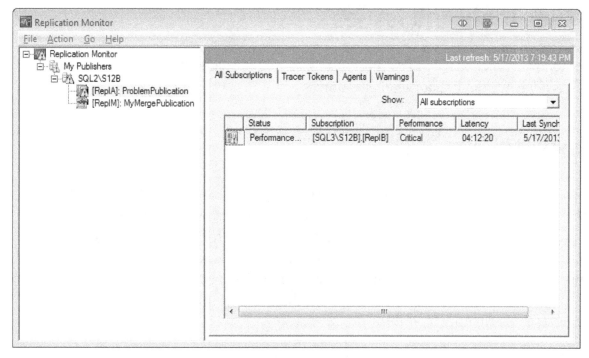

Figure 14-38: The subscription's performance showing as critical.

But what about the PAL?

If you paid attention in Chapter 7, you might be surprised now. That chapter clearly states that the account executing the Distribution Agent needs to be a member of the PAL. According to the official documentation in Books Online, this is a requirement. In fact, this requirement is mentioned in many places throughout the documentation. However, in a few situations SQL Server 2012 seems not to enforce this requirement. For example, as we saw in our troubleshooting exercises in this chapter, we received no errors requiring that logins be added to the PAL. This is most certainly not intentional and therefore you should always add the Distribution Agent account to the PAL, just to make sure that the next Critical Update or Service Pack you install does not shut down your replication setup. Refer back to Chapter 6 for details on how to add an account to the PAL.

Other Tools and Issues

The following sections list a few more issues, as well as techniques that you should be aware of when troubleshooting replication.

Tracer tokens

One important tool in the DBA's toolbox is the tracer token. We already covered tracer tokens in Chapter 13, so here we will repeat only the highlights. Tracer tokens allow you to measure the latency between the Publisher and the Distributor as well as between the Distributor and the Subscriber. However, they can also be used to check for problems. If you create a tracer token and it gets replicated to the Subscriber in a reasonable amount of time, you can be fairly confident that everything is working correctly. Figure 14-39 shows a successful tracer token run.

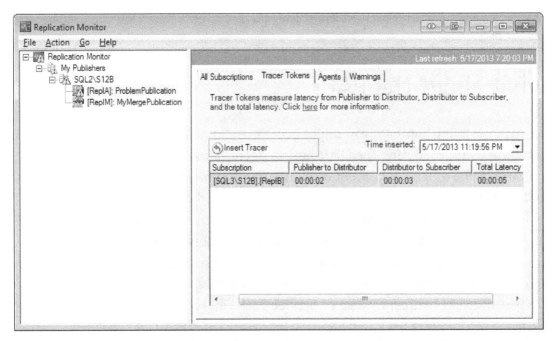

Figure 14-39: Tracer token confirming that the subscription is working properly.

So, if you are unsure whether data is moving, just create a tracer token and in a few seconds you will know. If you regularly use tracer tokens, you can even detect trends such as increasing latency. That can help you identify problems before they become too painful.

Always check the details

You should also be aware that on rare occasions Replication Monitor can show misleading information. For example, the subscription information shown in Figure 14-40 indicates that everything is working as expected. However, if you look closely you will see that the latency value is 00:00:00, a value not likely to appear in a live system.

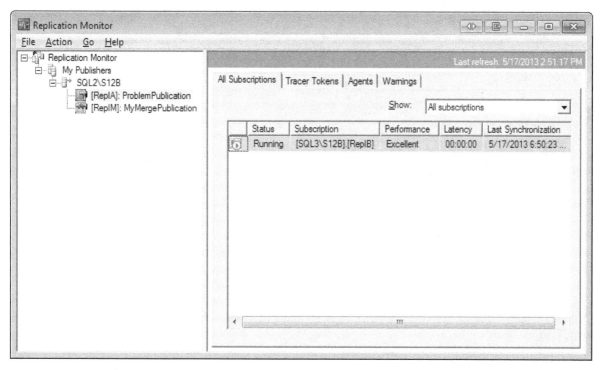

Figure 14-40: Replication Monitor showing misleading information.

If such a value shows up, it might just indicate that there is currently no data that needs to be replicated. On a production system, however, it almost always means trouble.

In my case, the subscription was marked for re-initialization using an existing snapshot. However, the existing snapshot was already expired, so the subscription never finished its initialization step. If you double-click the subscription, the **Subscription** dialog box will open and reveal that the initial snapshot is not yet available, as shown in Figure 14-41.

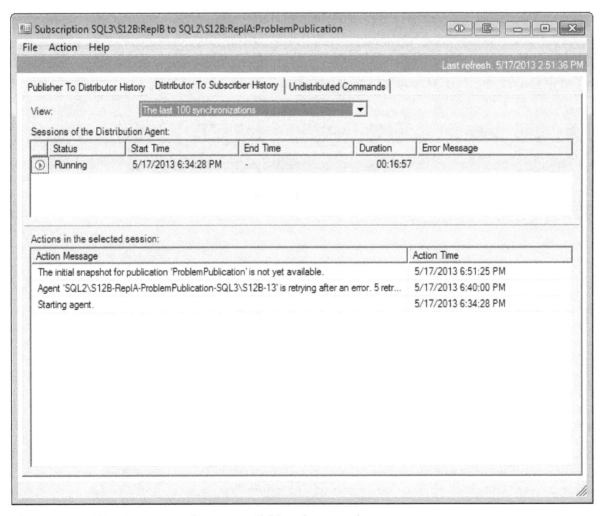

Figure 14-41: Warning message for an unavailable or lost snapshot.

To resolve this issue, you need to manually start the Snapshot Agent, as we did earlier in this chapter. You might also have to reinitialize the subscription after the Snapshot Agent is finished. Sometimes in this situation the subscription gets stuck and does not use the new snapshot on its own.

Replication Monitor is a helpful tool when it properly notifies you that there's a problem; however, if it shows that everything is in great shape, make sure you look twice, so you don't miss a subtle hint indicating that there is a problem.

Data problems

If there is a problem in the replicated data, the Distribution Agent will keep trying to resolve it. For example, Figure 14-42 shows the **Distributor To Subscriber History** for `ProblemPublication`. It has a bunch of error rows with start times about two-and-a-quarter minutes apart. The error is the same for all of them: "The row was not found at the Subscriber when applying the replicated command." This error is caused by a mismatch between the data in the publication database and the subscription database, potentially caused by a delete being executed at the Subscriber. Remember, while the subscription database is technically read-write, the target tables of a subscription to a transactional publication should be handled as if they were read-only.

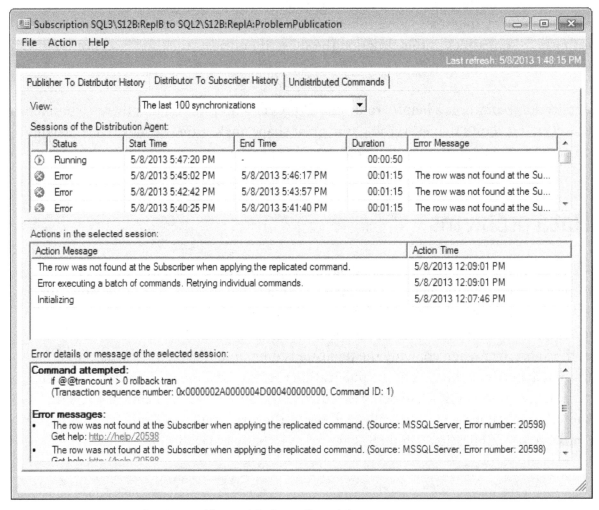

Figure 14-42: Errors indicating problems with the replicated data.

This error prevents the Distribution Agent from continuing because it could cause inconsistent data on the Subscriber. Instead, the Distribution Agent keeps trying, in the hopes that the error magically disappears. Each execution takes about one and a quarter minutes, as you can see in the **Duration** column in Figure 14-42. During that time, the replication agent shows that everything is working smoothly, which is what Figure 14-43 shows.

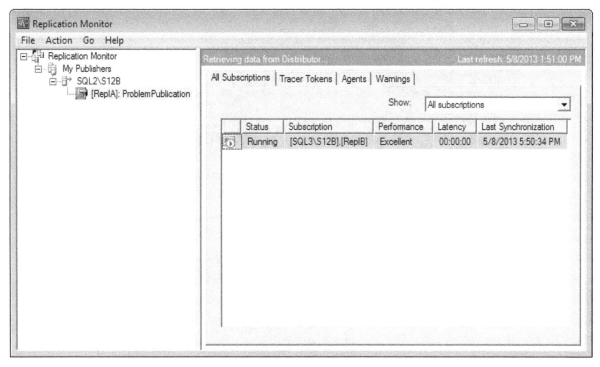

Figure 14-43: Replication Monitor indicating that everything is up and running...

However, during the remaining minute of the retrial interval, the Replication Monitor display looks vastly different, as shown in Figure 14-44.

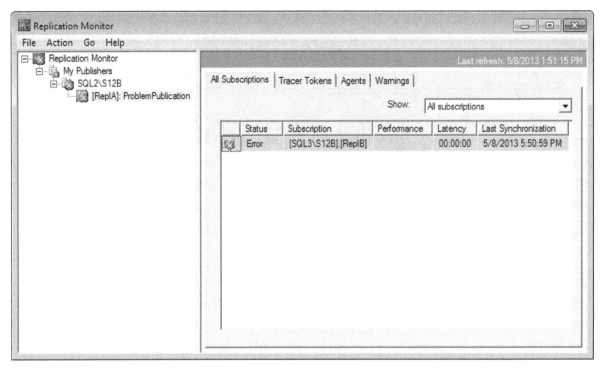

Figure 14-44: ... or maybe not.

So, if you happen to look at the Replication Monitor while the issue is occurring, you'll see what is shown in either Figure 14-43 or Figure 14-44. Which results you receive depends on whether the process is currently retrying or not. That means that, if you only briefly look at the tool, you'll get to see the error in less than half the cases, based on the times in my example.

Most problems, however, such as the one mentioned above, will show up in the **Subscription** dialog box (Figure 14-42) associated with a specific subscription. Therefore it is a good idea to get into the habit of opening the dialog box regularly. Remember, you access the dialog box by double-clicking the subscription itself in Replication Monitor.

To troubleshoot this and other data-related problems, review the error message itself, such as the one shown at the bottom of Figure 14-42. Notice that it contains a link to a Microsoft help page, which provides an explanation of what went wrong. There you will also find tips of how to resolve the issue. This link is displayed only when using Replication Monitor. The job history shows the error, but omits the link.

Summary

This chapter did a walk-through of a few troubleshooting scenarios found in a transactional replication setup. It focused on problems you might encounter during the SQL Server replication setup and provided a few ways to identify problems that you might encounter after your replication setup has been running for a while.

The takeaway from this chapter is that Replication Monitor, while being a good, and often helpful, tool to get a general feel for the health of your replication installation, does not always make problems obvious. You have to be able to read their subtle hints and then go elsewhere to get complete information. Most of the time this "elsewhere" is the SQL Server Agent job history of one of the Replication Agent's jobs.

The chapter also briefly mentioned that you should use tracer tokens or a similar tool to regularly monitor the latency of your installation. This not only provides you with information about performance, it also provides an early warning if the continuous data stream is blocked by, for example, a data error.

This chapter also concludes this book. I hope you found it to be useful and had as much fun working through it as I had writing it. The book covered transactional replication and merge replication. It also introduced tools for monitoring and troubleshooting. From the beginning, we also paid special attention to following the "least privilege" principle when setting up replication to help ensure that you're creating secure replication installations from the get-go.

Index

SQL Server
and .NET Tools
from Red Gate Software

SQL Compare® Pro $595

Compare and synchronize SQL Server database schemas

→ Eliminate mistakes migrating database changes from dev, to test, to production
→ Speed up the deployment of new database schema updates
→ Find and fix errors caused by differences between databases
→ Compare and synchronize within SSMS

> "Just purchased SQL Compare. With the productivity I'll get out of this tool, it's like buying time."
>
> **Robert Sondles** Blueberry Island Media Ltd

SQL Data Compare Pro $595

Compares and synchronizes SQL Server

→ Save time by automatically comparing and synchronizing your data
→ Copy lookup data from development databases to staging or production
→ Quickly fix problems by restoring damaged or missing data to a single row
→ Compare and synchronize data within SSMS

> "We use SQL Data Compare daily and it has become an indispensable part of delivering our service to our customers. It has also streamlined our daily update process and cut back literally a good solid hour per day."
>
> **George Pantela** GPAnalysis.com

Visit **www.red-gate.com** for a 14-day, free trial

 **SQL Prompt Pro**   **$295**

Write, edit, and explore SQL effortlessly

- → Write SQL smoothly, with code-completion and SQL snippets
- → Reformat SQL to a preferred style
- → Keep databases tidy by finding invalid objects automatically
- → Save time and effort with script summaries, smart object renaming, and more

> **"SQL Prompt is hands-down one of the coolest applications I've used. Makes querying/developing so much easier and faster."**
> **Jorge Segarra** University Community Hospital

 SQL Source Control   from **$295**

Connect your existing source control system to SQL Server

- → Bring all the benefits of source control to your database
- → Source control schemas and data within SSMS, not with offline scripts
- → Connect your databases to TFS, SVN, SourceGear Vault, Vault Pro, Mercurial, Perforce, Git, Bazaar, and any source control system with a capable command line
- → Work with shared development databases, or individual copies
- → Track changes to follow who changed what, when, and why
- → Keep teams in sync with easy access to the latest database version
- → View database development history for easy retrieval of specific versions

 # Deployment Manager   from **Free**

Automated deployment for your applications and databases

→ Deploys your whole application – ASP.NET sites, dependent assemblies, and databases – in one process

→ Makes deployment repeatable with a minimum of custom scripting

→ Shows you which version of your software is running on each dev, test, staging, and production environment, from a central dashboard

→ Works with local, remote, and Cloud-based servers

→ Uses public/private key encryption to keep deployments over the Internet secure

> **"Our old deployment process was cumbersome and stressful – now it's almost fun."**
> **Mattias Geigant**
> Developer, BEAB

SQL Backup Pro

$795

Compress, verify, and encrypt SQL Server backups

→ Compress SQL Server database backups by up to 95% for faster, smaller backups

→ Protect your data with up to 256-bit AES encryption

→ Strengthen your backups with network resilience to enable a fault-tolerant transfer of backups across flaky networks

→ Control your backup activities through an intuitive interface, with powerful job management and an interactive timeline

→ Get integrated backup verification with automated restore + DBCC CHECKDB

→ Quickly, simply, and securely upload and store a copy of your backup offsite, in hosted storage

> **"SQL Backup Pro cut the backup time for our most mission-critical database by 92%, and provided us with 95% compression. Built-in network resilience has also reduced our failure rate to zero. I'm absolutely amazed at how well it performs."**
>
> **Kiara Rodemaker**
> Manager, IT Accounting Services, Czarnowski

 # SQL Monitor

from **$795**

SQL Server performance monitoring and alerting

→ Intuitive overviews at global, cluster, machine, SQL Server, and database levels for up-to-the-minute performance data

→ Use SQL Monitor's web UI to keep an eye on server performance in real time on desktop machines and mobile devices

→ Intelligent SQL Server alerts via email and an alert inbox in the UI, so you know about problems first

→ Comprehensive historical data, so you can go back in time to identify the source of a problem

→ View the top 10 expensive queries for an instance or database based on CPU usage, duration, and reads and writes

→ PagerDuty integration for phone and SMS alerting

→ Fast, simple installation and administration

→ Add your own T-SQL scripts with the custom metrics feature to expand SQL Monitor's range

> **"Being web based, SQL Monitor is readily available to you, wherever you may be on your network. You can check on your servers from almost any location, via most mobile devices that support a web browser."**
>
> **Jonathan Allen**
> Senior DBA, Careers South West Ltd

 **SQL DBA Bundle**   **$1,895**

Seven essential tools for database administration

Backup & Recovery

Protect your data with highly-compressed, fully-verified, and encrypted backups, and ensure reliable restores with backup verification.

Performance Monitoring & Tuning

Monitor your servers in real time and obtain the performance data and alerts that are important to your business.

Change management

Get a simple, clear rundown of your schema and data changes, and sync database changes automatically.

Storage & Capacity Planning

With four levels of backup compression, you can make the most of your storage space. Monitor data growth easily, so you can plan how best to deal with it.

Troubleshooting

Get an alert within seconds of a problem arising, gain insight into what happened, and diagnose the issue, fast.

Productivity

Save time writing SQL in SQL Server Management Studio or Visual Studio, with code-completion and customizable SQL snippets.

Documentation

Automatically generate database documentation with a couple of clicks in SSMS, so you can save time and keep your team up to date.

The SQL DBA Bundle contains:

SQL Backup Pro   SQL Monitor   SQL Multi Script   SQL Compare Standard
SQL Data Compare Standard   SQL Prompt   SQL Doc

The tools in the bundle can be bought separately with a combined value of $3,565, or purchased together for **$1,895, saving 45% on the individual tool prices.**

Visit **www.red-gate.com** for a 28-day, free trial

SQL Toolbelt $2,195

The essential SQL Server tools for database professionals

You can buy our acclaimed SQL Server tools individually or bundled. Our most popular deal is the SQL Toolbelt: fourteen of our SQL Server tools in a single installer, with a combined value of $5,930 but an actual price of **$2,195, a saving of 65%**.

Fully compatible with SQL Server 2000, 2005, and 2008.

SQL Toolbelt contains:

→ **SQL Compare Pro**

→ **SQL Data Compare Pro**

→ **SQL Source Control**

→ **SQL Backup Pro**

→ **SQL Monitor**

→ **SQL Prompt Pro**

→ **SQL Data Generator**

→ **SQL Doc**

→ **SQL Dependency Tracker**

→ **SQL Packager**

→ **SQL Multi Script Unlimited**

→ **SQL Search**

→ **SQL Comparison SDK**

→ **SQL Object Level Recovery Native**

> **"The SQL Toolbelt provides tools that database developers, as well as DBAs, should not live without."**
>
> **William Van Orden** Senior Database Developer, Lockheed Martin

Visit **www.red-gate.com** for a 28-day, free trial

ANTS Memory Profiler $495

Find memory leaks and optimize memory usage of your .NET applications

→ Zero in on the causes of memory leaks, fast
→ Visualize the relationship between your objects and identify references which should no longer be held in memory
→ Optimize your application's memory usage

ANTS Performance Profiler from $395

Identify performance bottlenecks within minutes

→ Drill down to slow lines of code with line-level code timings
→ Analyse both your .NET code and SQL queries in a single profiling session
→ Optimize .NET application performance

Visit **www.red-gate.com** for a 28-day, free trial

.NET Reflector

$95

Decompile, debug, and understand any .NET code

→ See inside assemblies, libraries, and frameworks so you can understand how they work, even if you don't have the source

→ Decompile, search, and analyze any .NET assembly in C#, Visual Basic, and IL

→ Step straight into decompiled assemblies while debugging in Visual Studio, so you can debug 3rd-party code just like your own

SmartAssembly

$595

Prepare your application for the world

→ Obfuscation: Obfuscate your .NET code to secure it against reverse engineering. Multiple layers of protection defend your software against decompilation and cracking.

→ Automated Error Reporting: Get quick and automatic reports on exceptions your end-users encounter, and identify unforeseen bugs within hours or days of shipping. Receive detailed reports containing a stack trace and values of the local variables, making debugging easier.

Visit **www.red-gate.com** for a 28-day, free trial

SQL Server Execution Plans (2nd Edition)
Grant Fritchey

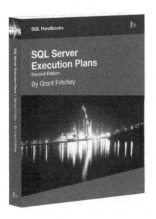

Every Database Administrator, developer, report writer, and anyone else who writes T-SQL to access SQL Server data, must understand how to read and interpret execution plans. This book leads you right from the basics of capturing plans, through how to interrupt them in their various forms, graphical or XML, and then how to use the information you find there to diagnose the most common causes of poor query performance, and so optimize your SQL queries, and improve your indexing strategy.

ISBN: 978-1-906434-93-9
Published: October 2012

SQL Server Concurrency:
Locking, Blocking and Row Versioning
Kalen Delaney

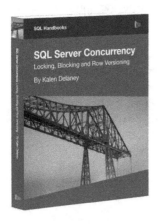

Your application can have impeachable indexes and queries, but they won't help you if you can't get to your data because another application has it locked. That's why every DBA and developer must understand SQL Server concurrency and how to troubleshoot excessive blocking or deadlocking.

ISBN: 978-1-906434-91-5
Published: September 2012

SQL Server Backup and Restore

Shawn McGehee

A DBA's tasks from day to day are rarely constant; with one exception: the need to ensure each and every day that any database in their charge can be restored and recovered, in the event of error or disaster. In this book, you'll discover how to perform each of these backup and restore operations using SQL Server Management Studio (SSMS), basic T-SQL scripts and Red Gate's SQL Backup tool.

ISBN: 978-1-906434-86-1
Published: May 2012

The Red Gate Guide:
SQL Server Team-based Development

Phil Factor, Grant Fritchey, Alex Kuznetsov, and Mladen Prajdić

This book shows how to use a mixture of home-grown scripts, native SQL Server tools, and tools from the Red Gate SQL Toolbelt, to successfully develop database applications in a team environment, and make database development as similar as possible to "normal" development.

ISBN: 978-1-906434-59-5
Published: November 2010

Printed in the USA
CPSIA information can be obtained
at www.ICGtesting.com
LVHW060646100923
757544LV00030B/311